William Minturn

Travels west

William Minturn

Travels west

ISBN/EAN: 9783337208448

Printed in Europe, USA, Canada, Australia, Japan

Cover: Foto ©Andreas Hilbeck / pixelio.de

More available books at **www.hansebooks.com**

TRAVELS WEST.

BY
WILLIAM MINTURN.

NEW EDITION.

London:
SAMUEL TINSLEY,
10, SOUTHAMPTON STREET, STRAND.
1877.
[All Rights Reserved.]

TO

MY DEAR FRIEND

DR. FREDERIC LABADIE LAGRAVE,

AS A SLIGHT MEMENTO

OF MY PROFOUND RESPECT AND

SINCERE AFFECTION.

PREFACE TO THE SECOND EDITION.

To one perhaps not at present fully accustomed to English ideas it appears, to say the very least, unfortunate that without attempting to discuss the aim of a book, and give the reader some idea of the author's purpose or object, and how far he has succeeded in that respect, English critics should proceed to endeavour to extinguish a young writer before he has had time to raise his head above the sod of the literary world. They ask why the author wrote such a book—why he wasted so much paper and ink—and what is the *raison d'être* of his production, etc., etc. These critics seem to forget that the smallest voices often tell the greatest truths. They seldom endeavour to discover whether the writer had any other aim than that of seeing his work in print. Or else they compare his book to that of some acknowledged "litterateur." What an honour! Our poor young writer, groping stumblingly in the darkness, finds himself suddenly brought forward and placed in the foremost rank next to acknowledged leaders, and then those that placed him there call on him and the world to remark his littleness!

Returning from a three months' trip to California and the West, I looked through the different libraries for books on the subject of Western travel. I discovered, among others, Sir Charles Dilke's book; but I found that he only gave some thirty pages to the United States. I also found Miss Kingsley's book; but apart from its literary merits, it did not seem to me to represent to the casual reader the true state of affairs in the Great Republic; and, above all, it did not seem to me to give the *true* colouring to the country or the people.

I do not pretend to have given a better book to the public than either of those I have specified; but I do think I have given a more scrupulously exact and analytical picture of the manners, customs, etc., of the American Western populace than either Sir Charles Dilke or Miss Kingsley have given; for while the first writer lost himself in speculations about the pre-historic lakes and the lost tribes of Indians, and the second writer gave herself up to seeing the country in a poetic way, and describing what she saw in a charming manner, I went as an American into the hard facts of American Western life. I searched out the cancers existing in American Western society; I tried to discover flaws in the existing state of the Western commercial system; and I told, plainly and truthfully, what I discovered, without even sparing those whose goodwill might be of service to me. I had the audacity to take the Chinaman's part against the Western-man, and to explain the tyranny exercised over the Celestials by my

Christian countrymen. But all these things are passed over without notice by my extremely sagacious critics, who, instead of dwelling upon matters of public interest, devote valuable time and space to criticising faults of style and other minor blemishes common to inexperienced writers.

However, one critic at least, and he a Frenchman, recognized the aim I had in view in attacking the Chinese Companies, and expressed his sympathy with my plea for the Celestials in the following terms:—

"The author of this book has crossed the United States from New York to San Francisco. He has travelled as an inquisitive and intelligent tourist. Going along he has taken notes of his remarks, his reflections, his conversations.

* * * *

"In a book of this kind we seek less of a literary entertainment than of a shorthand document, an official report of the state of places, men, and manners of a world which to us will always be new.

* * * *

"The author dwells on the situation of the country and the society of the Mormons, on California in general, and on the Chinese population of the State in particular. These are the three most profitable parts of the book for the reader. Not that the author fails to show himself *naïf* and trifling as is his wont.

"So he exclaims (page 152) that 'the horrible vice of polygamy' has nevertheless an aspect a little less repulsive than certain venial sins which are committed in such 'Christian' towns as New York, London, and Paris. The Mormons do not seem to him destined to last long; but Mormonism has been one of the greatest pioneers of civilization. Twenty years ago, what was Utah? A desert. To-day it is a State covered with prosperous towns, manufactories, and cultivation. On a tract of five hundred English miles there are not less than two hundred and twenty schools. Mr. Minturn, who is tolerant, does not demand the persecution of the Saints. Much scandalized at having such eccentric countrymen, he confides the task of their conversion to what he calls 'the most powerful trinity of modern time.' The following are the three persons of that trinity to whom Mr. Minturn, with full confidence, trusts: the railways, electricity, and the press.

"He has also seen San Francisco. There are few spectacles better calculated to strike an American. In the streets, always full of a motley crowd, the signboards are painted with Chinese letters, in Spanish or Italian. The names of the towns and places, up to the style of cooking, all remind the Anglo-Saxon of the race of the first conquerors of America. Nowhere is Catholicism more ardent. Nevertheless, Mr. Minturn, more sceptical than usual, insinuates that the predominant religion of California is Dollarism — the most tolerant of beliefs.

"In San Francisco are the head-quarters of the six great companies which, formed after the model of the famous East India Company, *exploit* the Chinese labourers of the coasts of the Pacific and Australia. The agents of these companies traverse the interior of the Empire in all directions. If they detect an old indigent couple burdened with children, they single out the most gifted and the most robust of the boys, and lay an infallible trap for the father of the family. A creature of the agent of the companies tries to pick a quarrel with the old Chinese, and gets him into prison under some accusation. There remain, therefore, at one stroke a dozen famished children who have nothing to eat, because the miserable father supported them all with his daily labour. Then the agent of the companies in his turn comes upon the scene. He is the *deus ex machina* who appears at the unravelling of tragedies. He offers bail to liberate the old father; he even gives a great sum on condition that such and such boys should follow him beyond the sea, and serve him for so many years. The son has signed. On his part the agent pledges himself to bring back to the native place the bones of the emigrant, if by accident he should die before the end of his engagement. This is the most important clause of all. The Chinese cannot bear the idea of being buried far away from his fathers in the land of the barbarians.

"Mr. Minturn makes of those companies a sort of Society of Jesus, or the Holy Office.

Not an action, not a secret thought of these slaves disseminated in the depths of the mines or the forests of the Pacific coasts, escapes the species of Council of Ten which holds its See in San Francisco. The power and influence of the companies would deprive the Chinese guilty of certain offences of the just chastisement of the laws. These companies have secret tribunals without appeal, which would pronounce even capital punishment. The fear of a certain death prevents the Chinese from disclosing the existence of these dark and formidable jurisdictions. I am myself absolutely ignorant as to how much truth there may be in these singular statements.

"The whole chapter under the title, 'The Chinese on the Pacific Coast' is, I repeat it, very instructive. I am bound to notice what the author says of the food of the Chinese, who do not live exclusively on rice, as some people assert, but who fetch from the mother-country all they consume. The sobriety and endurance of the sons of the Celestial Empire are well known. They work for prices which defy competition from the Americans of all races. They amass slowly, dollar by dollar, fortunes which often become very considerable. Neither the Persians nor the Arabs can be compared to the Chinese in industry, sobriety, and economy.

"The Chinese excel in imitating and reproducing instantaneously everything they have seen done. Hence the astonishing facility with which they catch the secret of nearly all our trades. The manufacture of cigars in San Francisco has passed altogether into their hands. The same with the boot trade, etc. What can a Chinese of the Pacific coast not do? Cooks, washers, hairdressers, barbers— they excel in all the manual arts. We have not seen them yet as preachers, doctors, judges, or newspaper writers; but the time seems not far distant, so Mr. Minturn jokingly assures us, when these professions, too, will have to meet the universal competition of the Celestials.

"Not only in San Francisco, but in all the other towns of the coast, the Chinese live in separate quarters. Entering during the night in San Francisco into 'Little China,' one would imagine oneself in some populous town of the Celestial Empire. Thousands of coloured lamps are suspended before the houses and shops; the streets are plunged in a sort of twilight obscurity. Everybody knows in what frightful quantities the Chinese live together in their houses, and what unpleasant odours emanate from their quarter. You know the playhouses where the Celestials of all classes gather, eight or nine round a table, in a heavy atmosphere; their yellow faces get animated, their black eyes sparkle; and nothing has a more picturesque effect than those beings clad in dark garments, gesticulating and making faces in the subdued light of a few lamps. I do not mention the opium-smoking establishments: these two vices are not as serious as one would think.

"The Chinese, who number not less than one hundred and fifty millions in the States of the Pacific, and go on increasing, will soon give to the world the spectacle of the greatest fight for existence which has ever been seen. The American labourers from all parts cry out already that they are ruined by 'the work at reduced prices of the Chinese.' The final victory will belong to the 'best,' according to the theory of Darwin, says the author. Therefore the 'best' in the industrial struggle are those who can produce the most and consume the least."

"Jules Soury."

I would take this opportunity to thank M. Jules Soury most warmly for his criticism—a criticism which for style, acuteness, and thoroughness might put to shame some of the infallible critics of the English press, who might also imitate with advantage the French habit of signing their often too careless criticisms.

One of my principal objects, then, has been to defend the "Chinese American;" and I will now close this preface to the second edition by saying that by more reading and by more proofs that have since been brought to my cognizance, I can say with certitude that the old slavery in the South is far surpassed in cruelty and tyranny by the modern legal slavery of the West.

CONTENTS.

CHAPTER I.

PAGE

Departure from New York—Suburbs of Jersey City—Political Ignorance of the Masses in the United States—Aspect of the Country going West—Night in a Sleeping Car—Inconveniences of the Temperance Movement—The American Birmingham—Cincinnati—St. Louis—Commercial advantages of its Site—Peculiarity of the Water—St. Louis Champagne—Turkish Baths 1

CHAPTER II.

Overflow of the Mississippi—Iron Mountain—Pilot Knob—Angling; Small Profits and Slow Returns—Water Snakes—The National Beverage—Train Transporters of the Mississippi—Chas. Dickens's Eden—Inchoate Cities—Wooden Houses with Mock Fronts—Poplar Bluff—Little Rock—Hot and Cold Springs of Arkansas—Texarkana—Cheapness of Telegraphic Communication—Cattle Yards of St. Louis—*Cafés Chantants*—Theatres—Parks—Churches—St. Louis Transfer Company—Daniel Boone 26

CHAPTER III.

Springfield · Lincoln's Monument—Chicago—A Temperance Town—Anecdote of Daniel Boone—Growth and Commercial Importance of Chicago—Burlington—A Railway Critic—Omaha—Very Low Church — Coloured Church — The Black Hills Expedition. . . . 60

CHAPTER IV.

Papillon — Elkhorn — Waterloo — Fremont—Banks of the Platte River—Rogers—Schuyler—Richland Columbus — Pawnee Indian Reservation — Lockwood — Grand Island — North Platte City — Irregular Growth of Western Cities—Julesburg—Grazing Country—Cheyenne—Grand Conception of Horace Greeley—Mountains of Colorado—Small Towns—Grand Scenery—Highest Inhabited Point on the Continent—Variety of Flowers—Virginia Dale—A Western Man of the "Heroic Age"—Laramie—A Female Jury . . . 79

CHAPTER V.

Benton City—The Hog Back—A Paint Mine—Summit of the Rocky Mountains—Sage-brush and Alkali Beds — Red Desert—Bitter Creek—Descriptive Names — Green River — Romantic Scenery — A Pioneer of Western Civilization—Aspen—A Deserted Railway City—Bear River—Mormon Settlements—Bear Lake Valley—Echo Cañon—Mormon Fortifications—Echo City—Weber Cañon—Devil's Slide—A Ride on the "Cow-Catcher"—Ogden—Salt Lake and the Dead Sea —Aspect of the Country about Salt Lake . . . 10

CHAPTER VI.

Salt Lake City—Expensive Proselytism—City Irrigation—Subdivision of the City—The one Grand Theatre in the United States—The Tabernacle—View from Fort Douglas—Density of the Water of Salt Lake—Mormon Society—Museum—General Impressions concerning Mormonism—Residences of Brigham Young's Wives—Mormon Hospitality—Agriculture the Chief Employment—Good Government of Utah Territory—Corinne—Social Independence of American Ladies—Promontory—Opening of the Pacific Railway—Magnificence and Economy Combined à l'Américaine—General Observations on Mormonism—Utah Twenty-five Years Ago—Utah at the Present Day—View of the Great Salt Lake from Sand Ridge—Site of Salt Lake City determined by Customary Miracle—Population—Prospects of Mormonism 136

CHAPTER VII.

The American Desert; its Bad Pre-eminence—Nevada—Discovery of Silver—Rapid Increase of Population—Aboriginal Tribes—Topography—Mining the Chief Industry—Silver Mines the Most Important—Copper, Iron, Salt—Tecoma—Pilot Peak—Humboldt Wells—Valley of the Humboldt—Richness of the Soil—Humboldt River—Elko Game Country—Five Mile Cañon—Hamilton—Mining District—Most Important Mines—Attractiveness of a New Mining District—Small Profits of Miners—"Good Society" in a New Mining District—Rise of "Vigilance Committees"—Great Cave of Nevada 158

CHAPTER VIII.

Nevada properly a Stock-raising and Agricultural Country—Comparative Unprofitableness of Mining Speculations in Nevada as in California—Hard Work and Poor Pay the Miner's Lot—Austin—"Rough" Persecution—Chinese Patience—Battle Mountain—Resse River Valley—Winnemucca—Desert Country—Fancy Names—Great Desert of Nevada—Sage-brush and Alkali—Social Conveniences of the Pullman Palace Car—White Plains—Micage Verdi the Unmusical—Boca 189

CHAPTER IX.

CALIFORNIA: Expedition of Hernando Cortez—Sir Francis Drake—Spanish Missionaries—Traces of Spanish Occupation—Climate—Scenery—Fertility—Summit—Rivers—Railroad over the Sierra Nevada—Mean Temperature of California—Area—Agricultural Products—Construction of the Railroad—Summit Valley—Soda Springs—Great American Cañon—Dutch Flat—Mining Towns—Blue Lode—Romantic Railway Truck—Cape Horn—Engineering Difficulties—Grass Valley—Political Economy. SACRAMENTO: Placerville—Stocton; its Rapid Growth—Grand View from Mount Diablo—Extent and Fertility of Joaquin Valley—Niles—Enchanting Scenery—Oaklands—Distant View of San Francisco 216

CHAPTER X.

Aspect of San Francisco—Woodward's Garden—Seal Rocks—Golden Gate Park—Indigestible Economy—From

Merced to Coulterville—Dudley and Hubbards—New
Acquaintances—Bower Cave—The American " Race "
—Yeo-Semite Valley—Mirror Lake—The Clothes Line
The Nigger " Lady of the Lake "—Perverseness of
Guides — Snow's *Hospice* — Cloud's Rest — Departure
from Yeo-Semite 241

CHAPTER XI.

Pioneer Laundry—Ferry Boats—A Wayside Inn—*Digito
Monstrari*—Sonora—The U.S. Mail—Muscular Christianity—Intemperance of Miners—Calaveras Grove—
An Aristocratic Innkeeper—Charge on the System of
"Heads I Win, Tails you Lose"—How to see the
World — Big Trees — Postprandial Eloquence— Poor
Farming 285

CHAPTER XII.

Sunday Amusements—New Palace Hotel—San Franciscan
Hospitality—Reckoning without One's Host—Starr
King—Chinese Opera—Home, Sweet Home!—Chinese
Society—An Opium Den—Leper's Den . . . 303

CHAPTER XIII.

The Chinese on the Pacific Coast 318

CHAPTER XIV.

Oaklands—Restaurants—Growth and Civilization of San
Francisco—Its Natural Advantages—Bird's-Eye view
of the City—Mission Dolores 340

CHAPTER XV.

Nappa City—Lunatic Asylum—White Sulphur Springs—A Civic Dignitary of California—*Memoirs pour servir*—Popular Ignorance—Petrified Forest—Hot Sulphur Springs—Odious Comparison—Discounting the Future—The Geysers—Californian Wine—Santa Rosa—Return to San Francisco 351

CHAPTER XVI.

Travelling Bores—"Great Mill"—The Pullman "Chicken"—Won by a Foul—Proficiency of the Pullmanites in the Noble Art—Second Visit to Chicago—Detroit—Central Freight Depôt—The Canadian Side—Falls of Niagara—A Short Essay on the Sublime and Beautiful. 369

TRAVELS WEST.

CHAPTER I.

Departure from New York—Suburbs of Jersey City—Political ignorance of the masses in the United States—Aspect of the country going West—Night in a Sleeping Car—Inconveniences of the Temperance Movement—The American Birmingham—Cincinnati—St. Louis—Commercial advantages of its Site—Peculiarity of the Water—St. Louis Champagne—Turkish Baths.

On the morning of the 5th of May, 1875, I was invited by my brother to accompany him on a journey from New York to St. Louis.

I immediately accepted the invitation, and having made a few parting calls, drove in haste to the Courtland Street Ferry, where I arrived just ten minutes before the appointed time.

My brother, however, was nowhere to be found.

After I had spent some time in scanning all persons within sight, I asked the ticket agent at what time the St. Louis train started.

"Inside of five minutes," was the answer.

I mentioned to him that I had expected to meet my brother, whom I described, and inquired of him whether he had seen a gentleman of such appearance. He said he had; and that Mr. M—— had left word that if any one asked for him, that person should wait.

Just a few seconds before the boat left the slip to make connection with the train on the Jersey side, my brother arrived. I mentally contrasted this national characteristic of just catching the boat or train, when it is almost in motion, with the German or French habit of going to the depot three-quarters of an hour, or even a whole hour, before the starting of the train, often when the journey is only for a short distance, and on a matter of but slight importance.

A Frenchman or a German on his travels makes up his mind to be comfortable at all hazards, and he knows that there is no greater enemy to comfort than hurry; and the thought that strikes his imagination with a fear approaching to horror—that he might arrive at the depot just in time to be too late—impels him to the folly of losing so much precious time

The gentlemen who were kind enough to allow me to form one of their party, were going West on important business; and it was a mere act of civility on their part that I was invited to accompany them.

The ferry-boat took us over in about five or seven minutes; and, after the usual amount of bumping against the sides of the ship, the boat was finally secured to the bridge, and presently we found ourselves in the depot of the Pennsylvania Railway Company—an enormous structure, adequate, apparently, to the receiving and disgorging of any number of trains.

We had a compartment in one of the Pullman Palace cars; indeed, the whole of our party proper took up nearly one-half the car. This was the first Pullman car I had seen, and I was told that it was an exceptionally handsome one. I examined it with some curiosity. Most of the panelling was in polished walnut, mahogany, citron, and other rare woods. The centres of the panels and the corners of the seats were decorated and finished with artistic bronzes. The car was roomy, and all the appointments were excellent.

We found awaiting our arrival at the station a number of other gentlemen with whom we were to travel, and by whom I was warmly welcomed. Soon the whistle blew, the bell rang, the train moved forward with an easy gliding motion, and we were off on the first stage of our journey westward.

The *trajet* through the outskirts of Jersey City was extremely interesting to me, who had but recently returned from a prolonged sojourn in Europe. Magnificent warehouses, worth, no doubt, millions with what they contained, were shouldered and surrounded by buildings of one or two stories, in any one of which a lamp carelessly used would have sufficed to cause destruction to their wealth-containing neighbours.

The broad streets were ornamented with a profusion of old tin pans, battered into all sorts of shapes or no-shapes, a quantity of broken bottles, and a sprinkling of bits of crockery-ware which had doubtless seen better days. The enormous squares, marked out with only a house here and there,—say about four hundred yards apart,—presented a strange deserted appearance. Looking at the bridges and railway offices as we sped rapidly along, I thought them comparable to the best to be seen elsewhere.

Our party consisted of Mr. S. W., Mr. T. W., his nephew Mr. W., a lawyer, my brother, and myself. A few days previous to my leaving New York I had had the pleasure of hearing Mr. Charles T. Adams speak at a dinner given to Senator Schurz on the eve of his departure for Europe. I had been much struck with his firmness and assurance of manner, his general aptitude in the treatment of his subject, and the warmth which he threw into it. I now asked Mr. S. W., who was formerly of Boston, how it was that a man like Mr. Adams, who, by reason of his independent fortune, would find it unnecessary to steal, even if his high character did not render it impossible for him to do so—a man, moreover, of much greater intelligence than the average statesman, and whose training and habits of mind peculiarly fit him for a public station, and whose work, by virtue of his patriotism, would result entirely to the benefit of the country,—why such a man is not chosen to represent either the State or some portion of it.

He assured me that if Mr. Adams decided to open an account with any shopkeeper in Boston, not one would hesitate to credit him to any amount, without other surety than his known integrity; but if that same man were asked to give his vote for Mr. Adams for a position requiring the strictest integrity and and a lifelong devotion to the public interests, he would most decidedly refuse it. I asked the cause of this antipathy. He answered that some people were silly enough to regard Mr. Adams as an aristocrat, and to prefer a man who would flatter them, and pick their pockets, to men who, like Mr. Adams, would probably talk to them very roughly and tell them some unpleasant truths, and then devote themselves wholly to working for their good. There was also, he said, a lamentable ignorance among the greater part of the population, who imagined that if a public man stole a thousand dollars from the rich man, while he stole only one hundred from the poor man, he was injuring the richer to a much greater extent than the poorer victim; not remembering that a thousand cents was as much to the latter as a thousand dollars to the former.

The truth of this statement was afterwards proven to me very clearly as I went further West, and saw more of the people.

We had some pleasant conversation on subjects somewhat abstract. I sought his opinion on the point whether the bad representation of the country was caused by the want of a landed gentry whose interests as owners of the soil would be of the same kind at least as those of the workers of the soil: I cited by way of illustration a district in which there was a large town, and argued that the proprietors and workers of the soil in that district would have a much better right to a voice in determining its interests than those who were mere distributors of its products, and who could influence a large number of satellites, such as saloon and bar-room loungers. Mr. S. W. seemed to think that we should have rather a slim chance, if we tried, to found a landed power. I inquired the reason why Americans objected to all aristocratic forms in society, while they permitted the unchecked growth of such powerful monopolies—possessing all the leading traits of aristocracies—as telegraph, railroad, and similar organizations. He said the only real aristocracy we ever had—the slave-holding aristocracy of the South—was now completely destroyed, and it would be very hard to replace it.

During the first hour from New York, we passed through a slightly monotonous country; as we went, however, further "into the bowels of the land," the scenery became more inviting, the landscape more picturesque, the valley dotted here and there with well-built villages, in which pretentious "city halls," modest school-houses, and aspiring church steeples rose maje ally above all other structures. The eye caught a pleasing glimpse, as we whirled along, of many a pretty country residence, the prevailing colour being a light drab, with edgings or trimmings of a dark brown shade, and the style of buildings decidedly *melée*.

I ventured a remark on the admiration of the French for their country, as shown by their speaking of it always as *La belle France*. My neighbour said that only about one-third of France was really "*belle*," and that, as a general rule, those who spoke continually in this eulogistic manner were inhabitants of *La basse Normandie*, or other parts of France equally wanting in natural beauty.

I mentioned the artistic knowledge of one of our largest capitalists, who knew more about the worth of pictures than some of the first picture-dealers in Europe. Mr. S. W. said that he had asked this capitalist whether he had any celebrated landscapes by foreign artists. He answered that no foreign artist could paint landscapes to come up to the American artists' productions; "Indeed," he said, "they have no such scenery."

We got to Philadelphia about eight o'clock.

My brother asked the porter in attendance, where the refreshment room was:

phlegmatic answer,—"If you go ahead you will see the man bawling it out down there."

A quarter of an hour to hustle down "gunpowder" and hot water, oysters that looked more like clams, ham and eggs, etc. We were standing on the station platform, having a little chat,—I was leaning against the side of the car, when all of a sudden I was made to take a footbath without the usual formalities, namely, the removal of one's shoes and stockings. It seems that some gentleman had been washing his hands, and had afterwards pulled up the plug in the basin; thus my unfortunate extremities, which I am careful as a cat to keep dry, received the full benefit of baptism gratis. *Qu'il est doux de voyager!*

We were soon off again. The lamps were lit, and the car was turned into a very good substitute for a drawing-room. At ten o'clock we began to prepare for that most momentous of all American railroad experiences—a first night in a sleeping coach. For many years I had heard of the delicacy of movement, of the ease and comfort of sleeping in a Pullman car; but surely those who had spoken in this way had never been over the Pennsylvania Railroad. There was a continual noise as of a regiment of gigantic iron horses riding down upon us at full gallop; indeed, one might easily have imagined oneself on horseback, as the car jumped in the most frightful manner. This was rather too much for the first night. About eleven o'clock, arriving at a large hotel, I got out—I was going to say dismounted—and made my way towards a spacious refreshment saloon, where the savoury odours from the steaming pots made one's heart leap with joy. I hastened to the evident master of ceremonies, and producing my flask, I said,—

"Will you please give me a little brandy, sir?"

I thought I must must have stepped on the man's foot, for he no sooner heard my question than the right side of his mouth drew itself up towards his right eye, while his nose moved downward. With his left eye he stared at me aghast, and passed on without giving me any answer.

Seeing a beauteous maiden in attendance, I hoped to meet with more kindness from her soft heart. The same question brought forth the same response, only the spasmodic efforts were not quite so marked. At last, in desperation, I attacked a buxom old lady who was pouring out a dark boiling liquid for the delectation of weary travellers, and which was recklessly described as hot coffee—but then people are not critically exact under the circumstances.

"If you please, ma'am, can you get me a little brandy?"

She looked at me aghast for a few seconds, closed her mouth, opened her eyes, and hissed between her teeth.

"We are not allowed to keep any, sir."

A small boy offered to conduct me to a place where I could procure some. I had to wade through mud a distance of forty yards or so, to obtain my precious elixir, at a most fearfully disgusting bar. Pleasant for any elderly person who had been taken sick on the train, and absolutely needed some stimulant, to have to go through all this trouble to procure it! This extreme difficulty in some localities, and the wonderful ease in others of obtaining stimulants, whether necessary or otherwise, is one of the most striking peculiarities of the entire West; and, indeed, the same may be said of the United States as a whole.

Not caring to sleep, some of the gentlemen congregated in the small room, generally used as a smoking resort, where in various costumes of *deshabille* we chatted until about twelve o'clock. After that we went to bed, and happily went to sleep.

I woke next morning to find that we were in the midst of a pouring rain. Country extremely monotonous. We got to Pittsburg at half-past eight o'clock. I thought, for the moment, we had arrived at London or Birmingham. I did not know we were near the town until we were in it, for we seemed to be shooting into an immense cloud of smoke. Saw the first grain elevator: altogether a rather picturesque building; being made of different coloured slate, and being smeared with smoke, it looked like an ancient tower. It reminded my brother of an incident that occurred when he was crossing the Atlantic: having met with an iceberg, everybody being on deck, and the sun throwing a shower of rays through its transparent mass, everybody was entranced, and some one remarked, " How like an old Gothic cathedral!"

" Do you think so?" says Mrs. ——; " now it looks to me just like one of our grain elevators."

After the substantial part of our meal, we told the waiter to bring us some cakes, saying that we were just going to send a telegram, and would come back for them. When we came back—no cakes. When we mildly remonstrated, a coal-coloured representative of American liberty said we had been gone so long, he thought we must be half-way to New York by that time. I felt very much like reconstructing that imp of darkness. However, having gobbled down our cakes, we departed in peace, feeling very much as if some small boys had been shooting marbles down our throats.

The bridge and its surroundings at Pittsburgh, where you first see the steamboats, with the wheel at the back, and get the first view of the *levées*, is truly a marvellous sight, but far from beautiful. As you wind along the other side of the river, the scene is more suggestive of a busy populous town in the infernal regions, than of anything earthly. Every object the eye falls upon is black,— houses, roads, buildings, people's clothing, children's faces. Even the sky itself was black, and everything had been rendered blacker by the morning rain and the fog which had risen from it.

As one of the most important industrial centres of the country, Pittsburgh deserves a moment's attention.

Situated at the confluence of the Alleghany and Monogahala rivers, at the head of the Ohio, here has been formed a congeries of factories and foundries, in the very heart of the region containing some of the richest deposits of bituminous coal (besides iron ores) to be found on the continent. Coal is supplied from this point to the whole Mississippi Valley, to the extent of 1,600,000 tons a year. Numerous mining companies, iron and steel works, extensive machine shops, manufactures of steam boilers, engines, rods, spikes, rivets, files, wire, and foundries for casting cannon, here give employment to a vast army of toilers. Here also are copper, smelting, and rolling mills, cotton mills, white-lead and glass works. The atmosphere is so densely filled with smoke, from the great number of factories, foundries, and miscellaneous works, that this city well deserves the name given it, "The Birmingham of America." It is connected by steamboats with the whole Mississippi Valley, and by railroads and canals with Philadelphia and the West. Amongst its public buildings are a fine Court House, perhaps the largest Catholic cathedral in the country, about one hundred and fifty churches, numerous aqueducts, railway and other bridges, the United States Arsenal, many colleges and schools. Much "useful" information of this kind may, of course, be found in the guide-books "at large;" but as that kind of literature is rather bulky, and apt to be somniferous, I give the results of my observations and enquiries in such matter, without much regard to their novelty.

During the day, we passed through an extremely fertile and beautiful country. The farms seemed to be well managed, the fences in excellent condition, and in some places even there were hedges. The farm-houses which we saw from the car window seemed to be kept in good order, and were large and commodious, the out-houses and stables being near the main buildings. We also passed two or three stations which were evidently the stopping-places of large water-cure or "Thermal" establishments. Gorgeous omnibuses, painted with their names, "European Hotel," "Continental Hotel," and so forth, were waiting to receive passengers.

A quarter of an hour before we came to each considerable town, boys would traverse the train, with the latest newspapers, which they scrupulously sold at never more than two or three hundred per cent. profit. At one time a small "darkey" made his appearance with a violin which he held upside down, keeping the big end pressed hard against his abdomen, and ducking and accompanying himself on the instrument at one and the same time. That night our slumbers were perfectly peaceful, and I declared the next morning, with perfect good faith, that I would choose never to sleep in anything but a Pullman car for the rest of my days, or rather nights.

The next place of importance which I shall have time to notice, is one of the great rival cities of the West—Cincinnati.

The metropolis of Ohio is situated on the right bank of the Ohio river, opposite the mouth of the Licking, and immediately above the mouth of Mill Creek.

The upper part of the city is 540 feet above the level of the sea. One of the most populous cities of the Western States, it is reckoned about the fifth in size and importance among the cities of the Union. It is chiefly remarkable for its rapid growth, extensive trade, and productive industry. From its central position between Pittsburg and the mouth of the Ohio, it has become the principal gathering and distributive point in the valley of that river.

The city is beautifully situated in a valley three miles in diameter, intersected from east to west by the Ohio, and environed by a range of hills with a well-defined circular form, rising by gentle acclivities about 400 feet above the level of the river. The most beautiful views of Cincinnati are obtained from the summits of these vine-clad hills. The greater part of the city is built on two terraces or plains, of which the first is 50 and the second 180 feet higher than low water mark. The front margin of the latter, originally a steep bank, has been graded to a gentle declivity, so that the drainage of the city is effected by means of the streets, directly into the river. To turn a river into a sewer may not be considered a very striking proof of civic wisdom; but American rivers have a great capacity for digesting sewage, and the convenience of the plan is considerable. The upper terrace slopes gradually towards the north, and at the average distance of a mile terminates at the base of the Mount Auburn range of limestone hills, adorned with handsome residences, vineyards, and gardens, and forming a well-built and extremely beautiful suburb.

The city extends about four miles along the river, without including the suburban villages. The central portions are compactly and handsomely built; spacious warehouses and dwellings of brick and stone line the wide and well paved streets, many of which are shaded by large trees.

At about ten o'clock on the following morning, we beheld the towers and steeples of St.

Louis, and on descending from the train the first object that caught our view was Mr. Ead's magnificent bridge. Of all the bridges I have seen in various parts of the world, none do I consider so monumental, so grand, and of such fine architecture as this. It is capable of bearing two trains of cars passing each other, two street cars, two omnibuses, and any number of foot passengers, without the slightest danger being incurred. The heavy stone pillars, and the minuteness and gracefulness of the iron work, I have never seen equalled during my travels in America.

In the omnibus which we took at the station, there was a Russian peasant from the Black Sea, as systematically greasy and dirty as we could have hoped to have met him in the bosom of his native Russia. He spoke a horrible German *patois*, and informed me that he was going to meet a number of his countrymen, who had bought a large tract of land, farther west, where they were working.

On entering St. Louis proper, one is struck by an appearance of age and solidity nowhere else to be met with in American cities. This imperial city of the west stands in a most imposing situation on the right bank of the Mississippi, 20 miles below its confluence with the Missouri, 174 miles above the mouth of the Ohio, 744 miles below the Falls of St. Anthony, and 1194 miles above New Orleans; thus drawing, supplying, and distributing its rapidly increasing share of the products of a vast extent of country. By the Mississippi and Missouri rivers, and their affluents, it is the converging point of nearly 15,000 miles of steamboat navigation. Its river craft, plying between this and other points, numbers about 700 vessels, one-third of which are steamers and the remainder barges, etc., all of which are valued together at about 7,000,000 dollars.

The city extends in all about seven miles by the curve of the river, and about three miles or more back. The site rises from the river by two plateaux of limestone formation, the first twenty and the second sixty feet above high water. The ascent to the first plateau is somewhat abrupt, while the second rises more gradually, and spreads out into an extensive plain, affording fine views of the city and river. The city is well laid out, the streets being for the most part sixty feet wide, and with but few exceptions intersecting each other at right angles. According to the census return of 1870, St. Louis had a population of over 310,000, and over 1,000 manufacturing firms with an invested capital of nearly forty-eight millions and a half.

The Lindell Hotel, at which we stopped, is one of the finest establishments of the kind that I have ever seen, either here or abroad.

After breakfast we went out to visit the Iron Mountain Railway and its appurtenances, and were very much struck by the land owned, and by the marked regularity and good order in all the workshops and engine-houses. We were then taken by Mr. Allen, the president of the road, to see the new Custom-House, which is built so that trains arriving under ground can come right up to the cellars and receiving rooms. It is built of massive blocks of granite; with heavy iron supporters. We were then shown the future Central Depôt. We passed by some large grain elevators, and were driven round some of the small parks, and then taken to one of the Beer Gardens, for which St. Louis is celebrated, where we had a draught of cool refreshing beer, the recollection of which reminds me of the peculiar water we had found at breakfast. I had noticed that the glasses were filled with a perfectly white liquor, which I took to be milk, or rather, upon closer examination, thought must be weak butter-milk, or perhaps lemonade. I had a glass of this fluid by my plate. I told the waiter to take it away and bring me some water.

"Water, Sah!—why, that's just fresh water; I just put that there with some in it."

We called the head-waiter, and protested; but he assured us that the St. Louis people had drunk that same kind of water from the time of the foundation of the city, and that, though it was quite possible to filter it, and arrangements could have been made to do so at the reservoir itself, the St. Louis medical men of the highest standing had recommended its being left alone, deciding that it was much more wholesome in its natural state than it would be after filtering. From that time forward we got Seltzer water, and drank nothing but that, and St. Louis champagne,—which, by the way, is delicious, and greatly superior to a good deal of the foreign article.

That afternoon we drove to Shaw's Garden. This garden, which was laid out, completed, and given to the city by Mr. Shaw, is very pretty, resembling the old Hampton Court style of garden, or, rather, the old French and German gardens. We drove, too, through the park, which Mr. Shaw had also presented to the municipality, and which will no doubt be, one of these days, a very beautiful drive, but is now still in its infancy, the trees and plants being small, and the whole place, indeed, having an air of barrenness.

After dinner, my brother and I strolled through the market. This is a solid building, such as one sees in French provincial towns, and the whole traffic of the place seems to be carried on with certain French characteristics; indeed, most of the names over the stalls were French, as are likewise many of the names of the streets here. A large portion of the real estate of the city is in the hands of French people, or descendants of French owners. One evidence of this is seen in the fact that for a considerable distance around St. Louis the land is sold by the arpent, and not by the acre. Indeed, in more than one sense St. Louis has many French traits.

We were serenaded all that evening by some electioneering companies or bands, who kept promenading first up one street and then down another; also by two or three *cafés chantants*, that kept up a continual blast till eleven o'clock, at which hour we retired to our virtuous couches, and enjoyed slumber equal to that in the sleeping car, if not superior.

The next morning we were up betimes, and having sufficiently stuffed ourselves with hot cakes and coffee, we made our way to the office of the Iron Mountain Railway, where we were kindly received. Young Mr. T. W. and myself then went to the City Hall.

This is a massive building with a fine dome of granite and brick, the brick painted so as to resemble the stone. The interior, the stairs, the walls, and the pillars are very strong and massive. The dome commences at the first floor, the first gallery being supported by a circular line of pillars. Around this gallery are pictures representing scenes in the lives of celebrated Missouri statesmen. The second gallery, which is the beginning of the dome proper, is given up to national subjects, namely, the landing of Columbus, Washington crossing the Delaware, the arrival of Penn, and so forth. On the top is an emblematical picture of the United States. Around the inner part of the gallery ballustrade are seen the very effective arms of Missouri, in four different places, facing each other.

From the dome we had a magnificent view of the city and river. We could see many steeples, towers, and high smoke-jacks of the steamers, aspiring grain elevators, etc. We could see the bridge in all its grandeur.

After a view from the dome of the City Hall, one is not astonished that the St. Louis people claim for their city the title of the Metropolis of the West.

Being somewhat heated by our climb, we made our way towards another monumental structure, though of rather smaller size, namely, a Gothic soda-water fountain, at which with foaming glasses we slaked our thirst.

Returning to the railway office, I got my brother to go with me to the hotel, where we had a Turkish bath. And such a Turkish bath! Indeed, it could not have been better at Constantinople,—perhaps not so good. Above the baths, there is a most luxurious barber's shop, where I amused myself in perplexing one of the coloured attendants by asking him to shave me. If you know me, you will pronounce this no easy task. The poor man hunted vainly for something to vent his wrath upon, and at last—having soaped all over my face where the beard ought to be—he discovered an abnormal growth of three long hairs, which he immediately decapitated. His perplexity was very amusing to me at first, but I am convinced he made me pay double for the trouble I had given him, and it was the dearest shave I have ever had in my life. That evening we spent very much as we had spent the preceding ones, and went to bed at an early hour, having an excursion to make on the morrow.

The next morning we made our way to the Iron Mountain Railway Depôt, where we were ushered into a special Pullman car, which became, as it were, our residence during our journey towards the south.

We "inaugurated" the trip with a bottle of St. Louis champagne; then a "hoot" and ringing of bells and "gone to Texas."

CHAPTER II.

Overflow of the Mississippi—Iron Mountain—Pilot Knob—Angling; Small Profits and Slow Returns—Water Snakes—The National Beverage—Train Transporters of the Mississippi—Chas. Dickens's Eden—Inchoate Cities—Wooden Houses with Mock Fronts—Poplar Bluff—Little Rock—Hot and Cold Springs of Arkansas—Texarkana—Cheapness of Telegraphic Communication—Cattle Yards of St. Louis—Cafés Chantants—Theatres—Parks—Churches—St. Louis Transfer Company—Daniel Boone.

MOST of the day, we ran along the Mississippi, and then turning inland, soon found ourselves in the midst of one of those wonderful floods which most of us have read of from our youth up, but which are very hard to realize until we have seen one. All the valleys and fields were covered with water; here and there one would see a chimney rising out of these apparent lakes, or a fence running down to their edge, or a farm-waggon with the seat just above the surface; sometimes an oak tree nearly submerged, while great logs and bushes and torn-up trees floated about everywhere. In some places the water precipitated itself down a valley or over some high ground, producing a temporary Niagara. This was one of the most extraordinary sights I had ever seen. The train passed along with the water on all sides of it; indeed, more like a "ship in the desert" than a mere train of cars, carrying matter-of-fact people on matter-of-fact errands.

The earth was washed away in many places, and the roofs of houses and loose planks were floating everywhere. We passed through De Soto, a place of about 750 inhabitants; Mineral Point, numbering about 600 souls; Biskmark, rejoicing in a population of 60; and at last arrived at the celebrated Iron Mountain.

This is one of the grandest natural curiosities of the world. It is a mamillary-formed mount —or, less technically, a mount presenting the appearance of the human breast—and is composed almost entirely of pure iron ores. It rises 230 feet above the surrounding country, and covers an area of 500 acres. Five miles distant from Iron Mountain, the conical shaped Pilot Knob rises 581 feet above the plain, covering an area of 360 feet. Like the former, it is almost entirely a "mountain" of iron, and is estimated to contain upwards of 14,000,000 tons of iron ore, which differs from that of Iron Mountain, being more compact, containing less silica, and breaking with a steel-like fracture.

Properly speaking, Iron Mountain is not a mountain, but, as I have said, a large oval hill. Mining excrescences appear everywhere on its surface. Besides this elevation, many of the surrounding chains are supposed to be rich in mineral deposits, especially iron ores.

The town of Iron Mountain, with its many chimneys and buildings, is like a miniature metropolis. Here are several large iron furnaces (producing the best charcoal iron), one steam flouring mill, one waggon factory, and two general stores. According to the census of 1870, it had a population of 2000. Here we saw several lines of freight-cars loaded with metal ready to be sent to market. We had dinner at Arcadia, a place a little farther on; after which we passed through magnificent forests, fertile fields, beautiful valleys, containing many well-cultivated farms, and through the pretty villages of Des Arc and Gadshill, and arrived at Piedmont about six o'clock.

Here we had a very good supper. This place is situated in a charming valley, enclosed by pretty hills, one of which we climbed, and were rewarded with a superb view for many miles around. On coming down, we expected to push on to Poplar Bluff, but the flood had so washed away the road that it was quite impossible to get farther for the moment. We therefore went to sleep in the car, expecting to wake up *en route*. On the contrary, we woke in exactly the same spot in which we had gone to sleep. We had for breakfast much the same as we had had for dinner the day before. This naturally diminished our admiration for the local cuisine. After breakfast they loaded a platform car with labourers, and my brother and one of the party, an engineer by profession, went with them to the place where the road was washed away. Mr. S. W., another of the party, and myself, took a walk along the track, dextrously trying to shoot the bull-frogs which were in possession of the water on both sides of the road.

In one place we saw a very lean man with a very lean horse, and a very heavy plough, right on the side of a very steep hill, covered with stumps and underbrush; and close to him, although it was in the middle of the day and in the spring of the year, there was a great bear of a man with a two-foot beard, perched on the root end of an enormous tree, which was half immersed in water; next to him was his wife, and all along the tree, his children, and the remainder of his household. All were engaged in the exercise of Isaac Walton's gentle art. They had succeeded, thus far, in catching three or four miserable "shiners," each about two or three inches long; no doubt they felt assured that they were serving themselves and their country to the best of their ability. As we went farther on we met three or four more of the same interesting kind of individuals, walking homeward along the track, with three or four little fishes, held together by means of a crooked end of switch passed through their gills. At last we came to a beautiful piece of clear water, which aroused in me an inclination to bathe. I asked one of the gentlemen of the party, who was somewhat of a naturalist, whether water-snakes were known so far north. He assured me there was no danger, and I was about to take my clothes off for a plunge, when I saw a little eel, as it seemed, at the place where I intended to enter. I called my companion's attention to it, and he told me it was very lucky I had seen it, as it was a moccasin, a charming specimen of the *Trigonocephalus Piscivorus*,—a species of "thanatophidia," extremely interesting in a general way, but less so to bathers. Afterwards, I found, on inquiry, that moccasins are to be seen in great quantities in all the waters of those parts; in the breeding season, ten or twenty may sometimes be seen piled up in heaps, some of the snakes being from two and a half to three feet in length.

We walked back to Piedmont, and as we were very warm, I made for what I took to be a lager beer saloon, seeing in front of it a great many barrels, one on the top of another. On entering, I saw men seated at a table with large glasses full of a yellow coloured liquor, which I took to be cider or white beer. I went up to the distributer of beverages, and asked him for a glass of lager. I was received with a stare and a grimace very like, dear reader, what I have described before.

Seeing this look upon his countenance, I smiled and said,—

"I suppose you have no lager; in that case, give me a glass of ale."

Still the same dull stare.

"Then give me some of the cider those people are drinking."

"Cider? Oh! that's whisky."

"What had you in those barrels?" I enquired.

"Whisky. We never drink anything but whisky here," he hastened to explain, in case I might have entertained any erroneous and derogatory impression to the contrary.

I asked him whether I could get a glass of ale anywhere in town. He answered,—

"Oh no, I don't think you could get any this side of St. Louis."

We went to the dry-goods store and general emporium of the place. I was surprised to find all sorts of commodities,—ready-made clothing, ready-made boots, different kinds of tea, perfumed soap, writing-paper, hosiery goods, etc., etc. I wanted some three cent stamps; I bought one, and gave in payment a five cent piece, and received no change. It was afterwards explained to me that they never gave change for five cent pieces, and that I could have had three stamps for ten cents, or five for fifteen cents; useful information for economical travellers.

About seven o'clock the train from St. Louis arrived; also our friends and the workmen, who had been making repairs. We got the latest newspapers, which was some satisfaction. One of the conductors had been very courageous in saving a man from drowning at the gap.

We had some fresh eggs at supper, and some fish—both luxuries in those parts—and we spent a very pleasant evening chatting.

At about nine o'clock Mr. Allen determined to change the route; in consequence of which, we turned back as far as Bismarck, of which place, as I got there at eleven o'clock and was in bed, I cannot venture a description. The next morning we arrived at the Mississippi river, which we crossed in a train transporter,— a vessel very suggestive of an enormous floating barn, having pigeon-holes on the top, and two or three chicken-pens in different parts of the boat. I was surprised to see a very good engraving of the Greek Slave in the steerman's room,—who, by the way, was a very clever fellow, and brought his huge ark to the docks with perfect ease, although the river at this point runs with a very rapid pace, and he had to turn the boat almost completely in the middle of the stream, so as to bring it in head first. The docks at this place are very large, and built for storage.

I saw here for the first time an American polecat. This creature looks very much like a young tiger.

After breakfast we took the train to a point on the river opposite to Cairo, which we reached by boat. This place is mentioned by Dickens as Eden. Commercially, it is rather important. There are two long lines of high stone-front buildings, and a large hotel, at which we had lunch. After lunch we went to visit the narrow gauge railroad which runs from this place to St. Louis. The cars are very prettily arranged, with two seats on one side and one on the other, and would no doubt accommodate a good many passengers. We then went to visit a large icehouse. The mode of taking in the ice was rather amusing. It was pushed down from the boats in wooden runners, which carried the blocks nearly two hundred yards, the descent being sometimes rapid and sometimes slow. In this way it passed all round the house, to the foot of another enclosed plain, where a darkey was waiting with a long rope furnished with iron hooks; he put five or six large blocks on the elevated plain and fastened the hooks to the last piece—that is, the piece nearest the bottom; then placing himself triumphantly on the topmost block of the pile, he pulled a cord which was suspended alongside of the elevated plain, and was immediately hauled up into the icehouse, some sixty feet above him. We then returned to the steamer. I noticed a very French look about the place; two or three of the people on board had French hats on, and the servants at the hotel had a foreign air; and the waitresses were dressed in good enough taste to be French.

We returned to the train the same way

we had come, and then left for Poplar Bluff. The country on this line appeared to be peculiarly fertile. One very remarkable feature in this region is the perfect regularity with which all the future towns are laid out, —long broad streets, with two or three large buildings, and a great many smaller ones in wood. There is also a very peculiar custom here in the way wooden structures are built, and that is, to run up a mock front two or three stories high, with mock windows and covered with enormous signs, while as a general rule the real building runs far back along the ground, but is seldom more than eight or nine feet high. This does not look so badly where in the town there are a great many similar houses side by side; but when, as often happens, they build a house of this kind right in the middle of the woods, as I saw one at Texarcana, the effect is strikingly grotesque.

One of the towns we passed through was really quite remarkable in this respect; and unless we had known this habit of the people, we should have been led from our favourable point of view, to take that incipient town for a flourishing city.

We arrived at Poplar Bluff at half-past six o'clock. Here we had a very good dinner. A quack doctor at this place, with the "enterprise" inseparable from his tribe, has covered the barns, cattle-pens, and broad fences with the kindest possible invitations to you to buy a box of his pills.

The wife of the hotel keeper was one of the most perfect women I ever saw—a very Venus of Milo in form and face and grace. I could have wished to knock one of her arms off, and place her on a pedestal, and thus give our New York Museum something with which to rival the Louvre. I spilled a lot of hot coffee over my clothes admiring her, and was with difficulty torn away from the house.

We then went to look at the cattle-yards. These are made in enormous squares like a city, the fences being nine or ten feet high, and having a strong board running flatly along the upper edge, so that one could walk around the cattle-yard on this elevated sidewalk without being annoyed by the somewhat iritable occupants of the enclosures below. Most of the cattle are small, but the breed is said to be very fine. The railway brings up great train-loads of them, and they are fed at different stopping places.

There I saw for the first time a Texas saddle. This saddle was made of a piece of bone covered with strong leather. The bone seemed to be from the back of some animal. The saddle comes high up in front, where the lasso is fastened; it is said to be hard to ride on at first, but becomes by frequent practice easy as a rocking-chair. As much, perhaps, may be safely predicated of any other saddle; the Texas model is certainly cumbrous.

Poplar Bluff is in Butler County, Mo., and contains a population of about 850. It is the junction of the branch line to Cairo. We left it at about a quarter past eight o'clock, and at about ten we had left Missouri and entered Arkansas.

The next morning we awoke in an extremely beautiful country of the highest natural fertility, and well cultivated.

Little Rock, the capital of Arkansas, situated on the south bank of the Arkansas river, 300 miles from its mouth, on the first bed of rocks bounding the alluvial valley of the Mississippi, sits gracefully upon one of the most beautiful curves of the river, and is reached by a very fine bridge at Baring Caves, directly opposite.

I do not think a more beautiful site for a capital could be chosen. One gentleman to whom I afterwards spoke about it, said that he had lived many years in France, and for the last three years at Little Rock, and that he much preferred the latter place for the pleasure of living there.

The town is wonderfully well built, and contains a very fine City Hall, the Governor's house and United States arsenal; the two former being in white marble, and fine specimens of Greek architecture.

The buildings of the town are very solid, and at the same time pretty and graceful, a certain sandstone, brick, and iron being the principal materials used. The stores are numerous and very fine; one, the Pharmacy, is the handsomest I have ever seen. All the store windows have French plate glass panes. We drove up to the cemetery, which is very pretty, and kept in perfect order. We then went to the United States arsenal, which is in the centre of a "block" of ground, the drilling park and gardens occupying much of the space. The pieces of artillery placed in different parts of the depôt, and at the office of the Iron Mountain Railway, are very fine. Here, near the depôt, is the scene of many gallant actions during the War of the Rebellion, and also of several fierce political party fights since. Little Rock was captured by the Union Major-General Steele, with an army of 12,000 men and 40 guns, after a stubborn resistance, at seven p.m., Aug. 26th, 1863; the Union men entering the town, sabre in hand, on the heels of the flying enemy.

The population of Little Rock is estimated at about 13,000, and is certainly increasing. Arkansas being a portion of the Louisiana purchase, the territory ceded to the United States by France in 1803 has, like Louisiana, some decidedly French traits, having been settled by the French at Arkansas Post in 1865.

Fifty-three miles from Little Rock are the Hot Springs of Arkansas, a celebrated resort for invalids. These springs are said to be an almost certain cure for rheumatism and some other disorders. Fifty springs, varying in temperature from $110°$ to $150°$ Fahrenheit, break out from the side of a mountain and flow into a creek which empties itself into the Wachita river, six miles distant. There are also chalybeate springs and sulphur springs in the same county, and these too are much frequented.

At Little Rock I met an old Paris acquaintance, whom I had last seen driving to the Khedive Museum at Cairo, Egypt, and whom I now encountered in this out-of-the-way place after the lapse of three years.

After leaving this pleasant town, the country was at first extremely beautiful, and then took an appearance of almost savage wildness. Cleaving our way through the woods, a wilderness of green branches, every once in a while we would come to cultivated fields, and then plunge again into the depths of apparently interminable forests.

We arrived at Texarcana at half-past seven o'clock, and dined. We then visited some cattle-pens larger than any we had yet seen.

This place is situated on the boundary line between Arkansas and Texas, and will be the northern terminus of the International and great National Railway of Texas. This town is a most wonderful growth; but a few years ago, there was not a house to mark its existence, and now it covers a very considerable tract of ground. The main street is very broad and has two public wells at each end of it, one being in Arkansas and the other in Texas. The shops are large, and appear well filled; and the people are not by any means so savage-looking as one might have expected to find them.

After dinner I sent a telegram to New York, at a cost of two dollars. It is only in an out-of-the-way place like this that you appreciate the wonders of electricity, and particularly of electricity at that price.

Just think of being in the main street of Texarcana, Texas, and sending a message to your mother in Fifth Avenue, New York in an hour for two dollars!

We left on our return journey at about ten o'clock that night. We spent a very pleasant evening; Mr. Allen told us of one of his ancestors who, although a clergyman, was an ardent revolutionist, and wielded a deadly weapon on many battle-fields as he did the Holy Scriptures from the pulpit, with all his heart and soul. Altogether, the evening was very charming, and we all went to bed content and well pleased with our trip.

We left Little Rock the next morning, and towards evening we arrived at Minturn, where most probably the inhabitants had not expected us so soon, otherwise they would have come out to meet us with due pomp and ceremony; as it was, we saw only two or three lazy-looking fellows, who scanned us with an insolent gaze. At the next station we had an excellent dinner, and got to sleep before arriving at Poplar Bluff. We woke up next morning within twenty miles of St. Louis, where we arrived about nine o'clock, very much pleased with our travels.

That afternoon we went to see the enormous cattle-yards of St. Louis, which are much larger and better arranged than any we had yet seen,—quite a bovine metropolis.

There is a very fine hotel here that they drove us to, very like a large club-house.

In the evening we had a faultless dinner, very pleasant and cheerful, and at which more than one bottle of native champagne was opened.

One of the principal stockholders of the St. Louis Bridge was present; he told us that though nearly every Railroad Company had morally accepted the argreement to use the bridge under certain conditions, yet, when the bridge was once built, they had thought fit to make objections,—in other words, to repudiate the agreement. What a pity it is that the citizens of so great a nation should disgrace themselves by descending to the practice of such mean prevarication.

The morning following, I took all my companions of the trip to the railway station, and saw them off on their several destinations.

I returned to the hotel, and having nothing to do, I thought I would explore one of the *cafés chantants*.

These places of popular amusement are built within an open balcony. On this the band is seated, and plays until there is a sufficient audience collected, when they pass down the middle of the theatre, take their seats, and the performance begins. The theatre I visited the first evening was prettily arranged, the predominant colour being blue; of the same colour also were the chairs of the boxes and reserved seats. The decorations generally were very rich. I was particularly struck by the plaster of Paris work round the first gallery, which consisted of bas-reliefs, busts, etc., connected with garlands. The dome also was very graceful, painted with small but well-executed figures of Euterpe, Melpomene, Thalia, and Clio. The performance began with a translation of a small German farce for three actors, which I had never seen before out of Germany. The parts were well taken, and it was altogether very well rendered. We then had a pretty little song from a charming little songstress, feats by two Japanese gymnasts, and other Variety entertainments. The theatre was out at half-past ten o'clock. What a pity that all theatres do not take the habit of beginning early and finishing early, thus permitting of so many persons attending who would otherwise be unable to do so.

The following day I spent in exploring the

upper part of the town. The appearance of age is carried out in everything. Whether from the smoke or from the peculiar style of architecture, even the most modern houses have an old, staid, respectable look.

They build what is known as the Philadelphia entrance, a good deal, which may have something to do with it.

All the public buildings, such as schools, churches, theatres, and banks, are well built, and some of the architecture is really surprisingly fine. The streets are extremely well laid out, and generally kept in good order. There is a great number of street cars running in all directions; the fare is seven cents, or five tickets for twenty-five cents,—which arrangement is rather awkward, unless you are an inhabitant of the town; still, the companies are very accommodating, and receive each other's tickets.

Having noticed a theatre sign in German characters, with the heading "Apollo Oper Haus" and "Der Freischütz," printed in large letters, I requested the company of Mr. W., one of the gentlemen of our party who was still staying at St. Louis. He accepted, and we took the street-car to the theatre, which is situated some distance from the main part of the city. It is a spacious building, surrounded by a garden, such as one sees in Germany. Some people were finishing their dinner as we came in, and dishes of *sauer kraut*, sausages and ham, with large glasses of beer, were on the tables. The waiters and guests all spoke German, and when I asked the price of admission, I was told a half "thaler" apiece, instead of fifty cents each.

The orchestra was very good, and played selections from Strauss and Yung'l for some time, before the acting began. One of the singers was ill, so, instead of "Der Freischutz," we had a mythological fairy play. The scenery was extremely good, and the actors very funny.

Two days afterwards I heard "Der Freischutz," which was very well done.

The day after, I went to the United States Garrison, also out to one of the large suburbs. Nearly all the environs of St. Louis are connected with it by street cars. They drive large Kentucky mules, or strong horses—sometimes three or four,—and go at a fine pace. During the summer weather they have open cars with cross-seats; the cars are covered with light awnings; the ride is thus rendered very cool and pleasant.

On this road there is a fine Catholic monastery built on a terrace, which rises about twenty feet above the road, with stone steps converging at the top, which produces a very monumental effect. Over the door is a very beautiful figure of the Madonna. In the afternoon I went to Lafayette Park, situated on one of the hills of the city, of which and the surrounding country you have here a very fine view. In the park there is a very extraordinary statue of Washington, representing him at a more advanced age than do most of his statues; also making him appear thinner and slighter, and bringing out the features with more force and distinctness; indeed, giving him somewhat of the exactness of feature which we see in Houdon's statue of Voltaire. There is also a statue of Benton represented in the act of saying, "I tell you there is an India in the West."

This park is most charmingly arranged, and although covering but a small space of ground, appears much larger than it really is, to those within it.

Intricate walks with high box hedges, cunning little grottoes with glass of various colours inlaid in the stone, pretty fountains and ponds stocked with fish; there were also ducks, geese, and a stork, which seemed quite as much at home on the top of the grottoes as it would have been on a chimney in Strasburg; indeed, more so, as the Prussians are not likely to dish it up. The wall of the park is very remarkable, being made in simulation of the old Anglian wall, built of stone and brick, and so constructed that at unequal distances there are open spaces.

I returned to the hotel another way, had a very pleasant dinner with Mr. W——, and then went to the principal theatre of the city. The style of the interior of this theatre is very peculiar, the ornamentation being in that hard polished stone which was used in the Roman theatres. The Stadt theatre at Berlin is decorated in the same manner; indeed, this theatre reminded me somewhat of the former, there being very little of painted decoration, and that little very good. The art of fresco painting seems to be carried to a high point in this city. Over the stage is a medallion of Washington, and there are three other medallions round the ceiling, representing the heads of Booth, Irving, and Poe. The play was a light comedy, and was very well performed; the scenery, too, was excellent.

I went to the grounds where the St. Louis fair is held; the space is very large, and has in it "bosquets," grottoes, small temples, and frescoed cupolas, and large buildings for the fair; also an enclosed racecourse,—all very prettily and artistically arranged. I took a long ride into the country in this direction. In the car there was quite a delegation from Chicago, and as their base-ball club had just been beaten by the St. Louians, they took a savage delight in running down the city, and everything connected with it.

On the subsequent day I visited Hyde Park, only lately established. It is most beautifully arranged, the ground here being very undulating, and admitting of much adornment. One side being much deeper than the other, they have here formed a glen; at the top of the park there is a quasi-natural lake, with lilies and other water plants in great abundance; the water bubbles out of the earth as from a natural spring, and is surrounded by graceful shade trees, all of them, however, of small growth, so as not to diminish the lake (or pond) by comparison. From the pond, the water pours downwards in a pretty stream, and rushes to another pond, where it sinks in a miniature whirlpool. All along the stream there are pretty walks paved with asphalt. The trees in this park are very old and fine. In the upper part of the park there is a large asylum for the deaf and dumb,—a very beautiful building, and well calculated for the purpose to which it is dedicated. I saw two or three of the inmates in the grounds.

Seeing an enormous Corinthian pillar in the distance, I directed my steps towards it; I was led to a considerable distance out of the city. The walk was very pleasant; I saw two or three lakelets with residences near them, and passed a large brick-making factory, where I suppose they must have turned out many thousands of bricks *per diem*, of all shapes and colours. I now arrived at the Corinthian pillar, and found that it marks the site of the city water-works. It is a perfect Corinthian column, over 200 feet high.

I returned to the hotel by another way, passing through a thickly populated quarter of the town, where the lower parts of the houses are occupied by third or fourth class stores, with large wooden trays run out on the pavement, containing cheap laces, pocket-books, finery, and other things innumerable. Long cords from the store fronts were attached to the edge of the awnings, and from these were suspended calicoes, cloths, ladies' jackets, shirts, scarfs, etc. There were boot-shops with a gigantic boot as a sign, and any quantity of foot protectors pendant, from the ancient Blucher down to the most modern pump; then a hat-store, with the upper story built in the shape of a hat, with windows in it through which you could see an old broken looking-glass and the head of a bedstead, the whole being surmounted by an immensely tall flagstaff. Every once in a while you came across a small wooden building with some such sign as the following placed over the door, "Ah Whang and Ah Ching—Washing taken in," and inside you might see two or three Chinamen ironing, blowing, the while, in an invisible spray from their mouths the starch water necessary to the operation—a very effective but not quite unexceptionable method of "getting up" fine linen—and their long pigtails slowly and solemnly swinging to and fro with every motion of their bodies. I also saw some choice representatives of the celestial people in the streets and in the market. These were the first Chinamen dressed in their national costume that I had seen in America.

After dinner I visited a theatre somewhat similar to the Alhambra in London; it was a large building, devoted to gymnastic and comic performances.

The following day being Sunday, I visited

two of the churches; and I have seldom seen such prettily decorated buildings, with such fine stained glass, or heard sacred music so well conducted in a Protestant church.

I spent two or three days more at St. Louis, but saw nothing more that I think worth describing. I then left for Springfield. I must, however, mention the St. Louis Transfer Company. This Company owns all the omnibuses, and has a monopoly of the hotel " arrivals." Its vehicles are enormous, and contain from twenty-four to twenty-six persons inside, and two or three next the driver, and any amount of baggage. This conveyance leaves the Lindell Hotel about an hour before the departure of each train, and then calls at all the other hotels, then at the railway offices, where all the baggage is taken down and chequed and put up again, and then, when everybody's patience has become as sensitive to further pressure as the proverbial camel's back, they mercifully drive to the station. This custom reminds one strongly of the *Omnibus de la Gare* in a French provincial town.

As we drove across the bridge, and left St. Louis enveloped in fog, with the sunlight breaking through here and there, I really felt as though I were leaving an old friend.

Gazing on this city, the scene of an activity the most intense, the centre of wealth already enormous and rapidly increasing, all that I had read of the strange adventures, the romantic exploits, of the early pioneers of Western civilization—the men of little more than half a century ago, for Daniel Boone died in 1820—seemed to fade into the region of dreamland. It is difficult to realize, under the smoky canopy of a hundred factory chimneys, the historical fact that it was close to this spot Daniel Boone sought, and found for awhile, the solitude of the wilderness he loved so much.

Of this celebrated pioneer, thus recalled to my mind, and who is perhaps best known to the European reader by the beautiful lines in the eighth canto of Byron's "Don Juan," a brief account may not be unwelcome here.*

Daniel Boone is the principal figure in that group of daring adventurers, to whom we owe it that the civilization of the far West is not only now beginning. Until his time all beyond the Alleghanies was *terra incognita* to the settlers. One or two bold spirits had

---

* As "Don Juan" is, very properly, a sealed book to the

followed the chase across that rocky barrier, and brought back alluring accounts of the fertility of the soil and the abundance of

youth of a moral generation, and I should be sorry to give an excuse to the inexperienced for consulting that pernicious work, I have extracted the lines referred to:—

LXI.

Of all men, saving Sylla the manslayer,
    Who passes for in life and death most lucky ;
Of the great names which in our faces stare,
    The General Boone, backwoodsman of Kentucky,
Was happiest amongst mortals anywhere :
    For killing nothing but a bear or buck, he
Enjoy'd the lonely, vigorous, harmless days
    Of his old age in wilds of deepest maze.

LXII.

Crime came not near him—she is not the child
    Of solitude ; Health shrank not from him—for
Her home is in the rarely trodden wild,
    Where if men seek her not, and death be more
Their choice than life, forgive them, as beguiled
    By habit to what their own hearts abhor—
In cities caged. The present case in point I
Cite is, that Boone lived hunting up to ninety ;

LXIII.

And what's still stranger, left behind a name
    For which men vainly decimate the throng,
Not only famous, but of that *good* fame
    Without which glory's but a tavern song—

game; but the dread of perfect isolation among hostile tribes of savages had heretofore arrested the advance of the settlers, and

    Simple, serene, the antipodes of shame
        Which hate nor envy ne'er could tinge with wrong :
    An active hermit, even in age the child
        Of nature, or the Man of Ross run wild.

LXIV.

'Tis true he shrank from men even of his nation :
    When they built up into his darling trees,
He moved some hundred miles off for a station
    Where there were fewer houses, and more ease.
The inconvenience of civilization
    Is, that you neither can be pleased nor please ;
But where he met the individual man,
    He show'd himself as kind as mortal can.

LXV.

He was not all alone ; around him grew
    A sylvan tribe of children of the chase,
Whose young unwakened world was ever new :
    Nor sword nor sorrow yet had left a trace
On her unwrinkled brow, nor could you view
    A frown on nature's or on human face ;
The free-born forest found and kept them free,
    And fresh as is a torrent or a tree.

LXVI.

And tall, and strong, and swift of foot were they,
    Beyond the dwarfing city's pale abortions,
Because their thoughts had never been the prey
    Of care or gain : the green woods were their portions,

Daniel Boone was the only sufficient leader for the few who were willing at all hazards to push westward.

Born on the banks of the Delaware in 1734, and accustomed from his boyhood to the hardships and the *joys* of the wilderness—the *gaudia certaminis* with Nature and savages—Daniel Boone's education was limited to the arts of reading and writing. But he was endowed in a pre-eminent degree with the physical, moral, and intellectual qualities indispensable to the task to which he believed himself providentially called; he speaks of himself as " an instrument ordained to settle

---

No sinking spirits told them they grew grey;
   No fashion made them apes of her distortions:
Simple they were, not savage; and their rifles,
   Though very true, were not yet used for trifles.

LXVII.

Motion was in their days, rest in their slumbers,
   And cheerfulness the handmaid of their toil;
Nor yet too many nor too few their numbers;
   Corruption could not make their hearts her soil:
The lust which stings, the splendour which encumbers,
   With the free foresters divide no spoil:
Serene, not sullen, were the solitudes
   Of this unsighing people of the woods.

LXVIII.

So much for Nature; by way of variety,
   Now back to thy great joys, Civilization!

the wilderness." He appears, indeed, to have united and carried to the highest point the conflicting virtues of civilized and savage life. Of almost feminine delicacy in his tastes and habits, no Indian chief could compare with him in patient endurance of hardship, in subtlety of design or skill in execution, whether as a hunter or a warrior; of inflexible honesty both in word and deed, he proved himself an overmatch for all the treachery by which he was surrounded; and when in the War of Independence the British Government called to its aid the tomahawk and the scalping-knife, it was chiefly through the efforts of Boone that the settlers escaped extirpation. Twice taken prisoner by his ferocious enemies, he was formally adopted into the tribe of the Shawnees, and so highly did his captors value their acquisition that they refused £500 offered for his ransom by the Governor of Detroit. Despite, however, all their precautions, Boone effected his escape just in time to save his little garrison at Boonesborough from the destruction that threatened it from the Shawnees.

In the long struggle with the Indians Boone lost two of his sons, and much of his property. But when the war was over, the colony secure, and crowds of settlers were pouring into

Kentucky, the land surveyors and the lawyers discovered that Boone had no legal title to his farm. Had Boone been naturally of a less peaceable disposition, he might perhaps have responded to the demand to show his title-deeds by pointing significantly to his rifle; he had not settled the territory for lawyers alone.* Boone, however, hating alike violence and chicanery, quietly retired from his farm. This, it seems, was the second time he had been ousted on the same pretext from his hard-won domains.

He removed to Upper Louisiana, where his reputation had preceded him, and the Spanish authorities made him liberal grants of land for himself and his followers. Here he followed hunting as a business, to pay off his debts in Kentucky; and having accomplished this, he might have hoped to pass the rest of his life in peace. But when Louisiana was ceded to the United States, it was found that Boone's detestation of lawyers and their parchments—perhaps, indeed, his incessant occupation—had again prevented him from obtaining

---

* Earl Warrenne being required by the Commissioners of Edward I. to show his titles, drew his sword, and subjoined that William the Bastard had not conquered the kingdom for himself alone.

a proper registration of his title, and for the third time his lands were confiscated. He was then seventy-four years old. If the making for oneself a position in the world is the grand test of ability and respectability, Boone had signally and disgracefully failed. Happily, Congress did not take this view of the matter, but eventually conferred on him a grant of 850 acres of land. Boone was then seventy-nine years old. On the banks of the Missouri, far, as he loved to be, " from the busy hum of men," he passed the remainder of his days in the most enviable calm, in pursuits the most congenial to his simple tastes.

It is a striking proof of the lofty predominance of Boone's character, that although he had outlived most of the generation that had witnessed his exploits, and could alone have appreciated the difficulties of settling Kentucky; though his name was associated with no great military achievements, no political question, no religious sect, and he had been for years lost to public view in "wilds of deepest maze," public honours were awarded to him at his death, September 26th, 1820.

In 1845 the remains of the great pioneer were removed from Missouri to the capital of Kentucky. It would have been more in unison with the tenor of his life to leave them undisturbed. Boone had himself marked out with particular care the spot where he desired to be buried. Resurrectionists have no sentiment. Embalmed in the verse of Byron, the memory of Daniel Boone will probably outlast the Kentuckian monument, and, very certainly, the rather dull biographies from which I have collected these incidents of his life.

As the train went slowly off, I looking out of the window into the dusky evening, seeing the smoke from the many steamers on the river and from the many factories in the city, it seemed to me that they mingled together, rising to one gigantic column, to take the semblance of the pioneer, his arms crossed on the muzzle of his gun, protecting the great metropolis. Thus were my last thoughts of St. Louis associated with Daniel Boone.

CHAPTER III.

Springfield — Lincoln's Monument — Chicago — A Temperance Town — Anecdote of Daniel Boone — Growth and Commercial Importance of Chicago — Burlington — A Railway Critic — Omaha — Very Low Church — Coloured Church — The Black Hills Expedition.

AGAIN I am on the iron-road, passing through a country of gold. I speak not of the ore, but of the fields of brilliant gold.

I made the acquaintance in the omnibus of a gentleman from the Eastern States, who showed me a melancholy trifle—a piece of the dress of Laura Keene, with Lincoln's blood upon it. As will be remembered, she had held his head after he had been shot.

We had a delicious dinner on board the train, in the *restaurant* car, as well served and with as good a bottle of champagne as we could desire; indeed, we even had our *café noir* and *petit verre* afterwards. We then went to the smoking-car and enjoyed our cigars. The smoking-cars in the West are much more luxurious than those in the Eastern States; each smoker has a separate cushioned seat to himself.

We arrived at Springfield, the capital of Illinois, about six o'clock, and repaired to the Leland House, which is a fine old building of its kind, with low ceilings and old-fashioned fireplaces.

We walked through the town by gaslight, and thought it extremely picturesque. The City Hall, the Court House, and Springfield Block are very fine buildings.

The residences are built in gardens, along fine broad streets, bordered with full-grown trees, like the Paris boulevards.

Lincoln passed the latter part of his life at this place, and we passed his home on our way back to town, where we had a very comfortable supper, accompanied by a bottle of Munn's "extra dry."

After breakfast the following day, I took the street cars to the Lincoln monument. At the time of Lincoln's death it was the intention to bury him in a vault in the new State House grounds, but Mrs. Lincoln objected, desiring that he should be interred at Oakridge Cemetery. In compliance with her wish the body was placed in the public receiving vault of the cemetery. Ropes were extended in front of it, and a guard of soldiers kept there day and night for over two weeks, out of respect to the deceased. In 1869 the present monument was commenced. It was to be executed by Richards of Springfield, at a cost of $171,500. The monument is in granite, the statue is of bronze. The sarcophagus is also of granite. The basement is filled with objects associated with his life, and on the walls are letters of condolence from various Societies of different nations. There is also a curious piece of stone which is said to have been taken from the wall of Servius Tullius, and sent to the President by some Roman citizens, after his re-election, in order to show their appreciation of his character, and also as a symbol of the parallel between his life and that of Servius Tullius. I give a translation of the inscription:—

"To Abraham Lincoln, President for the second time of the American Republic, Citizens of Rome present this stone from the wall of Servius Tullius, by which the memory of each of those brave assertors of liberty may be associated. Anno Dom. 1865.

They were both of plebeian origin; both did their utmost to elevate the condition of the masses; both were assassinated by those with whom they were contending, and whom they were governing, and both were succeeded by a deplorable state of affairs.

I got to the station just in time to take the

train. I here heard of the madness of Mrs. Lincoln. The coincidence seemed strange, just having quitted her husband's grave, and my mind still pondering on him and his life.

From Springfield to Chicago the scenery is somewhat flat, with far distant horizons, but the fertility is something wonderful. A noticeable feature of the country are the farm-houses, which look like little square boxes on a large whist-table,—an endless expanse, with hardly any trees to break the monotony. At half-past six o'clock we arrived at Chicago.

Wonder of wonders! a second Florence, with a magnificent lake instead of the muddy Arno. I was quite dazzled, what with the light and the high buildings. I almost thought that by some extraordinary accident instead of taking a steam car I had got into a pneumatic tube, and been shot through the earth into the very heart of Paris. We stopped before a magnificent building, which might have been a palace or a gorgeous Hotel de Ville, but which was nothing more than an ordinary hotel. The exterior decorations of this building are perhaps finer than the internal adornments, although the dining room is 250 feet long by 80 feet broad, and the ceiling beautifully frescoed. After dinner we went to the Adelphi theatre. This is a large stone building; the external ornamentation is very chaste, and the auditorium excellently arranged, both for seeing and hearing. The walls are very prettily decorated; on the curtain is an allegorical picture of the burning of Chicago: the United States supporting her daughter; Faith and Hope holding their arms out to the sufferer; a beautiful vase, filled with fruit, with two or three cherubs sitting on its edges, is arriving on a railway truck, while other cherubs are lugged in, distributing the contents of another vase already on the scene. The conception is very good, and very well carried out. The play was a translation of the *Courrier de Lyons*, and was very exactly rendered and well performed.

The next morning I went to visit the new park. This is going to be an extremely fine drive and promenade, although the country being very flat renders the formation of a park extremely difficult. The boulevards are very fine, consisting of a very broad road bordered with trees; in the middle of the road, flower-beds are kept in good order.

They have what are called trotting days; that is, days when trotting is allowed; the scene is then very cheerful and animated.

Afterwards we went to an hotel situated at

the border of the lake; there we had a refreshing glass of lager-beer, and a beautiful view of the lake. In the evening I went to M'Vicar's theatre. This is one of the most charming buildings. The auditorium forms an enormous semicircle; the large mirrors on each side of the stage, set in plaster of Paris frames, slightly gilded, reflect the whole audience. The play was Schiller's " Robbers," rendered by Mr. Pope, an American actor. In some places he was rather boisterous; but apart from his peculiarities he was certainly very fine in that magnificent scene of the last act, and, altogether, the leading character of the play has rarely been better taken.

We then went to the " Toledo Bier Hall," which had just received a grand orchestrion about thirty feet high by twenty broad, and very perfect in arrangement.

We were here regaled with songs of all nations; also with marches, overtures, fine operas, and some of Strauss's waltzes and Offenbach's quadrilles. This place is always full, as the beer is very good, and costs only five cents a glass. It is the particular resort of the Germans.

The following day we drove to Evanston in a buggy. Evanston is beautifully situated on the shore of Lake Michigan, twelve miles north of Chicago. Being within easy distance from the city, it is a favourite place of residence, the more so on account of its great educational advantages, being the seat of the North Western Female College, the North Western University, and the "Garrett Biblical Institute." Here, also, is the Illinois State Ladies' Home and the Greenleaf Public Library. This was the first time I had ever been in a temperance town; not a drop of liquor is to be had in the whole place, except from the druggist on pretence of sickness. The druggist refuses payment.

Here, I was introduced to a charming Massachusetts family, who had all the kind and pleasing manners of the Bostonians.

I spent the next day in visiting the objects of interest in the city: the canal, the drawbridges, the tunnel, store-houses, railroad terminus, etc.; and in the evening I crossed the river to what is called the Academy of Music, but which is really a charming *bijou* theatre. The orchestra seats are real *fauteuils*, quite separate from each other, and movable. Two knights in armour, holding torches, lighted the scene, and when the other gas was low, produced a very striking effect. The play was founded on an incident in the life of Daniel Boone, the Kentucky pioneer; and the picture of early Western life was very effective. As an illustration of the incidents of that life, the following anecdote, said to have been taken down from the lips of Boone himself, may be interesting. It is thus given by Abbott :—

"On one occasion, four Indians suddenly appeared before his cabin and took him prisoner. Though the delicacy of Boone's organization was such that he could not himself relish tobacco in any form, he still raised some for his friends and neighbours, and for what was then deemed the essential rites of hospitality. As a shelter for curing the tobacco, he had built an enclosure of rails a dozen feet in height, and covered with canes and grasses. Stalks of tobacco are generally split and strung on sticks about four feet in length. The ends of these are placed on poles ranged across the tobacco house, and in tiers one above another, to the roof. Boone had fixed his temporary shelter, so as to have three tiers. He had covered the lower tier, and the tobacco had become dry, when he entered the shelter for the purpose of removing the sticks to the upper tiers, preparatory to gathering the remainder of the crop. He had hoisted up the sticks from the lower to the second tier, and was standing on the poles which supported it, while raising the sticks to the upper tier, when the four stout Indians entered the door and called him by name.

"'Now, Boone, we got you. You no get away more. We carry you off to Chillicothe this time. You no cheat us any more.'

"Boone looked down upon their upturned faces, saw their loaded guns pointed at his breast, and recognising some of his old friends, the Shawnees, who had made him prisoner near the Blue Lick in 1778, coolly and pleasantly responded :—

"'Ah, old friends! glad to see you.'

"Perceiving that they manifested impatience to have him come down, he told them he was quite willing to go with them, and only begged that they would wait where they were, and watch him closely until he could finish removing the tobacco. With their guns in their hands they stood at the door of the shed, grouped closely together, so as to render his escape apparently impossible. In the meantime, Boone carefully gathered his arms full of the long, dry tobacco leaves, filled with pungent dust, which was as blinding and stifling as the most powerful snuff; and then, with a leap from his station, twelve feet high, came directly upon their heads, filling their eyes and nostrils, and so bewildering and disabling them for the moment, that they lost all self-possession and self-control.

"Boone, agile as a deer, darted out of the door, and in a moment was in his bullet-proof log-hut, which to him was an impregnable citadel. Loop-holes guarded every approach. The Indians could not show themselves without exposure to certain death. They were too well acquainted with the unerring aim of Boone's rifle to venture within its range. Keeping the log-hut between them and their redoubtable foe, they fled into the wilderness."

Colonel Boone related this adventure with great glee, the historian of his life tells us, imitating the gestures of the bewildered Indians. He said, notwithstanding his narrow escape, he could not resist the temptation, as he reached the door of his cabin, to look round in order to see the effect of his achievement. The Indians, coughing and sneezing, and blinded and almost suffocated with the tobacco dust, were throwing out their arms, and groping about in all directions, cursing him for a rogue and calling themselves fools.

Chicago is planted in a commanding situation, on the south-western shore of Lake Michigan, at the mouth of the Chicago river. The name is of Indian origin, and is first mentioned by Perrot, a Frenchman, by whom this section of country was visited in 1671. In 1803 a stockade fort was here erected by the United States Government, near the mouth of the river, and named Fort Dearborn. When the war with Great Britain broke out in 1812, the Government, apprehensive that a post among the Indians, so far from the frontiers could not be successfully maintained, ordered the commander to abandon it. The Indians destroyed the fort, which however was rebuilt in 1816.

The first settlement of Chicago, as is well known, took place in 1831, previous to which time it was a mere frontier post; in 1832 it contained about a dozen families, besides the officers and soldiers in Dearborn. The town was organized by the election of a board of trustees, August 10th, 1833, forty-three years ago, the total number of voters being just twenty-eight, one-fourth of whom are said to be now living in the city. According to the census of 1870, thirty-seven years from the date of the organization of the town, the population of Chicago was very nearly 300,000 souls.

On the 26th September, in the year which witnessed the election above named, a treaty for the cession of all their lands was made with the Patowatomies, 7,000 of the tribe being present, after which they removed west of the Mississippi. The first charter of the city was passed by the legislature, March 4th, 1837.

This city, perhaps the most remarkable in the world for its rapid growth, is built upon a plain sufficiently elevated to prevent inundation. The site appears to the eye a perfectly flat prairie; the level of the engineer, however, shows that the height of the ground, within the limits of the city, varies from five to twenty-four feet above the lake. Within a recent period, the elevation of the principal streets, and the buildings, has been raised from four to ten feet, the object of this costly and gigantic undertaking being to admit of a thorough system of draining.

The Chicago river and its branches, which unite about three-quarters of a mile from the lake, separate the city into three divisions, which are connected by bridges, placed upon a turntable or pivot, so that little, if any, inconvenience is experienced in passing from one part of the city to another. The main stream, flowing directly west, is about 100 yards wide, and forms one of the best harbours on the lakes. Vessels ascend the river and its branches a distance of four miles from its mouth, thus affording nearly eighteen miles of wharfage.

The Illinois and Michigan canal, completed in 1848, connects the Chicago and Illinois rivers, thus affording communication between the lakes and the Mississippi to the coal-fields of Illinois, and to the vast quarries of so-called Athens marble, regarded as the finest building material in the country. It is found on the banks of the canal about twenty miles from Chicago; is easily worked when first quarried, like the Caen stone, and, like it, becomes exceedingly hard when exposed.

In February 1852 there were forty-seven miles of railway completed and centring in Chicago. To-day it is the western terminus of eleven distinct lines of railroad, which intersect the country in every direction, and the number of the miles of each route is counted by the thousand.

It is undoubtedly the commercial capital of the north-west, notwithstanding that St

Louis exceeds it in point of population, which fact has indeed formed the text of several miles of local editorials, devoted on the one hand to crippling the force of the stubborn figures, and even, in some instances, to arguing them entirely out of existence; while those manufactured at St. Louis stoutly maintain the full advantage and effect of the figures of the census, and usually end in giving vent to a savage triumph over a fallen foe.

The Grand Pacific Hotel in Jackson, Quiney, Clark, and La Salle streets, and opposite the Government Square, represents the most liberal investment in land, buildings, finish and furnishing ever made for an enterprise of its kind, having cost, it is estimated, over 3,200,000 dollars.

Since 1854, this city has been the largest primary grain depôt in the world,—that is, a larger amount of grain is collected there directly from the producers than at any other point.

The tonnage of the great chain of lakes, which cover an area of nearly 100,000 square miles, is something enormous, and it is by no means comprehensively stated when expressed in figures.

From Chicago I went direct to Omaha, passing through Illinois and the populous state of Iowa. Much of the ride is very charming. In many places we passed through vine countries. The town of Burlington, Iowa, is beautifully situated, and seems a thriving place.

Burlington is an important railway centre, and is the county seat of Des Moins County. It is situated on the west bank of the Mississippi river, at the mouth of Hawkeye Creek, 255 miles above St. Louis, and 791 below St. Paul.

The city is located on an elevated plateau of some three miles in extent, between north and south hills—some of which are 160 feet high—being the seats of many private residences. Its streets are regularly laid out, well paved, and handsomely ornamented with many fruit and shade trees.

"This is another of the future metropolitan cities of the west." Thus the inhabitants speak of it, and indeed those interested in new Western towns generally speak of them in this way.

I was innocently reading a translation of a French book, "Other People's Money," by Gaborian, which I bought on the train. A gentleman behind me all of a sudden hit me with great force on the back, and enunciated with lightning rapidity the following words:—

"That's a nice book, ain't it? Ever read his other book—'113'? Did you ever read any of 'Ouida's' books? 'Under Two Flags' is a very nice book. You ought to read it. She is a Frenchwoman. They say she is the wife of a French general of Algiers. ''Spose you are going to Omaha? This is my station. Good-bye. I guess you'll like that book. Be sure you get 'Under Two Flags.'"

The train stopped, and he was off without my having uttered a syllable.

I made the acquaintance of two of my fellow travellers. One a thorough Yankee from Boston; the other a German. We had a very pleasant time up to Omaha, the country round about which is very rich and fertile.

We were kept an hour waiting for the train which was to take us across the bridge that here spans the Missouri river. This bridge is of an immense length. The bed of the river was quite dry.

We got to Omaha about nine o'clock. Going into the town, we found very nice little restaurants, in one of which we had a very comfortable supper. The Grand Central Hotel is a very fine building, and I here had the pleasure of meeting an old coloured waiter who remembered me as a boy.

The growth of this town is something marvellous. The fineness and solidity of some of the buildings are very astonishing, although of course the greater number of houses are hardly more than wooden shanties. This is one of the towns that began by the building of a lager-beer saloon. Indeed, many of the Western cities took their rise in this way, on the line of some railway. Then, gradually, the workmen, explorers, and settlers built up around it. I was told a very amusing story about one of the saloons. When the first visitors from the east went over the line, they stopped over Sunday at one of these places, and as the only building was a saloon, the clergyman of the party requested permission to use it for Divine Service. His request was politely acceded to, and a temporary division put up in the middle of the building. On one side the service was held; on the other there was gambling and drinking, but carried on decently and without noise. In the midst of a pathetic part of the sermon, a shuffling of cards was heard, or "That's your money ,Joe," penetrated to the ears of the entranced congregation. Sometimes a stealthy figure was seen making its way towards the rearward division; but that was all. I stayed at Omaha over Sunday. There was a numerously attended "Turner

Fest" in a large garden near the city, at which the performances were very good, and an incredible number of barrels of beer was consumed.

In the afternoon I went to a "coloured" church, where I heard a charcoal Father Hyacinthe, who offered to show me the way to heaven, and "predicated" with great force and eloquence. The singing was very good, much better than one generally hears at the same sort of service by whites. Some of the singing was very characteristic of the African race, such hymns as "Come, Lord Jehovah" being sung with great *gusto*. It evidently was a special favourite.

The streets are broad, and the city, situated on a very steep hill, is well laid out. It is the eastern terminus of the Union Pacific, and many other lines of traffic; and by the new bridge across the Missouri it becomes the western terminus of all lines centring at Council Bluffs. During the season of navigation, regular communication is had with St. Louis, and the way points by the St. Louis and Omaha Company's line of steamers. And very fine boats they are that perform this service.

Omaha is the county seat of Douglas

County, and is located on the west bank of the Missouri river, about fifty feet above high water mark, and at an altitude of 966 feet. It is nearly opposite the city of Council Bluffs, in Iowa, its rival; and 820 miles above St. Louis. According to the last census, the population was a little over 16,000.

I visited a very fine collection of Indian curiosities and specimens of minerals, quartz, etc. On returning to the hotel, I found the commander of the "Black Hills Expedition," whose *materiel* had been burnt up by the U.S. troops, and who had come to Omaha to consult with the Governor of the State. He was all covered with dust, and seemed in a state of great discontent and rage. This man had started on his own account, had provisioned a number of men, and had been stopped on the border of the Indian Reserve by the U.S. troops. The negotiations had not yet been opened with the Indians, and the Expedition had no business in the country.

The next morning I took the omnibus to the western bound train. In the omnibus there was a Philadelphian and his wife, and an Anglo-American from Newark.

CHAPTER IV.

Papillon—Elkhorn—Waterloo—Fremont—Banks of the Platte River—Rogers—Schuyler—Richland Columbus—Pawnee Indian Reservation—Lockwood—Grand Island—North Platte City—Irregular Growth of Western Cities—Julesburg—Grazing Country—Cheyenne—Grand Conception of Horace Greeley—Mountains of Colorado—Small Towns—Grand Scenery—Highest Inhabited Point on the Continent—Variety of Flowers—Virginia Dale—A Western Man of the "Heroic Age"—Laramie—A Female Jury.

The country west of Omaha for a considerable distance is of perfectly wonderful fertility. At Papillon we passed a small stream, called Papillon river, which empties itself into the Elkhorn, a few miles below the station. The population around this station has much increased within the last few years.

Elkhorn, which we passed fourteen miles farther on, is on the east bank of the Elkhorn river, and is of some importance in the way of freight traffic, as it is the outlet of Elkhorn River Valley.

The Elkhorn is a stream of about 300 miles in length. It takes its rise among the hills near the head waters of the Niobrara river. It is much used as a mill stream. The valley of this stream averages about eight miles in width, and is of the best quality of arable land. The stream abounds in native fish, and has also a great variety of fish from other waters. We were informed by Mr. Crowfut that a car-load of " fancy brands " had been accidentally emptied into the river, while *en route* to be placed in the lakes and streams of California, during the spring of 1873.

Wild turkey, along with deer and antelope, are seen here in considerable numbers, and ducks and geese seek the river during certain seasons of the year. The well-conducted farms and comfortable houses, surrounded by growing orchards and well-tilled gardens, are pleasing to the sight. Indeed, I believe there are no pleasanter valleys than this in Nebraska.

With scarcely a thought of Wellington or Napoleon, we passed Waterloo, a small station with its school-house, flouring mill, and a few cottages scattered around; and four miles beyond, we reached Valley, where we begin to mount. Between Valley and Fremont we see the Platte river for the first time. Fremont, the county seat of Dodge County, has a population of about 3,000. Here we had a very comfortable dinner, although we were only allowed twenty minutes for its consumption. The Sioux and Pacific Railway connects here with the Union Pacific, and runs through to St. John's, Iowa. Fremont is connected on the south side of the Platte by a waggon bridge which is said to have cost over $50,000.

We now go for many miles along the north bank of the river. Sometimes its course can only be traced by the timber growing on its banks. The scenery consists of broad plains, with here and there abrupt hills. The channel of this river is very often perfectly dry. Its average width, from where it empties itself into the Missouri to the junction of the North and South Forks, is not far from three-fourths of a mile; its *average* depth is SIX INCHES. In the months of September and October the river is at its lowest stage.

Farther on we notice a peculiarity—fields hedged with cotton-wood. Before coming to North Bend, we run close by the river's bank. The country around here is remarkably fertile.

Ragers, the next station, is still in the primitive lager-bier stage of Western cityhood.

Schuyler is an *entrepot* for cattle eastern bound. This place has 600 inhabitants. Passing Richland—another primitive place of saloon proclivities—we arrive at Columbus, which that emotional statesman, George Francis Train, calls the centre of the United States; being moved doubtless to make this discovery by the fact of its possessing the name of the great Christopher, and to which, with a fine sense of the fitness of things, he advocates the removal of the national capital. Very little doubt exists in the public mind that should George be elected President of the United States in 1876—which, as our first President was likewise named George, anybody with the smallest pretensions to that fine sense already spoken of, will be obliged to confess is an event by no means impossible —he will carry out his idea, and we shall then behold the capital of the Union located on these broad plains.

This place is the county seat of Platte County, and is situated at the junction of the Loup Fork and Platte rivers. It has a population of about 550, and is the head-quarters of the United States Pawnee Indian Reservation. The town seems to be prosperous. There are said to be numerous railroad projects from this place to the north and south. The farming country is well-watered by the Loup Fork. Game is said to be abundant in the valley of the Loup.

Passing Jackson—a small station—we cross a little stream called Silver Creek, and soon arrive at the village of the same name. To the south-east of this station is situated the Pawnee Indian Reservation, but not visible from the cars. It covers a tract of country fifteen miles long by thirty broad, most of which consists of the finest lands. Upwards of 2,000 acres of this land is under good cultivation. The tribe numbers nearly 2,000, and is provided with an " Agency " (Colombus, as stated above, being the head-quarters), where all the undeniable evidences of " advanced civilization " may be had at the market price per gallon.

Clark's—the next station—is surrounded by a fine agricultural country. Eleven miles beyond, we arrived at the melancholy station of Lone Tree,—I am unable to say whether or no it is a weeping willow. It is the county seat of Merrick County. It has a population of about 425 souls.

The old emigrant road from Omaha to Colorado crosses the river at this point, at old " Shinn's " Ferry. A bridge that would be an advantage to the town is now contemplated. Passing by Chapman's, we crossed broad plains which are rapidly filling up. Five miles farther west we passed Lockwood, a small side track station, and after another run of six miles reached Grand Island, where we had supper. The food here was not very good, nor was the hotel as neat as might have been desirable; however, we were allowed a full half-hour to enjoy our meal in—an allowance of time which we did not always obtain. The population of this place ranges from 1,100 to 1,200 souls; it publishes two newspapers, and is the county seat of Hall County.

The bridges of the rivers Loup Fork and Platte cause considerable trade to concentrate itself here. The Union Pacific Company's machine and repairing shops, round houses, and so forth, which are situated here, are large and well built. The station is named after Grand Island in the Platte river, two miles distant. This island is about eighty miles long by four wide, well wooded, of fertile soil, and by many thought to be the most beautiful in the river. It is reserved by the Government and guarded by soldiers. Buffaloes used to frequent this part of the country. They had a playful habit of frisking about the parade ground at Fort Kearney; the soldiers used to amuse themselves shooting them down on the parade ground itself, until they received orders not to do so.

Passing by Alda, the railroad runs through

a thickly-settled country. This valley was one of the earliest settled in Central Nebraska.

Thirty miles beyond, we arrive at Kearney Junction. Fort Kearney is five miles from the station. Settlers are said to be coming in and filling up the country. After another run of thirty miles we come to Plum Creek, once the site of the military camp of that name.

Ten miles farther, after leaving Cayote, we passed through heavy cottonwood timber. From this point westward the timber becomes smaller. In another ten miles' run we passed Willow Island, where we saw some old log-houses, their sides pierced with loopholes, and walled up with turf, the roof being prettily covered with the same.

It would be tedious to describe or even enumerate all the stations, or towns advancing to cities, which lie between Omaha and Cheyenne. North Platte City is perhaps the most promising. The population of towns created by the railroad, naturally fluctuates with the partial or arrested developments of their feeders. Thus it has happened that North Platte City, which in 1867 had a population of about 2,000, has now only about 800. It is, however, improving steadily, and with the completion of the railroad system of the districts will, no doubt, become one of the great cities of the plains. Cities, like other things, may grow faster than is good for them. When North Platte was at its highest point of seeming prosperity, it was also the centre and capital of all the rowdyism that failed to get farther west. Its future will be more gradual and healthy. Julesburg, once with a population of 4,000 " very rough," has become respectable, it is said, by becoming nearly deserted.

From Antelope—some distance farther on—is a vast grazing country. Crofut says: "By stocking this country with sheep, an untold wealth would be added." Perhaps; but before trying the experiment on a large scale, it would be well to have actual proof that the pasture and climate are really favourable to sheep. Similar visions of untold wealth from sheep-raising have not been everywhere realized.

Cheyenne—just midway between Omaha and Ogden—is now a well-ordered city of 3,000 inhabitants. It is famous, or becoming so, for moss agates, and likewise for saddles, which are of the Mexican type, and much celebrated for the ease they afford both to horse and man. In a country where everybody rides, we naturally expect to find a perfectly easy saddle, although in countries where everybody walks we have seldom found a tolerably easy shoe.

To the south lies Denver City, and between it and Cheyenne, Greeley, founded under the auspices of the late Horace Greeley. This last-named place is remarkable as yet for nothing but the impossibility of obtaining in it any alcoholic drinks honestly, and the perfect ease with which the same may be had by the aid of a little dexterous lying and a medical prescription. Hence a new kind of pander has come to the surface of society under the venerated name of " physician "; unless, indeed, we are to suppose that forms of disease imperatively requiring the use of alcohol as a beverage are terribly rife in this little town.

The idea of gathering into one town, as into a huge lunatic asylum, all the potential drunkards of the country, and enabling them to indulge their propensity under the respectable mask of sickness, can only rank second to that still grander idea—grander because more universal—which is embodied in the city of Mormon. But the principle may be still further extended. Why not have cities founded for and devoted to all the potential gamblers, and all afflicted with a craving for homicide, and still another for all who are bent on suicide ; in which several places the respective inhabitants might easily gratify their little foibles without breaking the law, or shocking any local prejudices, or forcing their objectionable practices and customs upon their unwilling neighbours.

Denver City, reached by a branch from the main road at Cheyenne, is the county seat of Arapahoe County, and the capital of Colorado —aptly called the " Switzerland of America." Says Mr. Samuel Bowles in the introduction to his pleasant volume " A Summer Vacation in the Parks and Mountains of Colorado," " The distinctive physical feature of Colorado is her wide elevated parks, lying among her double and triple folds of the continental range of mountains—like counties in Illinois or Iowa, or states in New England, 6,000 to 9,000 feet above the sea-level, surrounded by mountains that rise from 3,000 to 5,000 feet higher ; plains green with grass, bright with flowers ; mountains dreary with rocks, white with snow. The distinctive charm is the atmosphere, so clear and pure and dry all the while, as to be a perpetual feeling, rather than vision, of beauty; invigorating every sense, softly smoothing every pain, lending a glory to life and landscape alike, clothing every feature of nature with beauty, and giving the eye of every spectator the power to see it—this is the indescribable thing that lifts Colorado out of other lockings, and more than compensates, in the comparison, for what is peculiar to Switzerland.

"Here, where the great backbone of the continent rears and rests itself; here, where nature sets the patterns of plain and mountain, of valley and hill, for all America; here, where spring the waters that wash two-thirds of the western continent, and feed both its oceans; here, where the mountains are fat with gold and silver, and prairies glory in the glad certainty of future harvests of corn and wheat —here, indeed, is the centre and central life of America,—fountain of its wealth, health, and beauty. Switzerland is pleasure and health; Colorado is these and use besides— the use of beauty and the use of profitable work united."

The altitudes of the principal mountains, according to Professor Whitney, are: Mount Lincoln, 16,190 feet; Pike's Peak, 14,336 feet; Gray's Peak, 14,251 feet; Sapri's Peak, 14,200 feet; Mount Comoron, 14,000 feet; Mount Guizot, 13,223 feet; Vealie's Peak, 13,456 feet; Parry's Peak, 13,214 feet.

There are other peaks less high, but equally grand and majestic. A recent writer thus speaks of them:—

"The Alps, storied monuments of poetical legendary fame, cannot compare to these mountains in scenes of sublime and awful grandeur. Here, all of the vast scene is laid before you, the pure air bringing the distant mountains within your vision, as though anxious that the whole grand beauty of the scene should be visible at one and the same moment. The mind drinks the inspiration of the glorious vision at one draught, and filled with awe, wonder, and admiration, the bounding heart almost stands still, while the eager eyes gaze on the grandest panorama in nature. From the top of Gray's Peaks, either of them, a morning scene of glorious beauty is unfolded to the visitor, such as one rarely sees in any clime, for nature in her wildest moods has never excelled her handiwork in the panoramic view spread out in every direction. European travellers tell us that nowhere within the range of European travel can such scenes be found,—scenes so full of beauty, sublimity, and inspiration.

"Nowhere on the old continent do we ascend so high; from no point is the view so wide and comprehensive. From Alpine summits the tourist's gaze extends over one petty province to rest on another. Here the eye fails to reach the extent of even one portion of our country, and the far-distant horizon closes in the scene, by dropping an airy curtain, whose fleecy fringes rest on mountain peaks and vast plains, in far-distant portions of the same fair land.

"*The summit of the Rocky Mountains*, from one side of which the waters of numerous little springs ripple softly away, as though afraid to venture on the vast distance which lies between them and the waters of the Atlantic Ocean, their final destination. On the other side of the crest the scene is repeated, with this difference, that the waters stealing away through beds of tiny, delicately tinted mountain flowers, are destined to reach the Pacific Ocean on the other side of the continent. So close together in their infancy, so far away in their prime, or at their final grave—the ocean. This point is the apex, the centre of the North American continent, the crowning peak of that grand backbone, whose iron ribs are represented by the many spurs that branch away in earnest support of the whole grand system."

Six miles west of Cheyenne is a station with the very uncertain name of Hazard. I hazard nothing in saying that Hazard *has had* many a better pun executed upon its jest-inviting cognomen. Further attention it hardly deserves at present. In the future it may possibly rival the most promising cities of the plains. To what extent of growth, population, and wealth, a western town may attain, is certainly one of those things which, as Lord Dundreary says, "no fellow can find out."

At the next station, Otto, eight miles beyond, the ground begins to rise rapidly, and by consequence the heavy grading commences, as the train ascends the Black Hills.

We are now 6,724 feet above the sea. To the north of this place there is a fine valley, where Crow Creek finds its source in many sparkling springs. The valley contains very superior grazing-land, and likewise, in conjunction with the adjacent hills, affords ample game for the hunter.

Grand Cañon is five miles west of Otto, and 574 feet higher. Here are found great stone quarries, whence was taken the rock for the Company's buildings in Cheyenne; also for the stone warehouses there.

Buford, seven miles farther west, is a small side track. Heavy rock-work, snow-sheds, and fences, mark the road at this point. Here the country impresses you with a sense of wild and rugged grandeur. On either side, and quite near, great perpendicular masses of granite rear high their sombre sides, piled one on the top of the other in wild confusion. The scenery as we approach Sherman is peculiarly striking; the altitude gained, we seem to move along a level plain, covered with grass, rocks, and shrubs, until Sherman is reached, 8,242 feet above the level of the sea, the highest inhabited point on the continent. It is named in honour of General Sherman, in order thus to indicate the exalted fame which that great soldier attained in his country's service, and likewise because he is the tallest General in the United States army. Sherman is 549 miles from Omaha, and 1,365 from San Francisco.

Here the Company has a stone round house of five stalls, and likewise a repair shop. The train stops here but a few minutes. About twenty-five or thirty houses of logs and boards constitute the sole architectural adornments of the town. The commercial importance of Sherman is yet in its infancy, and is now represented only by one store, two hotels, and two saloons. The freight, however, that is taken up at this station for the east and west is very extensive, consisting of sawed lumber, telegraph poles, and wood obtained in the hills and ravines but a few miles distant.

From Sherman to Rawlings is 160 miles, the road running between the Black Hills and the Rocky Mountains range; presenting along the route varied and impressive scenery.

As the road leaves Sherman it turns to the left, and three miles farther on is Dale Creek Bridge, 650 feet long, and 126 high, spanning Dale Creek from bluff to bluff. When viewed from the bridge below, it has the appearance of a light, airy, graceful structure. The beautiful little stream, as you see it from the bridge, looks like a silver thread below us, the sun glistening on its surface with a thousand flashes of silvery light.

Anon, the dark walls of the Cañon shade it, as though they were envious or jealous of its beauty being rendered common property. A narrow green valley, half a mile above the bridge, is the site of the former Dale City, where, at one time, were gathered a population of over 600. Now, a few hundred yards beyond can be seen a solitary house, like a lone sentinel in front of a deserted camp. Here, as well as around Sherman, and indeed all over the Black Hills, are found countless flowers of every shape and hue; over 300 varieties have already been classified.

Fifteen miles to the south-west of Sherman is situated Virginia Dale, in Colorado. Some " yellow-covered novelist " has immortalized it by calling it the " Robbers' Roost," though failing to indicate the particular bar-fence or other object upon which they roosted. But aside from this questionable notoriety, Virginia Dale is the most widely known of any locality in these mountains.

This place was originally a stage station on the old Denver, Salt Lake, and California road, which was laid out and kept by a notorious cut-throat, Jack Slade by name, who was Division Superintendent of the old Stage Company from 1860 to 1863. It was the popular opinion that this Slade was at the head of an infamous band of desperadoes, who infested that region of country, and whose chief occupation consisted in running off with and appropriating the stock of emigrants, etc. At all events, he was a noted desperado, of the extreme early Western type, having, it is said, killed his thirteen men. The last of the exploits, east of the mountains, of this fiendish ruffian, was the wanton and cruel murder of Jules Berg, the person after whom Julesburg was named. Slade had had a quarrel with Berg in 1861, the upshot of which was a shooting affray in which Slade was worsted, or, in the slang of the desperadoes of that time, "forced to take water." In 1863, some of the drivers of the lines, friends and *employés* of Slade, decoyed Jules Berg to the Cold Spring Ranche, on North Platte river, which was then kept by a wicked old scamp called Antoine Runnels, but more commonly known as "The Devil's Left Bower," who was a great crony of Slade, who seems in the opinion of unprejudiced persons to have rightfully earned the title of "Right Bower" to that same fireproof individual.

The place where the tragedy took place is fifty miles north of Cheyenne, and twenty-five miles below Fort Laramie, whither Slade hastily journeyed from Cottonwood Springs (opposite McPherson Station) in an extra coach, as soon as he was notified of the capture of his old enemy. He drove at the top of his horses' speed, without stopping night or day, and arrived at Cold Spring Ranche early one morning.

On alighting from the coach, his cruel heart leaped with delight on finding his hated foe tightly tied to a post in the corral, in such a manner that he was rendered entirely helpless.

Slade went immediately to work, putting into effect the long-contemplated butchery over which he had gloated in imagination. He shot him twenty-three times, taking care not to kill him, cursing and blaspheming all the time in the most frightful manner, glutting his thirst for vengeance, and taking a demoniac delight in the pain he was inflicting. He returned to the ranche between "shots" for a "drink." While firing these shots he would tell Jules just where he was going to hit him, applying to him the most profane, bitter, and scornful epithets; adding at every shot that he did not intend to kill him for some time, but he was going to keep riddling him with bullets until he was tired of the amusement, and thus torture him to death. Unable to provoke a cry of pain or a sign of fear from the unfortunate but stoical Jules, he became infuriated, and thrusting the pistol into the mouth of the miserable man, blew his head to pieces with the twenty-third discharge, the brains and blood of the murdered man spattering over the face and clothes of his cruel murderer.

Slade then cut off the ears of his victim and put them in his pocket. Seven of Slade's friends stood by, and calmly viewed, like so many spectators of a play, the enactment of this brutal scene.

In the saloons of Denver City and in those of other places, he would take Jules' ears out of his pocket, throw them upon the bar, and openly boasting of the act, demand drinks on his bloody pledges; and these were never refused him. Shortly after this exploit, it became too hot for him in Colorado, and he was obliged to flee.

He next went to Virginia City, Montana, where he continued to prey upon society. The people of that country had no love or use for his kind, and after his conduct had become insupportable, the Vigilantes hung him, as he richly deserved.

His wife arrived at the scene of execution just in time to behold him in the very last agonies of death by hanging. She had ridden fifteen miles as fast as her horse could trot, with the avowed purpose of shooting Slade, to save the disgrace of having him hung, and she arrived on the scene, revolver in hand, only a few minutes too late to carry out her scheme—Jack Slade the desperado was dead.

At an elevation above the sea-level of 7,122 feet, is situated Laramie City, the county seat of Albany County, Wyoming Territory. The cars stop here thirty minutes for breakfast, which we all enjoyed with an appetite that only the incredible cordial of the mountain air can bestow.

Laramie City is regularly laid out at right angles with the road. A stream of clear cold water runs through the streets,—a practical and every-day sermon in favour of the temperance cause, which undoubtedly perceptibly affects the liquor interests in the town. The buildings are small and mostly of wood, with the exception of a few substantial structures of stone. The spirit of improvement, however, is abroad, for during the last year, severals stores, hotels, churches, schools, dwellings, etc., have been completed, including a court-house and jail. The spring, which affords ample water for the town, is very large, and lies at the foot of the Black Hills, a few miles to the east.

Laramie has the good or bad fortune to be the first place where a female jury was ever empanelled. History records that their first case was that of a Western desperado of the worst type, and while the jurywomen were considering their verdict—and let it be said to their honour that they did their duty without flinching,—the husbands of those in the jury-box who had "responsibilities" at home, besought the future citizen of this great country to be calm, not to swallow his fist if he could possibly avoid it, using the following words of a then popular song:—

"Nice little baby, don't get in a fury,
'Cause mamma's gone to sit on the jury."

Laramie Plains is a belt of fine grazing land, about twenty miles wide by sixty long, and is considered one of the best stock-raising sections in this part of the country. Beef can be raised and fattened on these plains at a cost not exceeding that of similar cattle in Texas,—where, as we all know, they get their own living and form the larger proportion of the "population." The well-known fact that thousands of buffalo roamed over these plains, furnishing the Indians with unlimited quantities of beef, before the white man drove both away, will go far to convince one that the laudations of this as a grazing country are not exaggerated.

Stock-raising now is almost the only industry noticeable, and a great many thousand heads of cattle, sheep, and horses may be seen in every direction.

Sixteen miles from Laramie City is Wyoming, on Little Laramie river. During the building of the road, large quantities of "ties" were received at this point, having been cut off at the head of the river and floated down the stream in high water.

Eighteen miles beyond is Look-out Station, where may be seen for twenty-five miles either way along the road vast herds of elk, deer, and antelope roaming over the rolling prairie country; seeing which you realize that you are away past the very outposts of civilization.

The unamiable name of Miser Station is applied to the next place, the country around abounding in sage-brush, a low-creeping shrub; upon observing which, a fellow-traveller desired to know whether it would not become longer as *thyme* went on. Many giggles greeted this execrable joke.

We are reminded of "The Lady of Lyons" and "Claude Melnotte" as we come to Como Lake, a beautiful sheet of water of no great expanse, lying to the right of the road; and, like Pauline, the traveller will look in vain for "the palace lifting to eternal summer its marble walls."

The lake is about one mile long and half a mile broad, and abounds in a peculiar fish, "a fish with legs." These *fish-animals* possess gills something like cat-fish, and are amphibious, being often found crawling clumsily about miles from the land.

At Carbon, eleven miles from Como, the first coal was discovered on the Union Pacific

Railroad. Two coal veins have been opened, each averaging about nine feet. The working capacity of these veins is about 200 tons per day. The coal is shipped eastward, much of it finding its way to Omaha, besides supplying the towns along the road. About 300 men are employed in the mines. The coal is raised from the mine and "dumped" into the flats which are standing on the tract. A stationary engine furnishes the hoisting power.

A well-informed writer thus speaks of this portion of the route :—

"Beyond, the country grows gradually barren; and after crossing the North Platte river, we enter upon 150 miles of desert,—a waterless, treeless, grassless, rolling plain, the soil fine, dry, and impregnated with alkali,—the air, pure, dry, and cool,—a section shudderingly remembered by slow-travelling emigrants, and memorable in the history of railroad construction, for the necessity of having a special water train to supply the workmen and the engines while carrying forward the work through it. Rightly named, Bitter Creek gathers the sluggish surface waters it furnishes, and carries them on to Green river, reaching which we enter upon new and better scenes. The water increases and freshens, the verdure improves; but that which attracts the traveller most is the novel and imposing forms of architecture that nature has left to mark her history upon these open plains. Long, wide troughs, as of departed rivers; long, level embankments, as of railroad tracks, or endless fortifications; huge, quaint hills suddenly rising from the plain, bearing fantastic shapes; great, square mounds of rock and earth, half-formed, half-broken pyramids,—it would seem as if a generation of giants had built and buried here, and left their work to awe and humble a puny succession. The Black, the Pilot, and the Church Buttes are among the more celebrated of these huge monumental mountains standing on the level plain; but the railway track passes out of sight of them all except the Church Butte, which, seen under a favourable light, imposes on the imagination like a grand old cathedral going into decay, quaint in its crumbling ornaments, majestic in its height and breadth. They seem, like the more numerous and fantastic illustrations of Nature's art in Southern Colorado, to be the remains of granite hills, that wind and water and especially the sand whirlpools which march in lordly force through the air—literally moving mountains.

—have left to hint the past, and tell the story of their own achievements. Not unfitly, there as here, they have won the title of 'Monuments of the Gods.'"

Speaking with one of my fellow-travellers on the future of the Indians, I was reminded of the very interesting chapter in Sir Charles Dilke's "Greater Britain" entitled "Red India."

"These Indians are not red," was the thought that struck him when he first saw the Utes in the streets of Denver. They had come into town to be painted, as English ladies go to London to shop; they might be seen engaged in daubing their cheeks with vermilion and blue, referring to glasses which the squaws admiringly held. Still, when they were met with peaceful, paintless cheeks, it could readily be seen that their colour was brown, copper, dirt—anything but red.

"Low in stature, yellow skinned, small-eyed and Tartar-faced, the Indians of the plains are a distinct people from the tall hooked-nosed warriors of the Eastern States. It is impossible to set eyes on their women without being reminded of the drawf skeletons found in the mounds of Missouri and Iowa; but, men or women, the Utes bear no resemblance to the bright-eyed, graceful people with whom Penn traded and Standish fought. They are not less inferior in mind than in body. It was no Shoshone, no Ute, no Cheyenne, who called the rainbow the 'heaven of flowers,' the moon 'the night queen,' or the stars 'God's eyes.'

"The plain tribes are as deficient in heroes as in poetry; they never have produced a General, and White Antelope is their nearest approach to Tecumseh. Their mode of life, the natural features of the country in which they dwell, have nothing in them to suggest the debased condition in which they dwell. The reason must lie in the blood, the race."

When you ask a Western man his views on the Indian Question, he says:—

"We can destroy 'em by the laws of war, or thin 'em out by whisky, but the thinning-out process is plaguey slow."

Among the men of the West, there is no difference in opinion in this question. Rifle and revolver are the Alpha and Omega of their policy with reference to this subject.

CHAPTER V.

Benton City—The Hog Back—A Paint Mine—Summit of the Rocky Mountains—Sage-brush and Alkali Beds—Red Desert—Bitter Creek—Descriptive Names—Green River—Romantic Scenery—A Pioneer of Western Civilization—Aspen—A Deserted Railway City—Bear River—Mormon Settlements—Bear Lake Valley—Echo Cañon—Mormon Fortifications—Echo City—Weber Cañon—Devil's Slide—A Ride on the "Cow-Catcher"—Ogden—Salt Lake and the Dead Sea—Aspect of the Country about Salt Lake.

AFTER passing several unimportant points, we came to Fort Fred. Steele, where we stopped. About two miles west of this place, the now abandoned and deserted Benton City once stood and flourished after its own fashion. Its history is an apt illustration of the birth, growth, decay, and final dissolution of that modern municipal ephemeron the railroad town, which, like many a better thing, is, as one may say, here to-day and gone to-morrow. And so it was with Benton. The road was completed to this point by the last of July, 1868. At that time, and during August and September, the place was all alive with business, the great quantity of freight destined for Montana, Idaho, and Utah, and the western country, had here to be unloaded from the cars, and then put in great waggons, to be hauled to the various points of destination.

This spell of business continued until the road was finished to Bryan, some distance beyond. This occurred on the first day of the following October. Then Benton knew that her sun had set. The varied population, who lived principally under canvas, "folded their tents like the Arabs, and as silently stole away" everything from one another that was portable; for a harder, rougher set of human beings—and there were 3,000 congregated there—it is said, could hardly be found. The predominating classes consisted of roughs, thieves, petty gamblers (between these two last named there may be a distinction, but there is certainly no difference), fast women, desperadoes, and "road agents,"—highwaymen in Western parlance being so designated. In its palmy days Benton enjoyed that peculiarly exhilarating spirit commonly called "a high old time."

As water had to be hauled from the Platte river, two miles distant, at an expense of one dollar per barrel or ten cents per bucket-full, the citizens shunned that unfamiliar beverage, and adding a little more money to the retail price of water, they slacked their thirst by unanimous consent with whisky pure and unadulterated—at least by the costly river product, the use of which was, in that locality, rigorously confined to external purposes.

As the road stretched, day by day, towards the westward, Benton gradually melted away to a mere skeleton of her former self, and now but a couple of battered and burnt chimneys, and here and there a few half-obliterated post-holes, mark the site of the once "flourishing" canvas city.

At Benton the bluffs of gray sandstone, worn by the rough usage of the elements, now become plainly visible in the distance, standing like grim sentinels at the entrance to the cañon of the Platte. They continue in sight until we come in the vicinity of Rawlings.

To the south, the celebrated "Hog Back" may be seen. This is a long ridge of gray granite, very high and narrow. It skirts the road for about fifteen miles, terminating in the highlands of Rawlings Springs.

This ridge is not above half a mile in width at the base, yet rises sharply about 1,000 feet, and at some points even 3,000 feet high. A pretty little valley, watered by a small creek, spreads out on the south side of the ridge, furnishing a pleasing contrast to the surrounding country.

Many years ago, this lovely vale, so green and fresh and peaceful-looking withal, was the scene of a bloody fight between the Sioux Indians and the Utes, their hereditary foes. The Sioux were encamped in the valley, reposing in fancied security. They were surprised by the Utes, who stole in upon them, favoured by the dim light of early dawn, and attacked them with savage impetuosity, slaughtering men, women, and children without mercy. Though surprised, the Sioux bore themselves bravely, and faced their foes with the courage of despair. But they were surrounded, and finally yielded to superior force. When trying to escape, they sought to cross the " Hog Back," but as every flying Sioux raised his head above the crest, he was instantly picked off and sent sprawling—a corpse—down the ridge. A mere remnant of the band made good their escape, in another direction, abandoning their dead and wounded to the tender mercies of the victorious Utes.

Rawlings is a place of, probably, between 500 and 600 inhabitants. The fine hotel, also a round house of fifteen stables, and a machine shop for division repairs, have here been built by the Company.

The face of the country at this point is rough and uneven, abounding in sage-brush and spotted with alkali. Close to the town rises a fine sulphur spring from under a bed of blue limestone.

Between thirty and forty miles to the northeast of this station are the well-known Ferris and Seminole mining districts. The ore is silver, and said to be very rich. Coal, wood, and water are abundant near the mines, and the prospect for the future of the district is considered bright.

To the north of this station, about two miles, a paint mine has been discovered, yielding a peculiar paint, which is said to be both fire and water proof. Two mills have been erected at the station for grinding the paint, with a daily capacity of three and ten tons respectively. The Union Pacific Railroad Company are using it to paint their cars.

Leaving Rawlings, the road winds through a narrow ravine, and then through a natural pass about 300 feet wide, which leads between two nearly perpendicular bluffs, over 200 feet in height, composed of yellowish-gray quartose sandstone, overlaid with carboniferous limestone. From all appearances, this bluff must have extended across the ravine at some immensely remote period. By the action of some large body of water, which has now wholly disappeared, these huge walls have been made, it would seem, expressly for the purpose of the railroad route, which they enclose, and which passes through a sagebrush and alkali country to a small station called Summit, where, however, the passenger trains do not stop; seven miles farther on we arrive at Separation, which derives its name from the fact that at this place the various parties of surveyors who had been together or near each other for the last hundred miles, separated to run different lines to the westward.

Fifteen miles from this point, we reach Creston, two and a half miles from the spot where is planted a flag which marks the summit of the Rocky Mountains,—the great "backbone" of the continent. According to General Dodge, we are now 7,100 feet above the sea-level. This point is about 185 miles from Sherman, 737 from Omaha, and 1,177 from San Francisco.

Taking this little flag-staff as your centre of observation, you gaze out upon a wide expanse, now arched and broken into ugly hollows and repulsive knobs, devoid of any signs of a rich vegetation. Away in the vast distance long lines of hills recede down from the sight, becoming smaller and smaller in the vast perspective,

The clear, cold, thin mountain air braces your lungs, yet it is far from refreshing; for here on the summit of the grandest range of mountains on the continent, the prospect of sky and earth is grey and uninviting, for sagebrush and alkali beds now meet the eye at every turn, filling the blue atmosphere with a certain harsh, repellent quality, so different from that balminess which permeates the radiant valley below, and renders life there so fresh and beautiful.

Gigantic masses of rock—seemingly the ruins of colossal fortifications—lie strewn all about us, presenting a mountain scene of wild magnificence, in keeping with this region of loneliness, ruggedness, and desolate grandeur.

We descend rapidly now towards the Pacific Ocean on an incline grade for the next 108 miles, in which distance the descent is over 1,100 feet.

Fifteen miles west brings us to Wash-a-kie, so named in honour of an old chief of the Shoshone Indians. When the fact was mentioned that at this station there is an Artesian well 638 feet deep, which, at about fifteen feet above the surface, yields 800 gallons of pure water per hour, an English gentleman who sat not very far from us, was heard to remark to his companion, "So they call this precious place Wash-a-kie, do they? I don't think you would 'ave a great deal of trouble washing a dozen keys, with such a quantity of water, *h*every *h*our in the day." And then, acting no doubt on the adage "If you want a thing well done, do it yourself," he set up a swelling peal of laughter at his own joke, while his companions and fellow-travellers, out of pure good-nature, forced to the surface a poor melancholy giggle, without any heart in it.

Nine miles beyond Wash-a-kie we reach Red Desert, so named from the colour of the barren soil. Round about here are several alkali lakes, upon whose surface nothing that has life can exist. Masses of shifting sand are lifted by every passing breeze, and then fall in drifting heaps, only to be caught up again and again by the capricious wind.

Thirteen miles beyond, our train stops at Table Rock, a station on the outer edge of the desert, with an elevation of 6,890 feet.

On the left-hand side of the road, your attention is attracted by a long line of red sandstone bluffs, lifting their great red sides, seamed and cut by the ceaseless action of the elements, to a height varying from 50 to 500 feet above the dead level of the surrounding country.

One of these bluffs, about 500 feet high, perfectly flat and even on the top, and extending for several miles along the road, gives the name to this stopping place. A brisk run of ten miles brings us to aptly named Bitter Creek, where the Company have a round house and a machine shop for repairs.

The country around this station is by no means of that fascinating character which could by any possible chance induce any sensible person to abandon home, wife, children, and friends, simply for the pleasure of pitching his tent here and making this section of country his future abiding-place; not, indeed, unless he had a decided natural liking for water strongly impregnated with that bitter caustic taste which alkali deposits always cause; not, indeed, unless he was particularly fond of sinking to his middle when he goes out for his morning walk upon the treacherous banks. In fact, this point has always been a terror to intending settlers. Excepting grease-wood and sage-brush, absolutely nothing in the shape of vegetation will flourish.

Sixteen miles beyond, we reach Point of Rocks, where an Artesian well 1,015 feet deep supplies an abundance of pure water.

Large train-loads of coal may be seen on the track, near this place, ready for shipment. The Wyoming Coal Company have here extensive coal-mines, which are worked to great advantage. In one bluff, five veins of coals have been found—one upon the other—which are respectively one, three, four, five, and six and a half feet in thickness. On the same bluff, just above the coal, is a seam of oyster shells, six inches in thickness. Professor Hayden says, "This an extinct and undescribed species, about the size of our common edible one."

At points near the road, the sandstone bluffs have been beaten by the capricious action of the elements into various fantastic shapes. The American aptitude for fanciful characterization has here been displayed in naming these bluffs: one is called " Caves of Sand," another " Hermit's Grotto," another " Water-washed Caves of the Fairies," and still another, " Sanko's Bower," etc. The above-mentioned authority, in his geological examition of this portion of the country, reported finding "preserved in the rocks the greatest abundance of deciduous leaves of the poplar, ash, elm, and maple." He also says: "Among the plants found is a specimen of fan-palm, which, at the time it grew here, displayed a leaf of enormous dimensions, sometimes having a spread of ten or twelve feet. These gigantic palms seem to have formed a conspicuous feature among the trees of these ancient forests."

There is a project on foot to build a railroad from this point north, to Bozeman, Montana, *viâ* Camp Stambaugh, Big Wind River Valley, and the Upper Yellowstone, a distance of 350 miles.

Twenty-five miles from this place, after passing three unimportant stations, we arrive at Rock Springs, a station that takes its name from a saline spring which boils out of the bluff, sparkling and clear to the eye, but bitter and deceptive to the taste.

As we speed onward from this point, the prospect opens to the view, the scenery becoming grander and more impressive as we proceed; then the frowning bluffs rise high over the narrow and romantic gorge through which we sweep with a tremendous roar and rattle, caused by the near proximity of the train to the walls of rock on either side, until we reach Green river, the end of the Laramie Division. Passenger trains bound west stop thirty minutes at this station.

Green river is now the county seat of Sweetwater County, Wyoming Territory; Atlantic City having formerly possessed that honour. The population numbers about 200 souls.

In "days of yore," the Mormons held a valuable franchise at this place, namely, a ferry; and as, excepting late in the fall, the river was seldom fordable, they did not fail to reap a golden harvest by charging travellers from $5 to $20 per team for taking them across the river, the charge varying with the ability of the owners to pay. Now, as it were in the twinkling of an eye, all this is changed. The Mormon monopoly has disappeared, and given place to one of far greater dimensions, whose charges, however, do not vary with the length of purse of each traveller. Where was once the humble ferry, plied by the "son of the faithful," a handsome bridge now spans the river, over which long trains of splendid saloon cars pass to and fro from time to time, conveying passengers by the hundred to their various destinations, and to and from the most extreme points on the continent.

The bluffs adjacent to this place, and which

skirt the road on one side, are of a peculiar formation, described by Professor Hayden as the " Green River Shales."

The sides of these bluffs rise in perpendicular masses to the height of hundreds of feet, and are of a greyish buff colour; the geological formations are very distinctly marked, and present not a little interest to the scientifically inclined tourist.

The hills topped with yellow sandstone and disposed in various battlemented forms, like so many massive towers, and in addition, the peculiar appearance of bands stretched along their sides,—the whole has contributed to make the scenery around this station very much celebrated.

Green river rises in the north-west of the Wind River Mountains, at the base of Fremont's Peak. Here, numberless little streams, upwards of 200 miles from the point where the railroad crosses the river, combine their accumulated forces to its source, whence it flows, with a broad rapid sweep, a distance of about 350 miles, and then empties itself into the Colorado river.

Green river is so named from the colour of its waters,—a deep, pronounced hue, which is imparted to the stream from the soil, composed of assimilated particles of rock, slate, etc., through which it flows. The water all the year round is of very good taste,—far superior, in fact, to any in these parts. The river and its tributaries are well stocked with fish of all kinds.

On leaving the station the train passes over a handsome bridge, the cars traversing heavy cuts; then along the river, by which we get a very fine view of the battlemented bluffs on the east side of the river. Twenty-nine miles beyond, after passing Bryan and Marston, we reach Grangers, by following due west the course of the Big Muddy; ten miles farther on we come to Church Buttes, noted for its moss agates.

This station derives its name from the singular shapes of the sandstone bluffs, which extend for many miles on the left-hand side of the road, and from it about ten miles. At the old Church Buttes station, on what is now known as the "old overland stage road," about nine miles to the south, "they rise," says a recent writer, "in lofty domes and pinnacles, which, at a distance, resemble the fluted columns of some cathedral of the olden time, standing in the midst of desolation; its lofty turreted roof and towering spires rising far above the surrounding country; but on a nearer approach the scene changes, and we find a huge mass of sandstone, worn and washed by the elements, until it has assumed the outlines of a church of the grandest dimensions, it being visible for a great distance."

A run of twenty-seven miles—Hampton and Carter intervening—brings us to Fort Bridger. This post was named after James Bridger, the renowned hunter, trapper, and guide, who lived in this part of the country upwards of half a century.

"Jim" Bridger is one of the most noted of all the plainsmen and early pioneers in our far western country.

Judge Carter of this place has written a short sketch of "Jim's" eventful life, from which the following is taken:—

"He was born in Richmond, Virginia, sometime about the end of the last century; and while he was very small, his parents emigrated to St. Louis, Mo., where shortly after their arrival, they both died of an epidemic then prevailing in that city. Having no one to look to, or to care for him, he engaged to accompany a party of trappers who were then fitting out for a trip to the Rocky Mountains.

"Entirely devoid of even the commonest rudiments of education, he crossed the then wholly unknown and trackless plains, and plunged into the pathless mountains. Greatly attracted by the novelty of the sport, at that time exceedingly profitable, he entered eagerly upon the business: being naturally shrewd, and possessing a keen faculty of observation, he carefully studied the habits of the beaver, and profiting by the knowledge obtained from the Indians, with whom he chiefly associated, and with whom he became a great favourite, he soon became one of the most expert trappers and hunters in the mountains.

"Eager to satisfy his curiosity, a natural fondness for mountain scenery, and a roving disposition, he traversed the country in every direction, sometimes in company with Indians, but oftener alone: he familiarized himself with every mountain peak, every gorge, every hill, and every landmark in the country. He pursued his trapping expeditions north to the British possessions, south to Mexico, and west to the Pacific Ocean. In this way he became acquainted with all the tribes of Indians in the country, and by long intercourse with them, learned their language, and became familiar with all their signs. He adopted their habits, conformed to their customs, became imbued with all their superstitions, and at length excelled them in strategy. The marvellous stories told by Bridger are numerous, but we have not space for a 'specimen.'

"In after years, when it became necessary to send military expeditions through the far western country, the Government employed Bridger as a guide, and his experience was turned to good account as an interpreter of Indian language.

"He is now living in the vicinity of Kansas City, Mo., but has outlived the sphere of his usefulness, there being no longer any portion of the west unexplored, and having reached the period of second childhood."

After passing Leroy, a small side track, five miles from Bridger, we reach Piedmont, a distance of ten miles farther on. The country here is rough and broken, and the railroad cannot be regarded as a straightforward affair, for, like a hare pursued, it doubles on its track in several places.

To the south the long range of the Mintah Mountains can be seen, well timbered with pine and cedar. We are told in one of the many guide books, that "the principal occupation of the citizens of Piedmont appears to be the burning of charcoal."

The next station—Aspen—is noted from the fact that, next to Sherman, it is the highest point on the Union Pacific Railroad. The elevation is 7,835 feet; being situated 977 miles from San Francisco, and 937 from Omaha, located on the lowest pass over the Mintah Mountains.

This station is named from the high mountain to the north, known as "Quaking Asp," so called from the particular species of poplar of that name, which grows in profusion in the gulches and on the sides of the mountain.

On leaving Aspen the train traverses three lengthy snow-sheds and one tunnel, and then runs rapidly, on a descending grade for about five miles, to Hilliard; two miles from which, to the right of the road, is the site of the once populous and prosperous, but now entirely deserted, Bear River City. A recent writer says: "At this point the roughs and gamblers who had been driven from point to point westward, made a stand, congregating in large numbers. They swore that they would be driven no farther; that here they would stay and fight it out to the bitter end. The town contained about 1,000 law-abiding people, and when the roughs felt that trouble was coming on them, they withdrew to the hills and organized for a raid on the town. Meanwhile some of the roughs remained in the town, and among them were three noted garrotters, who had added to the long list of their crimes that of murder.

"The citizens arose, seized and hung them. In this act they were sustained by all law-abiding people, also by the *Index*, a paper which had followed the road, but was then published here. This hastened the conflict, and on the 19th of November, 1868, the roughs attacked the town in force. This attack was repulsed by the citizens, though not until the Bear river riot had cost sixteen lives, including that of one citizen. The mob first attacked and burned the gaol, taking thence one of their kind who was confined there. They next sacked the office and destroyed the material of *The Frontier Index*, which was situated in a building close to the railroad, on the south side. Elated with their success, the mob, numbering about 300 well-armed desperadoes, marched over to the north side, up the main street, and made an attack on a store belonging to one of the leading merchants. Here they met with a volley from Henry rifles, in the hands of brave and determined citizens, who had collected in the store. The mob was thrown into confusion, and fled down the street, pursued by the citizens, about thirty in number. The first volley and the running fight left fifteen of the desperadoes dead on the street. The number of the wounded was never ascertained, but several bodies were afterwards found in the gulches and among the rocks, where they had crawled away and died. One citizen was slain in the attack on the gaol. From this time the roughs abandoned the city."

Like Benton City, this place also declined and finally disappeared, just as soon as the railroad was built past it; and now there is nothing left to mark its former site except a few old chimneys, some broken bottles, and a couple of beaten and battered oyster cans.

One mile beyond the next station, which is called Millis, we cross a trestle bridge 600 feet long, over Bear river. This noble stream, as well as the country around it, demands a moment's attention. About sixty miles to the south, among the Uintah and Wahsatch mountains, Bear river takes its rise, fed by many tributaries, and flowing with a majestic swell through a country rich in grand and beautiful scenery. Around Bear Lake—which is in reality but a widening of the river—there are several pretty Mormon settlements, which pleasantly dot the shore of the lake.

Bear Lake Valley is a point of great interest to the tourist, for here he can view a region of weird and picturesque scenery, strikingly diversified by rock, lake, and mountain.

This beautiful valley is situated in Rich County, the most northern county in Utah Territory, and is about twenty-five miles in length, varying considerably in width.

Nine miles beyond Millis is Evanston, where we stop thirty minutes for dinner. The Railway Company have here erected a twenty-stall round-house, repair shops, hotel, freight house, and passengers' waiting-rooms. The town now contains about 600 inhabitants. Evanston is the county seat of Mintah County, Wyoming, and is situated 957 miless from Omaha on the one hand, and San Francisco on the other, *just half way* between the Missouri and the Pacific Ocean.

Running through a beautiful little valley for about eleven miles, we arrive at Wahsatch, a deserted place now, since Evanston has usurped the honour, formerly enjoyed by this place, of supplying the hungry and thirsty traveller with the delectable though somewhat livid pie, the deceptive sandwich—innocent of meat, but rich in fat and gristle,—or the brown and boiling liquid impudently imposed on the public under the respectable guise of coffee.

Game in abundance is found among the

hills—deer, elke, and antelope. In the Uintah and Wahsatch ranges, brown, black, and cinnamon bears are common.

At the little station called Castle Rock—just beyond Wahsatch—the cars enter the celebrated Echo Cañon, after passing through the longest tunnel on the road, 770 feet in length, cut through hard red clay and sandstone.

Awakening a thousand thundering echoes, the train dashes through the deep and dark ravine, some seven miles in length, and at its head from one-half to three-quarters of a mile in width. On the right hand it is flanked by bold, precipitous, buttressed cliffs, from 300 to 800 feet high, denuded and water-worn by the storms which rage against them during the prevalence of the southerly gales. The opposite side, sheltered from furious winds and driving tempests of rain, is formed by a succession of swelling, verduous hills, or sloping masses of rock, profusely clothed with grass and mosses. In the hollow between them rolls a bright transparent stream. Incessantly at work, it has excavated for its waters a channel some twenty feet below the surface. At certain points a rocky ledge or a pile of boulders vexes it into madness, until, gathering itself up like an athlete, it clears the obstacle in one swift and sudden bound. About the middle the ravine narrows to a mere defile, where the stream grows wilder, fiercer in its rage, as the banks become steeper and closer. The lofty cliffs on the right are here broken up into a variety of fantastic outlines: pyramids and pinnacles, spires and towers, battlemented fortresses and ruined cathedrals—the whole resembling a fairy vision, embodied in stone, and which might furnish the imagination of poet or artist with inexhaustible material.

Near the end of Echo Cañon, and on the summit of rocky heights, a thousand feet above the valley, are the remains of the fortifications prepared by the Mormons against the expedition threatened by the Government in the early days of Mormonism. A sudden anti-Mormon frenzy had seized upon the East, and to pacify it, says Ludlow, it was suggested that troops should be sent to break up and scatter the Mormon settlement. But this was not done, the Mormons were not once attacked; only a body of our regulars, termed an army of observation, posted themselves at Camp Floyd, thirty-nine miles from Salt Lake City, and there remained, much to the mortification of the more eager Mormons. The feeling between troops and saints was, however, of a moderately cordial character, and every day was the occasion of some interchange of courtesies. Still, the fortifications were an established fact, and it is noticeable that the place selected for their erection is really a dangerous locality for warlike operations. The defile is very narrow, the bare red walls rise perpendicularly; and had Brigham Young been able to fulfil his intention of showering down upon our men grape and shrapnell from guns hung slanting over the edge of the precipice, sweeping them with similar missiles from each end of the defile, an army of the size of Johnson's would have been crushed with wonderful ease and celerity.

Nine miles from Hanging Rock is Echo City. The town is situated at the foot of the bluff, which towers far above it. As the cars enter this place from Echo Cañon, they turn to the right; and close to the base of the cliff, on the same side, stands Pulpit Rock, and the old stage ranche on the left, just where, to all appearance, one would say, "We must inevitably pitch off right into the valley and river below."

Eight miles below Echo we enter the Weber Cañon, which almost surpasses the Echo in sublimity and grandeur. All along the valley flows the Weber river, exquisitely clear, and cold, and beautiful.

Weber Cañon—twin sister in beauty of Echo Cañon—is certainly one of the striking features of the journey, and deserves a few moments' attention. For a distance of about forty miles the river rushes onward, foaming over some rocky obstruction. It passes between two massive walls,—great, gloomy mountains, which close the scene on either side. The river becomes a torrent ere long, fretting, and falling, and striking with mad impetuosity against every piece of rock which may chance to be in its way. Then it struggles fiercely to escape from the turmoil of its own concocting, which it finally succeeds in doing, gliding away towards the level plain with a smooth and tranquil flow, as though resting from the fatigues of the wild and headlong journey through the deep and gloomy cañon.

Two miles down the cañon are the Witches' Rocks, weird and wild-looking, and wearing a fanciful resemblance to those much-abused "powers" of the dark ages.

Some six miles farther on, and at the point called the "Narrows," may be seen a lone pine tree on the river bank. The traveller can hardly fail to notice it, for no kindred growth is near it, above it, below it, or on either side; and this memorial of a remote antiquity was ascertained, strangely enough, to be exactly 1,000 miles from the Missouri river by the Pacific Railroad. It bears a board, with the inscription, "One Thousand Mile Tree."

Just below this tree, the train crosses over to the left bank of the Weber, on a trestle bridge; then it follows the bank for a short distance, and crosses another trestle to the right bank again. Almost opposite the bridge, on the side of the mountain, can be seen the Devil's Slide, or serrated rocks. This slide of the satanic name is composed of two parallel ridges of rock, ten feet apart, and from fifty to two hundred feet high. Like two narrow slabs, standing on edge, these ridges seem as though they had been forcibly projected from the parent mountain, and run up its side nearly to the smooth and grass-covered top, where one might peacefully repose while considering the propriety of attempting a descent by the means of his dreaded majesty's privileged way.

Dashing along, we can but slightly note the varied beauty of the surrounding scenery, until finally we enter into the narrowing gorge again, where the great massive walls rise precipitately, and shut from the view the lovely fields clothed in the greenest of green. Between these lofty, perpendicular cliffs we thunder through, where scarcely, you would say, there could be sufficient space for the track and the fierce torrent which roars along beside it; then, turning a sharp point, we again emerge into an open space in the cañon, and stop for a brief moment at Weber. This station lies between two Mormon settlements, which, taken in connection, are called Morgan City. The architectural beauties of this place are by no means world-famous, the materials mostly in use being logs and sun-dried bricks, which are the components of structures of the simplest description. The villages are separated by the river, which runs through bottom land, much of which is under cultivation for a considerable distance.

Having attempted to describe the several points of interest, I will now relate some singular experiences in Western railroading. I will ask the reader to recall to mind the description of Weber Cañon and the places following it.

Just before entering Weber Cañon, the conductor of the Pullman Palace car very politely asked us if we would like to ride through the cañon on the cow-catcher. This being a rather novel idea, myself and comrade, the Anglo-American, accepted with alacrity. We climbed into the cow-catcher. A young lady who was with us sat right under the large lamp of the engine; myself next to her. I had taken this seat because, the outer places being pretty small and I being pretty large, I did not think I should have room enough. At last we started, hurrying through a most magnificent valley. As we went along, some of the horsemen seeing us would pretend to race with us, causing great amusement on both sides. One man being at full gallop was thrown all of a sudden on to the caravan, and to escape a collision had to turn his horse into a marsh, from which he had great trouble to extricate him, and only did so after having covered himself, his horse, and some of the caravan with mud; but they all seemed to take it good-naturedly. All the country in this valley has a pleasant, homely look. The fields are well tended, irrigation being very easy from the river. We passed through one tunnel and then came to the Devil's Slide, which I have already described. The name is very suggestive. One could easily imagine Mephistopheles amusing himself on a hot day sliding between these slabs, into the cool air, using his caudal appendage as a runner. The scenery all through this valley repays one for all the dreary desolate country which we had been carried through on our way out. The sensation of riding in front of the engine is very peculiar. As we were carried over the trestle-work bridges, it seemed as though we gave gigantic leaps. Sometimes, indeed, we seemed to be lifted bodily off the earth.

I give you a phlegmatic letter which was written from this place:—

"ON BOARD ENGINE 119, M.P.R.R.

"Just over the cow-catcher. Four berths. All well. Twenty-five miles an hour. Have beaten all the race-horses of the country. Are going to arrive at Ogden before the train."

On leaving the cañon we passed across an undulating plain, cultivated in some parts; and having passed the places already slightly noticed, we arrived at Ogden at about 6.30.

The town is mostly Mormon, the schools and churches being, to a great extent, under the control of the Church of the Latter Day Saints. It is the county seat of Weber County, and will in time become a place of considerable importance, owing to the fact that it is the terminus of the Utah Central Railroad, the length of the road to Salt Lake City being thirty-six miles. This branch road to the city of the much-married Saints, is controlled and owned by the Mormon people.

There had been a large fire the night before our arrival at Ogden, and we had the pleasure of seeing a good many Saints, each with at least three wives, the last one generally looking like the daughter of the first. Indeed, many of them diminish in age from seventy down to fifteen. I asked some of my fellow travellers if the suckling babes which some of the Mormon matrons carried were not also young spouses.

Here we took the railroad to Salt Lake City.

Skirting along the Lake, I felt a sacred awe come over me, such as I had felt on approaching Jerusalem. The Salt Lake reminded me very much of the Dead Sea in general appearance, and the atmosphere hanging over it, and the salinous appearance of the shore. The sight of the well-trimmed hedges makes one feel as though one were in England. All the gardens are very closely planted with peach trees, and have a cheerful and homely look. The houses are small, like the English cottages, and are generally built with unbaked brick plastered, or else of brick alone, there being but few wooden structures.

CHAPTER VI.

Salt Lake City—Expensive Proselytism—City Irrigation—Subdivision of the City—The one Grand Theatre in the United States—The Tabernacle—View from Fort Douglas—Density of the Water of Salt Lake—Mormon Society—Museum—General Impressions concerning Mormonism—Residences of Brigham Young's Wives—Mormon Hospitality—Agriculture the Chief Employment—Good Government of Utah Territory — Corinne—Social Independence of American Ladies—Promontory—Opening of the Pacific Railway—Magnificence and Economy Combined à l'Américaine—General Observations on Mormonism—Utah Twenty-five Years Ago—Utah at the Present Day—View of the Great Salt Lake from Sand Ridge—Site of Salt Lake City determined by Customary Miracle—Population—Prospects of Mormonism.

On arriving at the station we found a magnificent car filled with saints of consideration, and a whole open space in front of the station crammed with Mormons. It appears they had expected a train of fresh Mormons from Norway and Sweden, and had come there to look for wives.

The Mormons pay the *trajet* to Norwegians and Swedes out to Salt Lake, so as to get proselytes; very often these people take advantage of this, and get out within thirty miles from the city and go off in another direction with the funds entrusted to them.

As I was getting out of the car, a little wrinkled old hag looked up at me, and with a smile of compassion, said,—

"Poor young man! So far away from his home, and all by himself!"

We were driven through a crowd of Mormons to the hotel, where we had a good wash, and devoured everything that was put within our reach.

After dinner I and my friend the Anglo-American took a walk. The streets are broad, and running water passes along on each side of the road in wooden gullies; a system of irrigation by which every man may water his own garden. We visited the car and engine building; everything was in perfect order. In the second story a religious meeting was being held, and as we passed a pretty hymn was wafted out on the night air, sung in perfect symphony and cadence by evidently young maiden choristers. The city of Salt Lake is mapped out into compartments, each compartment having a Sunday-school building, where Sunday-school is held, and where, at regular intervals during the winter, "hops" find a "local habitation." Performances were going on at the theatre. This is a fine prepossessing building, being perhaps the only monumental and national theatre in the United States. Why not have one at Washington?

The shops were quickly illuminated, and young saints were walking about with two or three spouses on their arms, looking gay and contented, and not at all as if they desired to massacre anybody. We went to a restaurant, where we got a glass of real English ale on draught. Grass is kept growing on the top of the barrel to keep it cool.

The next morning we visited the Tabernacle. This great oblong building, somewhat in the shape of a tortoise, with a dome-like roof, surmounted by a flag-staff, is perhaps the largest hall in the world of a single span roof, unsupported by pillar or column, used for purposes of public meetings. It is 250 feet inside from east to west, with a width of 150 feet from north to south. Forty-six parallelogram pillars of red sandstone, nine feet deep by three feet wide, form the base, which is a strong lattice work of timbers, firmly bolted together and self-supporting. The ceiling is sixty-two feet from the floor, and is perforated with holes neatly stuccoed round, which serve the double purpose of ventilation, and a means by which scaffolding can be slung up to repair or whiten when necessity arises for doing either. The west end is occupied by a rostrum or "stand," an elevated platform, with three seats in the centre, in front, elevated one a little above the other, for the Church dignitaries. The space on either side of these seats is devoted to other members of the priesthood, such as Bishops, High Priests, Seventies.

The acoustic properties are very fine. There is always a great throng, as the attendance is enormous. There is one gallery which encircles the building, besides the seats on the floor. These seats are of wood, without cushions, so formed as to render the long occupation of them not unpleasant. The chancel is large, plenty of space being left for the choir.

The President's seat is covered with an old buffalo skin; the idea is peculiar and individual, and causes some admiration for the man,—his stern simplicity reminding one of his former life, and of that exodus across the desert.

The great organ—the third largest in the country, and *the largest* yet built in the United States—was made in Salt Lake, and is of fine design and of excellent make. The builder was Mr. Joseph Ridges, a Mormon artificer, of English birth. The great beauty of this building is its stern simplicity—its chasteness.

In the afternoon we drove to Fort Douglas,

a United States garrison, which is situated on the heights above the city.

From this point we get a most advantageous view of the city and its surroundings. The City Hall, Tabernacle, Theatre—all standing out in bold relief.

In the distance we have the river Jordan, and overshadowing all these, the Wahsatch mountains.

We were received with great politeness by the officers, and shown over the buildings. This place, although situated on a barren mountain side, has been rendered very pretty by the building of a small pond or lake, in the middle of which, rather inappropriately placed, is a statue of Eve; of course, one might take it for Venus rising from the wave.

We were very kindly invited to go on the excursion to the lake got up by the Mormons in honour of General Garfield, then a visitor at the city. We rode in open cars across alkaline plains, to the shore of the lake, where we embarked on a steamboat and were taken for a short sail. It is very hard to make any headway in this heavy water. We were served with all sorts of luxuries, and the people were genial and pleasant, the young ladies especially, but reserved—not at all what one is led to expect of them from the malicious reports which are spread abroad respecting the state of Mormon society.

Every one appeared to be in the best of spirits. Here a group portrait was taken, the hotel being made with balconies at each floor.

Every one tried to get into the most conspicuous position; some gentlemen who had taken particular pains to get into a very prominent place, striking a very impressive *pose*, were left entirely out of the picture.

That evening the *Messiah* was given at the theatre, everybody taking his part with care, and their efforts being crowned with success. This is a great move, and one cannot help but think that if there is something wrong in this society, it will be eradicated by the elevation of the general tastes of the people,—and what elevates the taste as does music?

The next day I was again invited to go on an excursion; this time to Utah Lake. This is a fresh-water lake, and the country around is extremely fertile and beautiful. All the villages seem to be in good condition and flourishing, the grounds well kept, and the residences pretty and neat.

At one of the villages or towns, we visited

the *chef lieu* of the country. We went to the top of the City Hall, from which we had a very fine view of the country round.

It is a strange thing on the part of new descendants of Englishmen, that although we were away from Salt Lake a considerable time, they gave us nothing to eat. When I say Englishmen, I mean that most of them being of English extraction, they have retained the type and manners wonderfully. Mr. Jennings, though, is more true to his Britannic descent, having both days brought with him some champagne and edibles, which the five favoured ones who partook of them greatly enjoyed. I had the pleasure of hearing General Garfield speak of his impression about the country; and if he feels sincerely, as I am convinced he does, what he then said, I only wish we could have more men like him to take care of public affairs. That evening we had a very pleasant dinner, at which we had the pleasure of having the officers as guests.

The next day we were taken to see some smelting works, and also taken a short distance on the narrow guage road which leads to a mine in the mountains. This road descends very rapidly. In coming down no steam-power is used. The following morning we visited the musuem, which is very interesting, containing some very fine Indian and foreign curiosities, large-sized photographs of all the principal scenes in the world, and the first boat ever used by a white man on the Salt Lake, also an original sewing machine made at Salt Lake City; and having visited some of the principal houses and residences, we reluctantly took our departure.

I must say that, so far as I could judge, although perhaps my opinion is not worth much, I saw nothing but was admirable during my stay there. To me the contemplation is simply wonderful; this band of common people —the very dregs of all society, perhaps even criminals—wending their way across a dreary desert, to the shores of a Salt Sea, and in the midst of cheerless rugged mountains, on an alkalinous plain, building a city which is as a garden of Eden, and forming a society which for order and completeness reminds one of those of the Greeks; and their faith, although disfigured by polygamy, is otherwise as pure and as sensible as are other religions. The army seems to me to be, morally, in a way to be gained over by the Mormons. I was told that Mr. Jennings is very far from being a docile follower of Emperor Young, and that the prophet is continually on his guard against him.

I must not forget to mention that we went to see the house which the President has built for his favourite wife. It is a very fine building. He must be a man of very great taste, and although approaching seventy, of a very sanguine temperament. We also saw the house of his discarded wife, who, out of spite, has her residence right under his nose. Most of the property on this hill belongs to Brigham, and the villas overlooking the road are principally occupied as habitations by his wives,—sometimes one wife living alone, sometimes two or three keeping house together. The residences are very pretty, and the gardens well tended. The entrance to the President's own house is through an earth wall some nineteen or twenty feet high, the gate being defended by two quaintly-shaped lions with extremely large mouths. Altogether, it was much more like the entrance of an old Neapolitan chateau, than that of a residence in the midst of the far west.

The hospitalities we received at this city left a very pleasant impression on our minds. To the north of us is the wonderful yellowstone country. There is a rather funny story said to be related by Mr. Langford, one of the early discoverers. At a certain point on the yellowstone river, the water runs down a steep and perfect grade, over a surface of slate rock which has become so smooth from the velocity of the rushing torrent, that at a distance of twenty miles the friction is so great the water is boiling hot! An egg may be cooked in it, inside of four minutes. This statement may appear to be in somewhat of the same condition.

We have now left most of our friends behind. Passing through this country one discovers the story of Mormonism everywhere. This people are essentially an agricultural people. You see none of the factories, etc., which you usually notice in the smallest western settlement. There is also a certain amount of order and quiet about the streets, indicative of good government, and which one lost so soon as one got out of Utah Territory. It seems a pity that a canal or stream could not be made so as to keep a continual flow from the Salt Lake, in that way producing a diminution of the quantity of salt; oysters and salt-water fish might then be placed in it. The diminution of the quantity of salt would gradually have an effect upon the ground, and then upon the water, and would be of very great advantage. We passed on this line Corinne, a very important Mormon city. It seems so strange, in the midst of this desert

10

to have one's mind drawn back to that wonderful production of that most highly civilized and refined woman, Madame de Staël.

My companion had a compartment with a lady who was out on a small excursion by herself. She had come from Denver, and was going to San Francisco. She asked about Salt Lake City, and said she would stop there on her way home. How strange this would seem to an European. A lady not more than thirty-five, travelling a distance of over 1200 miles without a companion!

Here we see the first Chinese settlements. They build their houses very near the railroad track.

Promontory, in Utah Territory, fifty-two miles beyond Ogden, and 1084 miles from Omaha, and 830 from San Francisco, is noted for one important fact in the history of the Pacific Railroad, namely, at this point the scene of the meeting of the two railroads took place, the one advancing from the east, the other from the west.

Here, on the 10th of May, 1869, the connection between the two roads was made, uniting the great East with the great West. Here, the two roads, one starting westward from Omaha, and the other starting eastward from Sacramento (the then western terminus), met and joined, and became one. Word went round the world, sent from this little spot, and carried by the electric telegraph over land and under sea, that "The Pacific Railroad is open;" the moment the connection was made, the fact was telegraphed to all parts of the Union, and then to every place of importance on the globe. The scene was impressive,—the occasion festive. From all quarters of the world came a multitude of persons to witness the grand event,—travelling, however, from opposite directions and meeting here. Two long trains of cars, one from Sacramento and the other from Omaha, stood fronting each other, their respective locomotives' occasionally spitting out a little steam, by way of defiance. Between the two locomotives, there was a small space, not yet bridged over.

The appointed time having arrived, Leland Stanford, President of the Central Pacific R. R., accompanied by the other prominent officers of the C. P. R. R., advanced to the end of the last rail, while on the other side, Vice-President Durant, of the M. P. R. R., assisted by the officials of the same Company, came forward to the termination of the road on their side. Both parties now paused, while a clergyman, advancing at right angles towards the centre of the open, unconnected portion of the road, stopped within a pace or two of it, and reverently invoked in a few eloquent and heartfelt words the Divine blessing upon this great work. Then the last tie, a beautiful piece of workmanship, of California laurel, with silver plates, on which were engraved suitable inscriptions, was put in place, and the last connecting rails were laid by parties of workmen from each Company. The last spikes were then brought forward—one of gold from California, one of silver from Nevada, and one of gold, silver, and iron from Arizona.

President Stanford then took the hammer, made of solid silver, and to the handle of which were attached the telegraph wires, and with the first tap of the silver hammer on the head of the golden spike, at the hour of twelve M., the news of this notable event was flashed to all parts of the civilized world. As each spike was driven home, appropriate speeches were made, and when the last spike was being hammered in, the assembled multitude looked on the scene with breathless interest, and when the final blow was given, the pent-up enthusiasm found vent in hearty cheers, which rent the air, and then, to finish up, three "times three," and a "tiger."

It must not be supposed that the above described tie, with its silver plates and the spikes of precious metal, were allowed to remain very long in the positions in which they had been placed, for while the invited guests were partaking of a sumptuous repast in the saloon cars, workmen set at once to work taking up the silver-plated tie and valuable spikes, and in their places put an ordinary pine tie, etc. This pine tie had to be replaced three separate times, on each occasion it having been chipped away by relic-hunters; each person who took a piece of the second and third ties no doubt religiously believing that they have a piece of the identical tie which took the place of the silver-plated one.

As the sun sank below the western summit of Promontory Point, the long trains moved away with parting salutes from the locomotives, the participants in the never-to-be-forgotten celebration speeding back to their far-distant homes.

Somewhat behind Promontory, the hills begin to rise, and attain almost to the height of mountains. From their summits may be seen, spreading out like a vast sea of molten silver, Great Salt Lake, brilliant and placid in the morning sun. With the aid of a glass,

Church, or Antelope, and other mountain islands could be seen, rearing their lofty peaks far above the silver fringe at their base, while their sides are covered by a mantle of the purest green.

Far beyond these islands, the white-capped Wahsatch Mountains rise; you almost think that you can point out the curve in their brown sides, where lies, safe in her mountain solitude, Salt Lake City.

Here among the hills we readily let our minds run into a dozen speculative dreams, concerning that most singular phenomenon in American social life, the great city of the polygamous saints, containing a population of over 25,000; a city prosperous and beautiful, situated in the midst of a surrounding territory of upwards of 100,000 souls.

If you talk with some earnest Mormon of a deeply religious nature, perhaps a doubt may arise in your mind, and involuntarily you might ask yourself the question, "Can they be right?" "Is it possible that this detestable social and religious system—enslaving women, physically, and holding man in the vilest of mental bondage—can have any foundation in right reason, in truth and wisdom, in real spiritual life, and in that 'peace of God which passeth all understanding'?" But a little reflection must inevitably lead us to the conclusion that a system so foreign, not only to American institutions, but to Anglo-Saxonism, must sooner or later give way and be swept out of existence before the advancing tide of American emigration and civilization.

And yet Mormonism will not have lived in vain; this "peculiar institution" has been the means of peopling the waste places, of building up beautiful cities where but yesterday, as it were, was the howling wilderness, making the desert to blossom as the rose; in a word, Mormonism has been the great pioneer of orderly industry, of patient toil, of some of the leading virtues of the Anglo-Saxon race.

And if in a latitudinarian spirit one should apply to this remarkable sect the maxim of Pope,—

"For modes of faith let graceless zealots fight,
His can't be wrong whose life is in the right,"—

we should certainly admit that this community has a pretty large share of right on its side. A people with only one vice appreciable by the general observer—and that vice a mode of religious opinion, in regard to marriage, reduced to practice—may be considered tolerably respectable, as communities go. The horrid vice of polygamy has somehow in Utah a less repulsive aspect than has the venial sin of prostitution in the purely Christian cities of New York, London, and Paris.

Yet, as I have said, the peculiar people is not destined to endure; at least, its peculiarity is not. Its one vice will die out; how many of its virtues will survive the extinction of that vice?

Twenty-five years ago, Utah was a wilderness; to-day, it is a land of thrift, industry, and wealth, its soil teeming with riches, its extensive population enjoying in peace and harmony the products of their labour. Prosperous towns and settlements (with 220 schools) extend a distance of about 500 miles from Idaho Territory on the north, to Arizona on the south.

A noble view of the Great Salt Lake is obtained from what is known as the "Sand Ridge," which the railway—the Utah Central —traverses for a distance of twelve miles.

Here the great expanse of the Lake, which is 120 miles long and 45 miles broad, may be seen to the best advantage. Dotted with many charming islands, wherein are found many rural retreats, and natural bathing places, it opens up to the gaze of the tourist scenery embracing the principal elements of loveliness and sublimity; a loveliness resembling, yet perhaps inferior to, the Bay of Naples, and a magnificence not unworthy the Swiss Alps.

During the summer months, sunset upon the lake is one of the most brilliant spectacles the eye could ever hope to see, so gorgeously rich is the colouring, when peak and cañon are bathed in the purple and golden twilight of departing day.

Within about five miles of the City of the Saints, the railroad reaches the Hot Spring Lake, fed by the celebrated springs. It forms a beautiful little sheet of water, nearly three miles long and upwards of a mile in width, whose placid surface is scarcely rippled by the flocks of wild ducks and geese floating so lazily upon it.

While varying greatly in the colouring of their descriptions, almost all travellers have recognised the skill with which the Mormon leaders selected the site and have gradually developed the plan of their city. But we should not wonder at the felicity of the choice, since, according to President Brigham Young, it was indicated to him in a vision by an angel, who, standing on a conical hill, pointed out the locality where the New Temple should be built. Consequently, when the Mormon patriarch first entered the Salt Lake basin, he looked for the angel-haunted cone, and discovering a fresh, clear stream rippling at its base, he named it City Creek. Some say the angel was the spirit of his predecessor, Joseph Smith, the apostle of Mormonism; others, that as early as 1842 the latter was favoured with dreams of these valleys and mountains, these lakes and rivers, and revealed them to his disciples. At all events, on the enforced exodus of the Saints from Nauvoo, they crossed the Rocky Mountains, and descended into this sheltered basin, to found their new city in a scene of picturesque beauty. On the 24th of July, 1847, the vanguard of the Mormon emigration, numbering 143 men, entered Salt Lake Valley; five days later, 150 more men arrived; and on the 31st of the same month, Salt Lake City was laid out.

The city is situated in an angle of the Wahsatch Mountains, and stretches up close to the foot of the northern hills; while, on the east, it comes within about three miles of the bold and rugged range. The highest summits of the Wahsatch reach an elevation of more than 7,000 feet above the level of the valley, and between 11,000 and 12,000 above the ocean level.

The city is laid out in square blocks of ten

acres each, the wide streets running at right angles to each other, following the cardinal points of the compass. Thus the city covers a space of about nine miles square.

It is a trite saying that the obvious is seldom the actual and real; and this is well illustrated by the census returns of Utah Territory and Salt Lake City.

Nine persons out of every ten will unhesitatingly give their opinion to the effect that the females in Utah far outnumber the males, whereas in reality the contrary is true, the males exceeding the females by 1277. The returns for Salt Lake City conclusively prove that "the twin relic" is sustained principally by foreigners. Among the native (American-born) population, the females are 78 fewer than the males, while in the foreign born population the females exceed the males in number by 686. In the native population of the city, there are 50 females to 51 males; in the foreign population there are 38 females to 31 males.

Thus we find that the peculiar feature of Mormonism, and which is so utterly un-American and opposed to the spirit of the age—I refer to Polygamy—is sustained and upheld in the main by foreigners. This fact alone is good and sufficient grounds to base the hope that time, with its gentle but irresistible influences, will finally settle the Mormon question. But should there be any meddlesome Federal legislation, conceived in a spirit of virtuous horror—the parent of bigotry and persecution—the result might be widely different.

Should the "stamping out" process ever be attempted,—and this is precisely what the Mormon leaders want to see adopted, well knowing that "the blood of the martyrs is the seed of the Church,"—then Mormonism would receive an impetus, which religious persecution alone can give, by which its forces would be concentrated and strengthened, its doctrines and practices brought more prominently than ever before the world, its wonderful material growth and prosperity set forth in its favour—and we all know what a weighty argument in these degenerate days is material wealth.

Under these conditions, undoubtedly great accessions to the ranks of Mormonism would be made, and the Mormon leaders, far from dreading a conflict with the United States Government, would welcome it as a source of profit to the Church of the Latter Day Saints.

The greatest enemy of every form of religious bigotry and social error is free speech and untrammeled discussion, and when the railroad, the telegraph, and the press—the most powerful trinity of modern times—made their presence known in Salt Lake City, the words "*Mene, mene, tekel, upharsin*" were written on the walls of the temple of Mormonism.

Prophecy, though always dangerous, may be indulged in here with some confidence. For if it be objected that the Saints will make another exodus whenever they feel the inconvenience of having neighbours, I reply that exodus is not establishment, and that they who could not hold what they had gained, will again lose under the same circumstances whatever they may be destined to acquire.

CHAPTER VII.

The American Desert; its Bad Pre-eminence—Nevada—Discovery of Silver—Rapid Increase of Population—Aboriginal Tribes—Topography—Mining the Chief Industry—Silver Mines the Most Important—Copper, Iron, Salt—Tecoma—Pilot Peak—Humboldt Wells—Valley of the Humboldt—Richness of the Soil—Humboldt River—Elko—Game Country—Five Mile Cañon—Hamilton—Mining District—Most Important Mines—Attractiveness of a New Mining District—Small Profits of Miners—" Good Society " in a New Mining District—Rise of " Vigilance Committees "—Great Cave of Nevada.

About twenty-eight miles beyond Promontory, we reach a little station called Monument, which is nearly on the outskirts of that great waste known as the American Desert. Here, at times—dependent on the direction of the wind,—the atmosphere becomes offensively charged with strong alkaline and saline odours, distinctive of this locality. At all times, even when the wind is most favourable, the air seems to be, if one may say so, in a state of perpetual pickle.

The arid waste called the American Desert extends over an area of about sixty miles square.

Desolate, bare, snow-white—not even Sahara so thoroughly deserves the designation of "desert." You walk upon alkali dust—a white, impalpable powder—which parches and chokes you, and it would certainly strangle you if you did not now and again relieve your throat with copious draughts of wine and water.

For a hundred miles the eye ranges over rough, broken places, over unsightly stones, over mountainous heaps of glaring, dazzling alkali; but no smooth, level lawn, no pleasant field or rolling meadow-land, no friendly habitation, no house of any kind, not a tree or a shrub,—in a word, NO GREEN THING WHATSOEVER.

In the waste places of Egypt the traveller finds relief in the oasis, which dots the desert with green and moisture; in those of Arabia he comes across an occasional date tree, or a well of cool, sweet water. But in the American Desert—true to our national radicalism—there is absolutely nothing but desert, not even earth, for the very ground which you traverse is soda—white, and bitter, and at times blinding, while the air and the few pools of water are as salt as the sea.

Several theories have been started to prove that this desert was once the bed of a great inland sea, perhaps a portion of Great Salt

Lake itself. And, indeed, there are many evidences in support of this supposition. The sloping plain sweeps off towards that body of water, and in some places bends down until its thirsty sands are kissed by the salt waves of the great inland sea.

At Lucinda—some eighty odd miles from Monument—we leave Utah Territory, and before our arrival at the next station, Tecoma, we have entered the great silver State, Nevada.

The region from which this State was formed was a portion of the territory acquired by the United States from Mexico under the treaty of Guadalupe Hidalgo, belonging, previous to its transfer, to the department of Alta, California. By this same treaty, Utah, and the Mormons with it, who had fondly thought they had escaped from the subtile, hostile influences of Anglo-Saxondom, came under the authority of the United States Government again, by the fiat of an inexorable fate brought face to face with the inimical social forces of a progressive civilization.

For ten years after the first settlement of Nevada, the population increased slowly, there being less than 1,000 inhabitants within the limits of the State in 1859. The discovery of silver that year attracted immigration to such an extent, that in 1861 there were nearly 17,000 inhabitants.

The principal aboriginal tribes of this State are the Washoes and Pah Utahs in the western, and the Soshones in the eastern part. These tribes, or nations, are divided into many small communities, or families, sparsely scattered over the country, and are generally peaceful and inoffensive. Some of the Indians are employed by the whites, and are found useful in many kinds of unskilled labour.

Nevada is mostly an elevated plateau, having a general altitude of more than 4,000 feet above tide water. It has numerous chains of mountains, from 4,000 to 5,000 feet above the common level of the State. These, for the most part, are covered with dense forests of pine, spruce, and fir, furnishing superior lumber. Between the ranges of mountains are beautiful and fertile valleys, in width varying from five to twenty miles, some of the most productive yielding from thirty to sixty bushels of wheat, and from forty to eighty bushels of barley to the acre.

The leading industrial pursuit is mining, the silver mines constituting the great source of wealth to the State. Gold was first discovered in 1849, near the Carson river, and the mines were worked with profit for several years, but have generally been abandoned for the richer silver mines.

As stated above, silver was discovered in 1859, near what is known as the Cornstock ledge, in Storey County. This is still the most valuable silver-bearing lode found in Nevada. It has been developed to the depth of more than 700 feet, and the famous Sutro tunnel project, now nearly completed, will, when finished, enable the lode to be worked to the depth of 3000 feet or more, with prospective profit. This tunnel will be 19,000 feet long, and its estimated cost is upwards of $50,000.

Copper and iron mines exist in some parts of the State, and lead and coal have been discovered. Salt is found in the greatest abundance. The salt bed at Sand Springs, in Churchill County, extends over several hundred acres, much of which is a stratum of pure coarse salt, nearly a foot thick; and in order to have it ready for immediate stocking, it is only requisite to throw it on a platform, that the water may drain off. About fifty miles west of this point is another and still more extensive salt bed, its superficial area being nearly twenty square miles, while in Nye or Esmeralda County, there is a bed covering more than fifty square miles, over nearly all of which the salt, clean, dry, and white, lies to a depth varying from six inches to two feet.

This mineral, so largely used in the reduction of silver ores, is an important source of wealth to the State.

Sir Charles Dilke, in reference to the Silver State, says: "The rise of Nevada has been sudden. I was shown in Virginia city a building block of land that *rents* for ten times what it *cost* four years ago. Nothing short of solid silver by the yard would have brought 20,000 men to live on the summit of Mount Davidson. It is easy here to understand the mad rush and madder speculation that took place at the time of the discovery. Every valley in the Washoe Range was 'prospected,' and pronounced paved with silver; every mountain was a solid mass. The publication of the Californian newspapers was suspended, as writers, editors, proprietors, and 'devils,' all had gone with the rush. San Francisco went clean mad, and London and Paris were not far behind."

Tecoma, the first station within the limits of the State of Nevada, is not especially remarkable, and would not call for special mention were it not the nearest point to some newly-discovered silver and lead mines, said to be very rich in these metals. These mines are located some five miles to the south of this station, in the Toano range of mountains. Much excitement has naturally been aroused among mining operators. A smelting furnace has been erected at the mines, and several hundred tons of bullion produced, with a fine prospect of continued production.

Almost due south, about thirty-six miles from this station, Pilot Peak—a great mass of crushed and shattered rocks—rears its lofty head some 2,500 feet above the barren plain. Its summit, when viewed from a distance, reminds the traveller of the appearance of a grand old keep or Moorish watch-tower, erected on some commanding eminence, overlooking the plains, for the purpose of noting the earliest signs of any hostile incursion.

This majestic pile has been visible for upwards of fifty miles along the route. To the emigrant, in pre-railroad days, it was a truly welcome sight, for, after his long and toilsome journey across the dreary waste, he knew by this landmark that he was nearing Humboldt Wells, or Thousand Spring Valley, where his patient, weary teams were sure of water, and food, and rest, and where he himself, and his comrades in hardships, might repose for awhile, encamped in a beautiful little valley, in the midst of which—some twenty in number—the celebrated Humboldt Wells are situated.

Unless these wells are specially pointed out to the traveller, he will scarcely observe them, for, with the exception of a circle of rank grass around each, there is nothing that marks their existence. When standing on the bank of one of these curious springs, you look on a still surface of water, perhaps six or seven feet in diameter, and nearly circular; there is no perceptible current, and you think you are gazing at an ordinary well, the result of man's handiwork, instead of a natural spring, inexhaustible, and of an unknown depth, since repeated soundings, with a fixed determination on the part of the investigators to touch bottom "this time," have failed to accomplish the purpose.

The most plausible theory yet advanced with reference to these wells or springs, is the one that supposes them to be the craters of extinct volcanoes, which at one period of the world's existence vomited forth upon the surrounding country flames, and cinders, and burning, molten lava.

The soil, and indeed the whole face of the land for miles and miles around, betrays abundant evidence of mighty volcanic eruptions.

Lava in hard, rough blocks, or decomposed and powdered, gigantic masses of granite and sandstone, broken, shattered, and thrown around in wild confusion, are a few of the signs, indicative of some of nature's terrific convulsions, far back in the night of antiquity.

The valley in which these wells are situated is about five miles in length, and about three broad, the surface of which is carpeted with a most luxuriant growth of verdure. The sudden transition from the parched desert, stretching over a space of a hundred miles, to these lovely valleys, grass-covered and watered so bounteously, seems like the magical transformation of a dream.

You step, as it were, from a desert into the very midst of green valleys, the atmosphere of which is full of fragrance from the countless thousands of wild flowers which flourish and bloom in these beautiful valleys.

The road runs down the valley for a few miles, and then we enter the main valley of the Humboldt, one of the richest agricultural and grazing valleys to be found in the State. The soil—a deep, black loam, moist enough for all purposes, without irrigation, is from fifteen inches to two feet in depth. This part of the valley, in length about eighty miles, with an average width of about ten miles, is nearly all of the quality described; all that it requires to make it one of the richest regions in this section of the country, is patient labour and ordinary skill in the science of farming.

The valley is almost totally unoccupied, only a few settlers being scattered here and there.

The valleys of Nevada are beautiful beyond description. Each one has its own peculiar attractions. Nature has bountifully bestowed on this favoured land every charm of scenery and climate, every substantial advantage.

We now follow the Humboldt river, a rapid stream, which takes its rise in the Humboldt mountains, emptying itself into Humboldt lake. The main stream has many varieties of fish, and at certain seasons of the year its waters are covered with wild ducks and geese. Owing to the parched soil through which it flows, the volume of the river is much diminished as it nears the lake into which it falls.

At Elko—some half-dozen stations off—we have a good substantial meal, for which we pay $1 currency, or 75 cents coin. This place is 1,307 miles from Omaha, and 607 from San Francisco, and contains a population between 800 and 1,000. It is the county seat of Elko County.

Inasmuch as a large portion of this town consisted of canvas tents, which are now giving place to structures of a more permanent character, one might say that it has almost passed its *linenhood*—a stage or condition of Western railroad towns which all who are familiar with the species will readily recognise.

The State University, which cost $30,000, is located here, just northward of the town. At no great distance from the town, there are a number of warm springs, which, on account of their healing qualities, are attracting considerable attention. In due course of time they will doubtless be the centre of a fashionable watering-place, when this region becomes a thickly-populated country.

Rapid mountain streamlets intersect this part of the State. Game in all varieties abounds, and causes this section to be much frequented by hunters, trappers, and sportsmen.

Twelve miles west of Elko we reach Moleen —a signal station. Here the valley assumes a new and more inviting appearance. Broad green meadowlands on one side; to the right, bold, high bluffs, covered with a luxuriant growth of bluff grass. In a little while, we leave the pleasant, open country, which is shut out from our view, as we enter Five Mile Cañon.

The scenery as we rattle along through this cañon presents many bold and impressive features. Near the entrance there are several isolated towers of massed rock, shooting upward to a height of nearly 200 feet. The river sparkles through the cañon, and occasionally you catch glimpses of the rich meadows through the open spaces between the bluffs.

After passing Carlin, the next station, we reach Palisade, where stages are in waiting to take passengers to the WHITE PINE Country, a distance of 110 miles, and where are located some of the most famous mines of Nevada.

The principal city in this district is Hamilton, and Treasure City ranks second. Around these two cities are located the chief mines of the district, such as the Eberhardt, California, Hidden Treasure, Consolidated Chloride, Aurora, Aurora South, Alturas, Summit and Nevada, Post Hole, Industry, Williard, etc.

The Eberhardt mine, which first attracted attention to this locality, was discovered in 1866, but it was not until the spring of 1869 that the mad stampede to this quarter of miners and speculators took place.

Some idea may be formed of the power to attract population which a new mining district possesses, when it is related that in 1869 about 400 people were at work in the White Pine country, and now its population exceeds 10,000. And yet, we know from statistics that this difficult, toilsome, and dangerous form of human labour yields the smallest *average* return to the actual workers in the gloomy mines.

What would our fierce, free miners of the west say, if they were informed of the mining laws in Scotland, and which were in full force and effect previous to 1775? According to these laws the persons employed in the mines were transferable with the estate. However, as the French say, "We have changed all that."

The rough miners of Nevada are decidedly free—especially with revolvers and bowie knives. It is related that a citizen of a new mining town was heard to complain bitterly of the tame and degenerate habits of city life in the following expressive words :—

"This place is too dull for me; only think how plaguey mean it is getting. Only one man shot yesterday, and it is doubtful if he will die! And now here is the best part of the day gone, and no prospect of a row. Oh! there is them Chinamen; perhaps something 'll turn up yet to make a little excitement."

Whenever the "roughs" are "hard up" for "a little excitement," poor John Chinaman is immediately remembered, and "a lively time" follows at once.

In the early days of Nevada—and this remark applies with equal force to all other Western communities in their infancy—the aristocracy consisted of the men most noted for the commission of deeds of violence and bloodshed.

To have killed "your man" was sufficient, indeed, for admission into the "best society;" but a mere paltry homicide unattended by any shocking or horrible circumstances—a sort of *sauce piquante* to the almost daily meal of murder—was certainly not enough to admit one to the highest honours.

The sweet-tempered, soft-mannered, amiable gentleman who could boast of having killed in cold blood his half-dozen men at least—and if they happened to be well known, all the better for the killer—was always a man of distinction in his burg, and commanded the admiration and respect of his fellows.

As the first death in the world, according to the biblical record, was a murder, so Nevada records the fact that the first twenty-six graves of white men in that State were those of persons who had been murdered.

An Irishman would have said that there were only two classes of society in that region, namely, the killers and the killed. With the exception of the Hibernicism, he would have been right.

In a rude state of society, where every man is his own lawyer, witness, judge, jury, and executioner, the knife or the pistol is arbiter between man and man, and undelegated force governs.

Wherever power manifests itself, fear, respect, and admiration are attracted. This probably accounts for the fact of the men of blood having the ascendancy in these infant communities.

"The desperado stalked the streets," says a well-informed and pleasing writer, "with a swagger graded to the number of his homicides; and a nod of recognition from him was sufficient to make an humble admirer happy for the rest of the day."

The deference that was paid to men of this class, especially those of wide and established reputations, and who were said "to keep their own private graveyards," was unmistakably marked and accorded with alacrity, not to say cheerfulness. When he appeared in public, apparelled in long-tailed frock-coat, patent leather well-fitting boots, and with dainty little slouch hat tipped jauntily over the left eye, the small fry roughs made room for his majesty; when he entered the restaurant, the waiters deserted bankers and merchants to overwhelm him with obsequious service; when he shouldered his way to the bar, the shouldered parties wheeled indignantly, recognised him, and—apologised. They got a look in return that froze their marrow; and by that time a curled and breast-pinned bar-keeper was beaming over the counter, proud of the established acquaintanceship that permitted such a familiar form of speech as,

"How're ye, Billy, old fel? Glad to see you. What'll you take? the old thing?"

The "old thing" meant his customary drink, of course.

I am indebted for the above sketch to the facile pen of the writer last quoted.

A few extracts from the periodicals of that day and locality, where the "old-fashioned, worn out" machinery of justice, in vogue in older communities was just barely tolerated as an experiment, will give us a glimpse of a state of things now happily fast disappearing.

The following newspaper accounts are clipped from the *Virginia City (Nev.) Enterprise:*—

"FATAL SHOOTING AFFRAY.—An affray occurred last evening in a billiard saloon on C Street, between *Deputy-Marshal* Jack Williams and Wm. Brown, which resulted in the immediate death of the latter. There had been some difficulty between the parties for several months.

"An inquest was immediately held, and the following testimony adduced:

"Officer Geo. Birdcall, sworn, says:—I was told Wm. Brown was drunk, and looking for Jack Williams; so soon as I heard that, I started for the parties to prevent a collision; went into the billiard saloon; saw Billy Brown running around, saying if anybody had anything against him to show cause; he was talking in a boisterous manner, and Officer Perry took him to the other end of the room to talk to him; Brown came back to me; remarked to me that he thought he was as good as anybody, and knew how to take care of himself; he passed by me and went to the bar; don't know whether he drank or not: Williams was at the end of the billiard-table, next to the stairway; Brown, after going to the bar, came back and said he was as good as any man in the world,—he had then walked out to the end of the first billiard-table from the bar; I moved closer to him, supposing there would be a fight; as Brown drew his pistol I caught hold of it; he had fired one shot at Williams; don't know the effect of it; caught hold of him with one hand, and took hold of the pistol and turned it up; think he fired once after I caught hold of the pistol; I wrenched the pistol from him; walked to the end of the billiard, and told a party that I had Brown's pistol, and to stop shooting; I think four shots were fired in all; after walking out Mr. Foster remarked that Brown was shot dead."

Here we have an officer of the law indulging in pistol practice at a drunken man, who had been disarmed by a brother officer, and it was "merely" remarked by Mr. Foster that Brown was shot dead,—an instance of the truth of the saying, "Familiarity breeds contempt."

In the following account the same gentleman, *Deputy-Marshal* Williams' again figures:—

"ROBBERY AND DESPERATE AFFRAY.—On Tuesday, a German named Charles Hurtzal, engineer in a mill at Silver City, came to this place, and visited the hurdy-gurdy house on

B Street. The music, dancing, and Teutonic maidens awakened memories of Faderland, until our German friend was carried away with rapture. He evidently had money, and was spending it freely. Late in the evening Jack Williams and Andy Blessington invited him downstairs to take a cup of coffee. Williams proposed a game of cards, and went upstairs to procure a deck, but not finding any, returned. On the stairway he met the German, and drawing his pistol knocked him down and rifled his pockets of some seventy dollars. Hurtzal dared give no alarm, as he was told, with a pistol at his head, if he made any noise or exposed them, they would blow his brains out. So effectually was he frightened, that he made no complaint until his friends forced him."

This efficient city officer, Jack Williams, had the common reputation of being a burglar, a highwayman, and a desperado. It was said to be quite an ordinary occurrence for him to stop citizens at midnight, in the streets of Virginia City, draw his revolver upon them, and rifle them of their valuables. Then cautioning them to keep their "mouth shut" about this "little private matter," on pain of receiving his leaden compliments "on sight," ordered them to "move on."

"More Cutting and Shooting.—The devil seems to have again broken loose in our town. Pistols and guns explode, and knives gleam as in early times. When there has been a long season of quiet, people are slow to wet their hands in blood; but once blood is spilled, cutting and shooting come easy. Night before last, Jack Williams was assassinated; and yesterday before noon, we had more bloody work growing out of the killing of Williams, and on the same street in which he met his death. It appears that Tom Reeder, a friend of Williams, and George Gumbert were talking, at the meat-market of the latter, about the killing of Williams the previous night, when Reeder said it was a most cowardly act to shoot a man in such a way, giving him no 'show.' Gumbert said that Williams had ' as good a show as he gave Billy Brown,' meaning the man killed by Williams last March. Reeder said it was a d——d lie, that Williams had no 'show' at all. At this, Gumbert drew a knife and stabbed Reeder, cutting him in two places in the back. One stroke of the knife cut into the sleeve of Reeder's coat and passed downward in a slanting direction through his clothing, and entered his body at the small of the back; another blow struck more squarely, and made a much more dangerous wound. Gumbert gave himself up to the officers of justice, and was shortly afterwards discharged by Justice Atwill, *on his own recognizance*, to appear for trial at six o'clock in the evening. In the meantime Reeder had been taken into the office of Dr. Owens, where his wounds were properly dressed. *One of his wounds was considered quite dangerous, and it was thought by many that it would prove fatal. But being considerably under the influence of liquor, Reeder did not feel his wounds as he otherwise would, and he got up and went into the street.*

"He went to the meat-market of Gumbert, and renewed his quarrel with Gumbert, threatening his life. Friends tried to interfere and get the parties away from each other. In the Fashion Saloon, Reeder made threats against the life of Gumbert, saying he would kill him, and it is said *he requested the officers not to arrest Gumbert, as he intended to kill him.* After these threats, Gumbert went and procured a double-barrelled shot gun, loaded with buck-shot or revolver balls, and went after Reeder. Two or three persons were assisting him along the streets, trying to get him home, and had him just in front of the store of Klopstock & Harris, when Gumbert came across towards him from the opposite side of the street with his gun. He came up within about ten or fifteen feet of Reeder, and called out to those with him, 'Look out! get out of the way!' and they only had time to heed the warning when he fired. Reeder was at the time attempting to screen himself behind a large cask, which stood against the awning post of Klopstock & Harris's store; but some of the balls took effect in the lower part of his breast, and he reeled around forward and fell in front of the cask. Gumbert then raised his gun and fired the second barrel, which missed Reeder and entered the ground. At the time that this occurred, there were a great many persons on the street in the vicinity, and a number of them called out to Gumbert, when they saw him raise his gun, to "hold on" and "don't shoot." The cutting took place about ten o'cloock, and the shooting about twelve. After the shooting, the street was instantly crowded with the inhabitants of that part of the town, some appearing much excited and laughing, declaring that it looked like the 'good old time of '60.' Marshal Perry and Officer Birdcall were near when the shooting occurred, and Gumbert was immediately arrested and his gun taken from him, when he was marched off to jail. Many persons were attracted to the spot where this bloody work had just taken place, looked bewildered, and seemed to be asking themselves what was to happen next, appearing in doubt as to whether the killing mania had reached its climax, or whether we were to turn in and have a grand killing spell, shooting whoever might have given us offence. It was whispered around that it was not all over yet,—five or six more were to be killed before night. Reeder was taken to the Virginia City Hotel, and doctors called in to examine his wounds.

"After being shot, Reeder said, when he got on his feet—smiling as he spoke—'It will take better shooting than that to kill me.' The doctors consider it almost impossible for him to recover, but as he has an excellent constitution, he may survive, notwithstanding the number and dangerous character of the wounds he has received."

Reader survived his injuries but two days. The now distinguished Gumbert was soon set at liberty, and never afterwards molested by the officers of the law.

As he walked the streets, his admirers pointed him out to strangers with the remark,—

"There goes the man who shot Tommy Reeder!"

A good authority states that between

200 and 300 men have been murdered in Nevada, and but two persons have suffered the death-penalty there.

But at the present time, after a due course of "Vigilance Committees," all this "pure cussedness," it is hoped, has for ever departed, and a respect for law and order duly installed in the hearts of the citizens. This reformation is sufficiently disgusting to the still large "rough element," who scornfully characterize it as "turning pious,"—a condition of mind totally incomprehensible to the mental perceptions of the desperado, and regarded by him as a species of hypocrisy, practised for gain and influence.

The desperado pure and simple is a sort of human wild beast, with a slight veneer of civilized polish covering the most fiendish, the most malignant passions. He is at once the cause and the justification of the existence of "Vigilance Committees."

The rise and growth of these peculiar and extra-official organizations, form a singular and instructive chapter in the history of our Western and Pacific States.

The discovery of gold and silver in these new countries attracted vast hordes of ruffians and desperadoes, in addition to the ordinary fortune-seekers, from all parts of the world.

These brutal elements of a debased civilization soon gained the mastery in almost every department of public life in these rude communities, and had indeed made deep inroads into the sanctuaries of individual rights. All that is dearest to the Anglo-Saxon heart lay prostrate at the feet of the vilest of the vile. This was too much for "human nature's daily food," especially Anglo-Saxon human nature. It rebelled. The organizing intellect of the race immediately came into play, and hence followed the various preliminaries resulting in the formation of the Vigilance Committee.

Somebody remembered the line,

"Eternal vigilance is the price of liberty,"

and aptly quoted it. In such times of intense public excitement the perceptions are sharpened, and the full force is felt of the scriptural saying, "A word in season, how good is it!"

When a man is desperately sick, nature sometimes works its own cure, after all the physician's remedies have failed. In the same way a vigilance committee (so-called) is a resultant of strenuous efforts on the part of a community to purge itself of the vile and criminal element which may be entrenched in power and place, paralyzing the arm of the law, poisoning the fountains of justice, and defeating by fraud, backed with force and terrorism, the expressed will of the people. Under these circumstances vigilance committees are not only justifiable, they are imperatively necessary to the existence of the social fabric itself. And with society no less than with the individual, the first law of nature is self-preservation.

There is a widely marked distinction to be made, however, between mere mob-law—and it must be sadly confessed that many vigilance committees were nothing or rather but little else—and the open and responsible organization of the best elements of society in sturdy rebellion against the tyranny and terrorism of the worst. As examples of this class, the first, and even more notably the second, vigilance committee of San Francisco may be cited.

When the famous Thirty-Three in 1856—the second Committee of San Francisco—opened books and called upon the citizens to enrol themselves in support of the Committee of Vigilance, within four days 9,000 able-bodied white men had pledged themselves to give the Committee all the necessary physical and moral support. The great majority of these names were those of merchants, bankers, property owners, taxpayers, and men of means and substance generally.

Here there could be no doubt about the *status* of the Committee—it represented the better and progressive elements of society in open rebellion against ruffians and desperadoes, firmly seated in places of trust and profit, elected by means of ballot-box stuffing, and other shameless devices.

Eastern Nevada rejoices in the possession of a great cave the location of which is about eighty-five miles south-west of White Pine. It is situated in a low ridge, scarcely sixty or sixty-five feet high, at the foot of which is a dark, rocky archway, which one little suspects to be the threshold to a vast cavern penetrating far into the bowels of the earth.

The bold explorer, after his eyes have become accustomed to the dim glare of many torches, with which the guides are well provided, finds himself in a low-pitched passage or natural hall-way, which extends for a distance of about twenty feet. Then it gradually grows wider and wider, while the roof becomes correspondingly high. This passage way leads into many chambers of great size; notably, one which has been aptly denominated the ball-room or great dancing-hall, its dimensions being about seventy by ninety feet, with an elevation of roof of upwards of forty feet, the even floor being covered with fine gray sand.

Here the light from the torches serves but to make " darkness visible," while the silence is oppressive, and unspeakable melancholy with clammy touch weighs heavily upon the beholder.

Opening into this chamber are several smaller ones which might be used as reception rooms or cloak and hat rooms for the guests who might make use of this subterranean dancing hall, until the neighbouring town can afford to build an adequate structure for the gratification and pleasure of all the devotees to the " light fantastic." That the dancers may have a plentiful supply of a cool and innocent drink to refresh themselves during the intervals between their excessive devotion to the German, the Lancers, or the Waltz, a clear, cold spring of the purest water gushes forth from the rock hard by. Additional chambers are discovered further on, pendant from the roofs of which are numerous beautiful stalactites, like so many icicles, varying in length and brilliancy, but dimly revealed by the torchlight. The floors have many circular incrustations—stalagmites, in technical language,—by which a mosaic effect is given to dark chambers. It has not yet been ascertained to what distance this mammoth cave extends; adventurous explorers have penetrated as far as 4,000 feet, at which point a deep chasm prevented farther progress.

The neighbouring tribes of Indians have a strange dread of this locality, and are seldom or never tempted to venture within the haunted recesses of this wonderful cavern.

They relate a legend that is current among them, to the effect that once a "heap" of Indians went in for a long way, and that not one ever returned. But another party ventured in some time afterwards, one of whom, only, escaped from the black, silent chambers, and he is now called "Cave Indian." According to this legend, he entered the cavern accompanied by some of his tribe; they travelled until they came to a lovely stream of water, where dwelt a vast number of Indians, happy in the possession of countless small ponies and beautiful squaws. Though strongly persuaded to make himself at home with this strange people "underneath the ground," to which end they offered to let him take his pick of the small ponies and beautiful squaws, still "Cave" could not make up his mind to entirely desert this "breathing world" for the uncertainties of subterranean society, and much preferred sunlight and air to small ponies and beautiful squaws, minus these pleasant accompaniments. So, keeping an eye to windward, he watched every chance and channel of escape, and finally succeeded in stealing away when all were asleep; and travelling for many days, as he supposed, through a more than Cimmerian darkness, and after he had undergone untold suffering, physical and mental both, he came to the rocky portal at the mouth of the cave, and thus he emerged again into "the light of common day." His people who went with him on his perilous and adventurous journey, still live in the cavernous paradise of small ponies and beautiful squaws, far beneath the green and sunlit surface of the earth.

The Indians place implicit faith in this story, and, moved by superstitious awe, avoid approaching even the dark portal of this cavern

"Measureless to man, where flows a sunless sea."

Quite a different story is told by the white people who dwell in the vicinity, namely, that the Mormons once held possession of this cave, and when the little "unpleasantness" occurred between them and the United States

Government, they made good use of it, as a secure hiding-place for the plate and treasures of the church and the valuables of the Mormon bishops and elders.

It is just possible that "Cave" and his companions may have entered the cavern when the Saints were in possession, guarding the sacred treasures of Holy Mother Church; the story which "Cave"—whom we have every reason to suppose is a gentleman of the strictest integrity and veracity; in fact, a "Cooper" Indian—related to his people about the ponies, and especially that part of it concerning the great number of beautiful squaws, might be regarded as giving some colour to this supposition.

On the hypothesis that this supposition is correct, and considering the very thorough work, for which the Mormons are noted, in all matters relating to the preservation of the Church or its property, and the very little regard for human life—especially Gentile and still less Indian lives—which they have manifested from time to time, it becomes a matter of no little wonder that our honest and truthful "Cave" escaped a violent end, and still lives to tell the tale of his adventures in the great Cave of Nevada.

CHAPTER VIII.

Nevada properly a Stock-raising and Agricultural Country—Comparative Unprofitableness of Mining Speculations in Nevada as in California—Hard Work and Poor Pay the Miner's Lot — Austin — " Rough " Persecution — Chinese Patience—Battle Mountain—Resse River Valley—Winnemuca—Desert Country—Fancy Names—Great Desert of Nevada—Sage-brush and Alkali—Social Conveniences of the Pullman Palace Car—White Plains—Micage Verdi the Unmusical—Boca.

The future of Nevada lies in stock-raising, to which a large portion of the State is well adapted, and already great herds of cattle may be seen browsing on the mountain sides. And it may be added that the real wealth of this region is less in the rich and numerous mines of precious metals, in which it abounds, than in its capabilities to produce food and other necessities of man.

Statistics clearly show that the great wealth of California is owing to the fact that it is *par excellence* a *wheat-producing* State, and in addition to this, its vast herds of cattle, its abundant fruits, and its enormous vegetation, all combine to make it a country specially adapted to meet promptly the physical wants of man, in return for the labour he bestows upon the cultivation of the earth.

Although mining for the precious metals is one of the legitimate industries of the country, and should be properly fostered, there is no calling so deceptive, so speculative, and which gives so small a return for the labour and capital expended; whereas in the cultivation of the earth or in stock-raising, with but slight drawbacks, the returns are certain and steadily on the increase, and to diligence and skill a competence and perhaps a fortune is assured, in a calling that is at once healthful and independent.

In support of these views I append the following statement of facts, derived from official sources, with regard to the yield of the Nevada mines in one district—the Virginia District—in which is situated the celebrated Comstock lode.

The estimated value of the precious metals which this district has produced during a decade, is upwards of $100,000,000. The gross annual yield is placed at $16,000,000. In commenting on this fact, a good authority says, "The sum is enormous, but the proportion of actual gain is very small. The net profit is understood to be not greater than half a million of dollars. Worse than the insignificance of the return is the prospect that, unless a desperate experiment is successful, these mines will have to be abandoned altogether. To avert this calamity, a tunnel is now being driven into Mount Davidson with a view to intersect the great Comstock lode at the depth of 2,000 feet. The distance to be driven is four miles. This is the now famous Sutro tunnel, to which I have already alluded.

The main point to be noted in the above is the extremely small return of profit—a trifle over three per cent. on the gross annual yield. And these mines are the largest and richest silver mines in the world. And now if we take into consideration the great number of mines that have proved failures, and strike an average, we must come to the strange and apparently paradoxical conclusion that our mines have been worked at a positive loss.

To the thirst for sudden wealth, which is sure to break out among all classes of men wherever new discoveries of gold or silver are made, is due the excessive amount of toil that is wasted on worthless mines—labour that would be so usefully, profitably, and healthfully employed in agricultural pursuits.

The cause for all this waste of human endeavour is not far to seek—it lies in the unsettled habits and diseased hopes of the gambler, who is the ripe fruit of the speculative blossom.

It takes years of wasted effort to cure the people of this mania for sudden riches, for it feeds on hope and,

"Man never is but always *to be* blessed."

This same mania is the parent of the numberless bubble speculations which finally lead to those financial revulsions called panics, or crises, and which are but the natural recoil from long-deferred hope, which maketh the heart sick to the very depth of despair and unreasoning fright.

How different and how much more satisfactory, both physically and mentally, is the condition of the tiller of the soil. He passes his days, it is true, in hard, grinding toil; but when he lies down at night his mind is free from the effects of fierce excitement; he rests contentedly untroubled by dreams of gold or silver, or rich placers, or labours with the pick, or washings of the golden sand in the pan. His labours are not only of far greater benefit and utility to others than are those of the miners, but it brings him greater reward in actual net again, than the miner receives for a similar amount of work, besides being a class of labour that is not a strain upon the nerves and mental faculties as well as upon the muscles.

Or imagine the life of the stock-raiser, whose time is almost wholly passed in the open air, upon horseback, visiting the different herds, which graze over an immense range of country. What a free and healthful occupation, the reverse of that of the miner, working by artificial light in a noisome atmosphere, in long, narrow chambers a thousand feet below the surface of the earth. Here they toil like so many imps of darkness, breaking with pick and gad into the rich ore rock, which is again broken into pieces of convenient size, ready to be packed in sacks and sent to the mills.

Besides the White Pine District, what is known as the Reese River District is likewise a section rich in silver deposits. This district is situated to the east of Virginia City. These mines are not remarkable for yielding great quantities of ore, but that which is found in them is of a very superior quality.

In the midst of the Reese River District stands the city of Austin, a mining town of considerable importance, with a population, including that of the adjacent country, of about 5,000, a large proportion being "very rough." A large number of Chinese form a portion of the population, engaged principally in domestic service or in the special and exclusive occupation of cleansing and "doing up" soiled linen. The sign "Ah Sing and Ah Ling:—Washing and Ironing," or a similar one, is frequently seen in Austin.

The Chinese here, like their yellow brethren in other places on the Pacific slope, are said to be neat, quiet, and orderly, adepts in learning, imitative to the letter, and excellent food for powder and shot, which, uncomplainingly, and with a bland smile, they receive into any portion of their anatomy— no preferences shown to any favoured region, such as the heart, lungs or brain—whenever the noble Anglo-Saxon feels that his peace of mind requires a certain amount of bloodletting—that is, the vital fluid of someone other than himself. The Chinaman should obtain the everlasting gratitude of the American people, a gratitude proportioned to the very great service that they have been in saving the lives of unnumbered persons, who must have inevitably fallen a prey to the savage instincts of "the roughs" in their cups, had not "John," with the most accommodating spirit, stood up and taken the bullets into his own body, glad only if he could save his pigtail, and dying delighted with the assurance from his companions in distress, that notwithstanding all the evils inflicted upon him by the "Melican man" with his "lilvolver," his bones will be shipped to his beloved China, and interred in its sacred soil with immemorial rite and usage.

A story is told by Sir Charles Dilke, in his "Greater Britain," illustrative of manners— very bad manners, no doubt—in Austin. A man riding on a mule in one of the main streets, heard a shot, felt a strange grazing sensation, for an instant only, on the top of his head, saw his hat fall into the mud, and picking it up, found a small round hole on each side. Looking up, he saw a tall bronzed and bearded miner, revolver smoking in hand, who smiled grimly and said, "Stranger, guess that's my mule." The stranger having politely explained where and when the mule was bought, the miner expressed himself satisfied with a "Guess I was wrong—let's liquor."

Nothing could be handsomer than this frank acknowledgment of error, followed up and clinched by the prompt invitation to "liquor."

At Battle Mountain, the sixth station from

Palisade, we stop for dinner; thirty minutes being allowed for the performance of that agreeable duty. It is, or rather it ought to be, always pleasant to perform one's duty, yet it cannot be denied that some duties are more pleasant than others; and among the latter are, undoubtedly, the discussion of excellent meals. It is a common remark of travellers over this road, that the food furnished at the regular eating stations after leaving Omaha is much superior to that to be had at the refreshment saloons prior to your arrival at the last-named point. And the viands with which the hungry and thirsty traveller renews his exhausted vitality at Battle Mountain, are by all odds the best that are found on the route.

This is now the point of distribution for the mining camps of Battle Mountain, Galena, and Copper Cañon in the mountains just to the south, as well as for Austin and the Reese river country.

From this station, a daily line of stages is run by the North-Western Stage Company to Battle Mountain mines, a distance of seven miles; to Galena, twelve miles; and to Austin, ninety miles.

The principal mining sections which are tributary to this station are situated off to the southward.

As we move on, we run along the base of the mountains towards the left, leaving the bright and shining river far to the right.

Pinte, the following station, is five miles beyond Battle Mountain. Reese River Valley joins the Humboldt at no great distance from Pinte.

Its main feature is its diversity in width, at some points being very broad—say, from eight to ten miles; at others, marked only by narrow ribbons of meadowland or sandy waste. Some parts of the valley are susceptible of cultivation, possessing an admirable soil adapted to most agricultural products of this zone. Other portions consist almost wholly of sand and gravel, whereon flourishes solely, in unrelieved solitude, that superfluous and all too-frequent bit of vegetation, about which we have long since more than satisfied our curiosity—I refer to sage-brush. Reese river, which flows through this valley, takes its rise some 200 miles to the south, fed by many tributary streams, whose sources are in the high mountain ranges that rise on both sides of the river its whole length.

The name of Battle Mountain is given to this whole range, because near by a desperate battle was fought with the Indians on one side and emigrants and settlers on the other.

The difficulty arose in this wise: a party of Shoshone Indians stole into the camp of the whites at night, and drove off a large portion of their stock. The alarm was given promptly, the brave and hardy pioneers assembled together, and determined to pursue the marauders. Armed to the teeth, fired with indignation, and desperate with a sense of unspeakable injury—for in a new country the robbery of cattle is regarded with greater abhorrence than the taking of human life—the plucky little band was soon on the war-path, in hot chase after the Indian despoilers. At this point they overtook them, where a slight skirmish ushered in a furious fight. From hill to hill, through valley and ravine, from rock to rock, the Indians were driven before the terrible onslaught of the whites, down to the very water's edge. The savages were here brought to a standstill and held at bay. They fought with the fury of despair. They asked no quarter and none was given. When night drew her curtain " o'er the scene, and pinned it with a star," the whites were in possession of the field and likewise of their stock. In this fight the Indians lost upwards of a hundred braves, which effectually broke the power of the tribe.

Eight miles west of Pinte, we come to a

station with the very suggestive name of Coin, "at which," a fellow traveller says, the train "don't stop because it don't pay."

A contagious titter runs round the party at this brilliant witicism, which puts everybody into the very best of humour.

Seven miles farther on we come to Stone House, which was once a strongly fortified trading post, well calculated to repel the attacks of the Indians. The Stone House is situated at the foot of a steep hill, close to a spring of pure water, of a most excellent taste. A deep, rock-bound gorge is formed upon the crest of the ridge, by parallel ridges, making a secure and natural fortification. Often in the early days the defenders of the Stone House were obliged to retreat to this gorge, which was but a hundred yards from the Stone House, and once safely entrenched, they could hold the place against the combined attacks of all the Indians of the Plains.

This has been the scene of many a well-contested fight, in which the native stubbornness of the Anglo-Saxon race finally triumphed over the fierce savages.

Thirteen miles west of Stone House is Iron Point, where "the trains," according to our informant—the same genius who made the wretched joke on Coin—"*stick* sometimes in the snow."

The next station, twelve miles farther on, bears the name of Golconda—rich in associations of hidden wealth—bringing to mind the great diamond mines which are popularly supposed to be located at Golconda, India.

Passing Tule, located nine miles beyond Golconda, we reach, after traversing a landscape remarkable for sameness and sagebrush, a pretty station with an equally pretty Indian name—Winnemucca, which is six miles west of Tule. At this place there once lived a chief of the Pinte Indians, who, having nothing better to bestow, gave his name to the station. The local traditions fail to discover to the mind of the curious student the reason why Winnemucca's name is thus immortalized beyond those of his predecessors in the honourable and no doubt pleasant position of chiefs of the tribe; but it is fair to presume that the reason why he is thus distinguished above his fellows is a good and sufficient one, whether we know it or not; and this mode of reasoning is convenient with a good many other moot points, which touch us very much nearer than the one under consideration.

We are now 1,451 miles out from Omaha, and the distance yet to be traversed ere our feet press the pavements of the Golden City—the proud and beautiful San Francisco—is just 463 miles.

In the vicinity of this place, many mines are in operation, yielding a considerable quantity of silver ore, though they are by no means remarkably valuable or productive. A good many mills and furnaces are kept going, and are said to be doing a very fair business.

This little town of, say, between 500 and 600 inhabitants, who occupy, for all purposes, structures of every kind, to the number of ninety odd, which include four or five hotels and the Company's shops, has had its ups and downs, in consequence of the advent of the railroad. For Winnemucca is now divided into two portions, the first being the old or pre-railroad town, and the second that part which grew up around the station, there being a distance only of about 300 yards between the two. It is said that that part of the town which boasts of its antiquity, and, after the fashion of elders, patronizes Winnemucca the younger, began its existence as a rough mining camp, with the usual accompaniments of gamblers, desperadoes, and other offscourings of eastern cities. Gradually these unlovely elements were eliminated,—the local records of the "vigilantes," if they could be reached, would be found to contain language far more pointed and practical, and would doubtless indicate the very tree just outside the town where "the red lightning of the people's vengeance" visited certain "parties" with death by hanging,—and as the better class of the population settled down into habits of industry and order, the camp changed by insensible degrees: buildings were put up of a more permanent character; that is, in place of tents and log huts, "stores" and warehouses came into being— often sent out from the large towns, ready made and fitted, requiring only a few nails and the labour of a couple of men for a brief time, to "set them up."

Twenty miles of easy railroading takes us past two unimportant stations—Rose Creek and Raspberry Creek—doubtless so named by some sarcastic railroad surveyor, because not only are there neither roses nor raspberries at either "creek," but the country is incapable of producing any. The faithful sage-brush and the not unfrequent bed of alkali are the best productions of this region. What were these things made for? "What were Indians and mosquitoes made for?" is the despairing enquiry of the Western man.

Another run of about twenty miles brings us to Humboldt, where we stop thirty minutes for supper; and a very good supper you get at this station, which is noted for having a fountain in front of it of ice-cold water, which flows, clear as crystal, from a mountain spring near by.

Passing Rye Patch and Oreana, some thirty odd miles from Humboldt, we reach a station called Lovelocks, remarkable only for the singularity of its name, suggestive of spit-curls, supposed to be all powerful in matters pertaining to Cupid and his darts.

As we leave this station, the country becomes still more desolate and bare, and we very shortly enter upon another waste place, known as the Great Nevada Desert, a region of concentrated barrenness, choking deposits of coarse dust, and an occasional clump of that loyal and steadfast shrub the sage-brush, which has so persistently kept us company for so large a part of our journey.

A couple of stations more—a matter of sixteen or seventeen miles—and we are at Brown's.

I mention the fact because it is somewhat of a relief to have done, if only for a short period, with the monotonous succession of sonorous Indian names with which the various stations are labelled, and the magnificent appellations given to mere stopping places. The average Western man exhibits an especial fondness for this kind of grandeloquence.

At Brown's—simple and unadorned Brown's, a title which leaves to the expansive imagination such a wide field to roam over in supplying the object of the possessive form, and which mental exercise has doubtless proved a positive boon to many a weary traveller oppressed with *ennui*, and the seemingly never-ending journey—we have a fine moonlight view of Humboldt lake, a sheet of water about thirty-five miles long and ten broad. This lake (so-called) is but the broadening of the Humboldt river, which after twisting and winding, like a great silver serpent, though the country for a distance of 350 miles, empties itself into this basin.

Bidding adieu to the friendly and familiar Brown's, we skirt the shore of the lake for about three or four miles, gazing with a feeling of quiet satisfaction upon the wide surface of this fine body of water, over which the newly-risen moon casts a broad band of silver, leaving in comparative gloom the face of the lake on either side of this bright belt.

This pleasant scene, however, is soon shut

out from our view by a high ridge of sand which intervenes between the road and lake.

We now speed on our way at a good round pace, and since the prospect is obstructed and the night is closing in, we seek for recreation rather from within than from without.

There is hardly a situation better adapted to the enjoyment of the pleasures of conversation than a Pullman Palace car at night, where friendly travellers, having banished from their minds, for the nonce, all cares and every unrestful thought, seek to please each other by relating their respective experiences, if they have been over the road before, or recalling suggested stories, touched with more or less humour and fancy, according to the natural bent and conversational powers of the persons thus cosily placed in pleasant companionship.

One is reminded of the taproom of an old-time village tavern, from the earliest period of English and American history, previous to the advent of Pullman Palace cars and Pacific railroads—the most orthodox and cosiest of all places of free and easy gossip, especially if by some unforeseen accident you were obliged to stay over-night at the ancient caravanserai; and if the night proved stormy and you heard the rain beating against the window-panes, so much the better pleased did you feel when stout Boniface piled still higher the great logs of wood upon the blazing hearth. Nearer together would the travellers draw around that immense fireplace where the crackling flames sent out a genial heat; and then the story-teller—was there ever a party of travellers seated at the inn fire in the old stage-coach days, without its story-teller?—would begin. The example was contagious, for no sooner had he finished than some one else was reminded of a story, and thus the tedium, which otherwise would have proved well-nigh insupportable, was relieved, and the evening wore away until bedtime.

In these times, however, the Pullman Palace car has usurped the place of the village taproom of bygone days, and we now do our story-telling while travelling at the rate of twenty odd miles an hour; the "pocket-pistol" and its accompanying cup do duty in lieu of hot toddy, and the coloured porter of the sleeping-coach administers to our wants—so far as the circumstances of the case will admit—instead of honest Boniface.

Having exhausted their budget of stories, jokes, personal experiences, and so forth, travellers nowadays have their beds made, while the cars are moving along with unabated celerity; after which they retire,—you can scarcely say to their quiet couches, there to sink into a calm repose, but you might hit nearer the mark if you said that they fell finally into a sort of slumber, "rocked in the cradle of a Pullman car."

And so we went to bed soon after leaving Brown's—or rather, it seemed soon after—to wake up the next morning in the Golden State, a land of many wonders, and of great interest, in manifold ways, to the traveller.

During our devotions to the drowsy god, we have passed White Plains, so called because the ground around the station, as far as the eye can reach, is white—that dirty white which a large admixture of alkali gives to the earth. The surface of the plains is innocent of vegetation of any description, and you learn from travellers who when going eastward have seen this part of the country by daylight, that you have lost nothing by slumbering through this delectable scenery.

Mirage is likewise passed while we sleep. Here, it is said, that wonderful optical illusion of the desert, from which the station derives its name, is seen. The toil-worn traveller through the dreary waste—thirsty, and hungry, and tired—is cheered by a distant though distinct view of bright, green meadows, beautiful streams of running water, and the cool shade of many large trees; yet all this scene of beauty, towards which the impatient wayfarer hurries yearning to enjoy it after the heat and thirst and misery of the desert, is but the " baseless fabric of a vision," which fades into nothingness as you approach it. This phenomenon, familiar to every one in books, and except in books known to comparatively few, occurs with peculiar brilliancy and effect in this region. But the most brilliant effects of mirage I ever witnessed occurred between Utah Lake and Salt Lake; a fairy city, with palaces and towers of fantastic beauty, groves and streams, more sharply defined than perhaps the reality would have been at such a distance, appeared suspended in the clouds,— an astonishing and lovely vision. Everything is remarkable in this country, from vegetation to desert; from the incomparably invigorating air to the alkaline blast that chokes you; everything is extreme, "big,"—in a word, American: *i.e.*, better or worse than the same things elsewhere;—why not, then, the mirage?

It would serve no purpose to mention all the stations between Mirage and the Californian State; they number some eight or nine, the most considerable of which is Reno, containing upwards of 1,000 inhabitants, engaged principally in mining. From Reno the Virginia and Truckee railroad branches off, going *viá* Carson City to Virginia City, a distance of fifty-one miles. The most inconsiderable among the eight or nine stations above named, is Verdi, named in honour of the celebrated musical composer. Diligent inquiry failed to reveal any facts tending to prove that there yet existed any Academy of Music, or other operatic hall or theatre, among the three or four log cabins, and two or three wooden shanties, which together constituted the total number of edifices of which Verdi—not the composer, but the place—could boast; however, it was ascertained that there was plenty of space for one, and it is conjectured that the inhabitants would offer no objection to the building of such a structure, which, if the proprietor found it a badly paying investment, might be profitably employed as a suitable place for sparring matches, a pistol-gallery, or possibly for the sittings of a future Vigilance Committee.

We soon enter the Golden State; and the first place we pass through is Boca,—an appropriate name, since "boca" is Spanish for "mouth."

CHAPTER IX.

CALIFORNIA : Expedition of Hernando Cortez—Sir Francis Drake—Spanish Missionaries—Traces of Spanish Occupation—Climate—Scenery—Fertility—Summit—Rivers—Railroad over the Sierra Nevada—Mean Temperature of California—Area—Agricultural Products—Construction of the Railroad—Summit Valley—Soda Springs—Great American Cañon—Dutch Flat—Mining Towns—Blue Lode—Romantic Railway Track—Cape Horn—Engineering Difficulties—Grass Valley—Political Economy. SACRAMENTO : Placerville—Stocton ; its Rapid Growth—Grand View from Mount Diablo—Extent and Futility of Joaquin Valley—Niles—Enchanting Scenery—Oaklands—Distant View of San Francisco.

CALIFORNIA presents not only numberless points of attraction to the tourist, to the commercial man, to every one, in fact, who needs a new home and a fresh start in life, but likewise to the student, who requires not to be informed that the history of California, since it came into the possession of the Caucassian race, dates back to the exploring expeditions of the Spanish conquistador, Hernando Cortez, in 1534 and 1535, that bold and hardy adventurer, who, notwithstanding many acts of cruelty, was yet distinguished by an admirable spirit of heroism, and an inextinguishable valour, which no hardship could weaken, no disaster daunt.

His own deliberate act—the burning of the ships—exhibits a wholesouled determination to conquer or perish, which finds no parallel for audacity in any annals of any other nation, before or since that day.

In this expedition Cortez discovered Lower California, and in 1542 Cabrillo, a Spanish discoverer, visited Upper California. In 1579, Sir Francis Drake cruised on the coast, and discovered Jack's Harbour, a few miles northward to the Bay of San Francisco. Various other Spanish voyagers landed in the neighbourhood of what is now San Francisco, and also in other parts of California, and in 1769 the Bay of San Francisco was discovered, or probably re-discovered, by Spanish missionaries.

Thus we see that California, more than any other State in the Union, has traditions of its own, and is connected with the most interesting and exciting portion of the history of Spain.

Throughout the whole of California, numerous traces of its Spanish occupation are plainly perceptible, not only in the names of towns, streets, and *plazas*, but likewise in the style of what is left of the old architecture, in the remains of old fortresses, and last, though not least, in the mode of preparing food, especially in the interior; the most conservative of all customs, preserved intact through countless generations by the most conservative of all human beings, the mothers and daughters of a nation.

It is strange—and yet not so strange, after due reflection—what little change takes place, even in the course of many centuries, in the leading traits of national cookery.

An investigation into and comparison of the *cuisine* of various nations, from the earliest dawn of history, might lead to important developments, quite as striking, perhaps, as any of the analogies obtained by the processes of comparative philology.

We may yet listen with delight to the clear, scientific demonstration of some deep, philosophical cook, lecturing on, perhaps, an abstruse point of resemblance between the mode of preparing a barn rat in the Southern States, and the very prevalent use of all varieties of that much-abused vermin among the Chinese,—arguing from this fact the evident relationship between the two nations. A slight example of this kind affords us a remote glimpse of the very great extent to which this new science might be carried by an ingenious and gifted mind, especially adapted to discern analogies where none exist.

But the majority of travellers are too much interested in the physical aspects of California —and they strike the senses with the force of inherent grandeur and beauty—to occupy themselves to any great extent with her past history and its suggestions.

Extensive wheat-fields, grand orchards, and beautiful vineyards—a climate so favoured that the agriculturist begins ploughing and planting in December, and continues his work till April, when he begins to harvest, and keeps at that until October, without the necessity of housing either animals or crops; beautiful groves, grand old forests, monster waterfalls, majestic rivers, and mountain ranges of giant proportions (to say nothing of the wonders of the semite)—these are but a very concise enumeration of the superficial advantages that here meet the eye of the traveller.

From Boca we begin gradually to ascend, and fourteen miles beyond Truckee, the next station, we reach Summit, the highest station on the Sierra Nevada mountains, an elevation of 7,017 feet above the sea-level. We have yet 245 miles to travel ere we make our destination, having journeyed 1,669 miles since leaving Omaha.

Great mountain peaks rise around us to an immense altitude,—bare, bleak, brown; they look down upon us from their enormous height, with a majestic calmness which is at once awe-inspiring yet singularly attractive.

The sight of these tall, massive piles of granite, bathed in the light of the early morning sun, impresses the imagination so strongly with a sense of the sublime that you involuntarily burst out into expressions of intense satisfaction, and you ask yourself the question, "Can I ever forget this? Will the memory of these emotions, which now fill my soul to the very brim, ever be effaced?" And then, you note—like so many diamond-points engraving the scene still more deeply on your memory—the dew-drops on the gray sides of the granite peak, glistening in the rays of the sun.

To our right, but far below, in a mountain gorge, the sparkling waters of the South Yuba, under the deep shade of many fir trees, skip and leap and waltz, over great rocks, through dense forests, frothing and foaming and posturing into countless shapes,—now as a noisy cascade, plunging headlong over immense boulders, with a deafening roar, sharp and ceaseless; then hurrying along with a quiet but rapid movement, stopping now and then to have a little quarrel on its way with some blundering obstruction, yet still continuing its journey to its final destination—the Sacramento river.

The head waters of the Bear river likewise take their rise in these mountains, and still farther on, to the left, the American river is seen. These streams, after many a devious winding, journeying through and watering a vast extent of country, meet at last, but far apart, after many wild wanderings, at the same resting-place—the Sacramento river.

Without doubt, the passage of the railroad over this mountain pass is one of the greatest triumphs of engineering skill, and one of the most wonderful achievements of human labour, which history has thus far recorded. Some notion may be obtained of the abrupt rise and still more abrupt descent in the road at this point—and from these facts the reader may judge of some of the difficulties of construction—when it is stated that the track going westward ascends 2,500 feet in 50 miles, and then descends 6,000 feet in 75 miles. Over one mile of tunnels in this locality testify to the amount of work done in blasting alone; the powder used for this purpose costing, it is said, over one million dollars.

If the traveller has sufficient and to spare of that most precious coin in these days of rapidity in all things—time, let him stop here for a few days, devoting himself to the congregated beauties and sublimities which these tall, majestic mountains, deep and solemn gorges, lofty peaks, glancing, foaming waterfalls, and smooth, crystal lakes, afford the beholder in such rich abundance.

The accommodation is said to be good at Summit House, but whether good or bad, the tourist will be obliged to make his headquarters here, since this is the only hostelry—unless indeed he has a natural preference to camp out upon the bleak mountain side, or by climbing a trifle higher, say 4,000 or 5,000 feet, he might enjoy the novelty of "posting" himself—in more senses than one—upon the SNOW-COVERED SAW-POINTS (this being an exact translation of the Spanish name of this chain of mountains, *Sierras Nevadas*), where, if he succeeded in reaching them, and there taking up his residence, it would be apt to be very permanent indeed.

As you stand at the foot of one of these frowning peaks, whose summit is covered with a sugarloaf cap of everlasting snow, and gaze upward—your head being in that position which the practised beer-drinker almost unconsciously assumes when draining a foaming tankard of ale—you begin to realize how extremely small humanity is beside the infinitely grand in nature.

The critical reader, were he here but for a short half-hour, would find in his heart ample excuse for the bad poetry and worse prose which has been written about these mountains, since everybody who visits them feels in duty bound to take everybody else into his confidence, and " pour forth his soul " in the *form* of poetry or prose, as the case may be; and we all know, or may know, from bitter experience, what a vicious and unprofitable practice is that of " pouring forth one's soul " in any form whatever; and, moreover, any well-informed reader, only ordinarily versed in human nature, knows that the contemplation of mountains, snow-capped peaks, black and gloomy glens, dense forests of giant trees, white cascades bounding and resounding, and the strong current of pure icy breeze (which almost takes one's breath away), has a very powerful tendency to induce one " to drop into poetry," or worse yet, prose-poetry, and thus " pour forth," *etcetera*; a practice much to be deprecated, as aforesaid. Instead of this, a few statistics about California will be light reading.

The mean temperature, taken in three separate places in the State, is as follows:—

    July, 82 degrees Farenheit.
    Oct., 56 ,, ,,
    Jan., 45 ,, ,,
    Apl., 58 ,, ,,
    May, 56 ,, ,,
    June, 56 ,, ,,

These figures abundantly prove that the climate is one of the most genial and inviting to be found upon the Continent,—neither too hot nor too cold for either indoor or outdoor work.

Extending along the Pacific coast for a distance of about 750 miles, from south-east to north-west, embracing a territory of varied climatic conditions, California is nearly twice the size of Great Britain, or, to be more accurate, contains an area of 188,986 square miles, or, to put it in acres, nearly 121,000,000, of which upwards of 90,000,000 acres, inclusive of swamp lands capable of reclamation, are fitted for some kind of profitable husbandry. The best authorities concur in the opinion that 40,000,000 are good arable land, and that the remainder is adapted to stock-raising, fruits, and so forth.

The soil and climate are eminently favourable to everything that grows, including man. The fruits of the temperate zone succeed well in almost all parts of the State, often attaining to a size and weight that seem fabulous; while along the southern coast such tropical products as figs, pine-apples, cotton, sugar-cane, indigo, and also oranges and lemons, are raised in abundance. Between 300 and 400 varieties of grapes have already been successfully cultivated, among them some of the choicest wine-producing grapes of Europe. The vineyards seldom produce less than 1,000 lbs. of grapes per acre, and in not a few localities the yield is as high as 20,000 lbs. per acre. A bunch of grapes is often three feet in length, and with a circumference in proportion.

The silkworm and mulberry bush are rapidly rising into importance, and the cocoons raised in this State have been pronounced by competent judges to be of superior excellence, and have been found to exceed the European in quantity by 50 to 100 yards of silk.

The cultivation of the tea plant, and also of coffee and tobacco, has now been begun under the auspices of some of the great Chinese labour-companies, with marked prospects of success.

After all, the two great distinguishing products of California are those that hold the largest share of power in the government of the world—gold and wheat.

The "big trees" of California have become proverbial; it is said that they are so tall that it takes two men and a small boy to look to the top of them. One man looks till he gets tired, then another commences where the first left off, and when the efforts of the second are exhausted without success, the small boy steps in and "tops off" the job.

At Summit the train enters a number of tunnels and snow-sheds in succession, so close together that you can scarcely tell where one begins and the other ends.

Of snow-sheds there are at this point an almost continuous line for a distance of about forty-five miles. These sheds, solidly built of heavy timber, were found necessary to protect the road from, not only the great snow-falls—often twenty feet deep—but likewise from the mighty avalanches which in spring rush down the mountains, and sweeping over the sloping roofs of the sheds, dive with a frightful plunge into the awful chasms, thousands of feet below the narrow ledge whereon the track is laid.

Emerging from the tunnels and snow-sheds, the train, like some huge snorting serpent, curves and winds around the base of lofty mountain-peaks; then shooting straight forward over the bleak ridge, affording on either hand snatches of scenery grand and impressive; then, without warning, it plunges into the gloomy recesses of a dense forest of giant trees, in whose deep shade we continue our journey until we arrive at Cascade, six miles west of Summit.

Here the tourist has in store for him one of the chief joys of physical existence, provided he is strong enough to enjoy it. For, all he has to do is to make terms with one of the rough but good-natured mountaineers, whose snug dwellings are nestled in the loftiest of the Sierra valleys, known as Summit Valley, and he may live in a region fit for the residence of the gods, as far as pure air and the luxury that pure air can supply are concerned; how great is that luxury, people " in cities pent " have but a feeble conception. This is a very paradise for stock-raisers and dairymen, whose habitations are found in this mountain valley, and who are rapidly bringing this place into celebrity, on account of the fact that they have demonstrated that beef and ham can be cured here all the year round. This fact, in connection with the nearness of the railroad, is bringing to this place a large and increasing business, and must ultimately result in making this point one of considerable importance.

Near the bottom of Summit Valley are situated the Soda Springs, which are large and numerous, and said to be the finest water for medicinal purposes to be found in the State.

Passing three or four stations, we come to Shady Run, at which point we are charmed with a view of the Great American Cañon, certainly one of the most striking and impressive scenes afforded the beholder in the whole Sierra Nevada chain.

Imagine a deep gorge, whose perpendicular walls rise to the enormous height of 2,000 feet; between these walls the American river rolls and rushes along through the cañon, which extends a distance of two miles; standing on the brink of the precipice and looking down into the awful depths below, you see the torrent coursing on and slipping away from the stony grasp of the huge cliffs, which seem bent on holding it a prisoner; but it escapes in a foaming rage and hurries, complaining and murmuring, on its way.

Half a dozen miles farther on, we come

to Dutch Flat. The town is located in a hollow close to the railroad. From the train, one can see a portion of the place. Among its buildings are many of a substantial kind, including churches, schools, and hotels.

It boasts of a population of about 2,500. Extensive and beautiful gardens, and fine groves of fruit trees, are attached to almost every home.

From this station the curious traveller may take stage, which leaves here daily, and visit several mining towns, which bear the respective appellations of Little York, You Bet, and Red Dog.

These towns are situated on what is called the Blue Lode, the best of the large placer mining districts to be found in the State. The Blue Lode begins somewhat below Gold Run—a station and mining town two miles beyond Dutch Flat—and runs through the entire length of one county—Nevada—and through a portion of Sierra County. It is evidently the bed of a former river, which has disappeared through some convulsion of nature.

The course of this river, which must have been considerably larger than any of the water-courses now existing in this locality, was nearly at right angles with the Yuba, and several other of these mountain streams, for they all run across it. The channel varies in width, being from one to five miles broad. In the bed of the river are found many petrified trees, such as oak, pine, manzanita, mountain mahogany, and maple,—precisely the same varieties that are now growing on the hillsides hard by.

At Gold Run, which contains about 200 inhabitants, you see that the miners have been at work, for on every side the ground is broken, the hills have been torn down by the process of hydraulic mining, and incessant activity is the order of the day.

We here begin to descend very rapidly, passing numbers of little hovels, which are inhabited by the thrifty Chinese, who collect a root, which grows here on the mountains in great profusion, called soap root, and which they prepare for the use of mattrass manufacturers.

The train rushes on, traversing a country given over entirely to the miner and all his devices, from the entanglements of which we emerge to catch a glimpse of the North Fork of the American river, rushing on with angry speed through a narrow gorge, far down, fully 1,500 feet below us. Some distance beyond, the North Fork of the North Fork—a true child of its parent—foams and dashes and jumps from rock to rock, making a wide detour, as though taking a mountain ramble, then joining the main stream.

Six miles beyond Gold Run, we pass a station which, if you did not know better, you might take to be a letter dropped here in the mountains, for it is called C. H. Mill, which, although this place is not a letter, it still contains a message of grandeur and sublimity which the least lettered can read, and which enchains the attention of all, "gentle or simple." For here the track winds round on a narrow mountain-ledge, running almost on the brink of a steep precipice, while from the car-window the traveller gazes into the awful depths of a chasm some 2,500 feet below the road-bed. At this enormous altitude, the American river, which streams through this chasm, appears like a mere silver thread as it dances along, gleaming in the sun.

This sublime scene is the celebrated Cape Horn, which causes one almost to shudder to behold it,—an effect startling to the nerves, yet filling the imagination with pleasant surprises.

You say, this is Switzerland over again, only grander, bolder, more impressive; in short, your patriotic ardour induces you to conclude that it is an American Switzerland, the national adjective serving to express to your mind, if not to that of others, that which was otherwise totally inexpressible.

Without removing your gaze from the far-distant silver thread, which seems to have a peculiar fascination, as the most attractive point in the scene, you notice, if you have sharp eyes, that, some distance beyond, the river is spanned by what appears to be a spider's web, but which in reality is a bridge on the road to a mining town called Iowa Hill, situated some twelve miles to the south of Colfax, the next station.

The train rounds sharply upon the mountain-ledge, turning to the right; on one hand are the huge masses of rock, vast and toppling, frowning and threatening; and on the other, the frightful abyss, stretching far, far below, almost directly beneath you. Unbidden the thought comes, "Should the train leave the track and roll off the ledge?" The very notion gives one the shivers, and makes one think that that would be even worse than to be caught between the devil and the deep sea.

By a strong effort, you banish all such unpleasant thoughts, and turn again to view the scene, which varies almost constantly.

We continue to wind round the mountain side, upon what would seem like a gallery cut out of the solid rock, and losing sight of the deep chasm and the thread-like river, we now are greeted with all the fresh beauties of a lovely valley, on the left, and which is still a thousand feet below us.

Old Californians who have returned home, tell us that the view of this famous locality, from the train going east, is far superior to that which we now enjoy. The train, seen from the river, looks, it is said, like some struggling monster working its way along, and screaming in angry tones which resound again and again over the country.

When this part of the road was built, it required no little degree of audacity even to ask the men to make their way up the precipitous cliff, and there at that enormous height make for themselves first a foothold and then a pathway for the iron horse.

The first workmen on this elevated rocky point—hardy industrious Chinese—were held and steadied by the aid of ropes, securely tied round their bodies. Thus they hammered away at the rock, until they made for themselves standing room, appearing like a swarm of ants on a loaf of sugar.

Five miles beyond we reach Colfax. Here,

we stop a while and satisfy the cravings of the "inner man." The table is excellent, like nearly all that are set on this line, and we do full justice to the unexceptionable fare that is placed before us.

Feeding on the sublimities has a singularly sharpening effect on the physical appetite, inasmuch as the brain is in constant activity and excitement, than which there is nothing more wearing upon the system; and since whatever waste is made in the physical economy must be replaced by food, Cape Horn and its surroundings are a direct source of gain to the hotel keepers, who should credit full twenty per cent. of their profits to the effects of the sublime scenery upon the physical man.

Colfax contains about 1,000 inhabitants, and seems to be very prettily and substantially built, being one of those few railroad towns —few in proportion to the many that blossom, as it were, for an hour—which have taken root, and possess a decided and secure future before it.

From this station a line of stages leaves twice a day for Iowa Hill, 12 miles; Grass Valley, 13 miles; Nevada, 17 miles; North San Juan, 29 miles; and other places at still greater distances. Four-horse express wagons carry the freight delivered at this station, very fast, to some of these places, considering the rough roads, while to many others a much slower process is adopted.

These are all fine mining towns, flourishing and thriving with the success of the particular class of mining to which, or rather the surrounding neighbourhood of, each is devoted.

From information derived from a fellow-traveller, I learn that the most important and attractive is Grass Valley, situated about thirteen miles to the north of Colfax, and containing upwards of 5,000 inhabitants. Its main importance is derived from the extensive quartz mines in its vicinity. Few, if any, towns have produced more gold from quartz than Grass Valley. It is adorned with many fine buildings, public as well as private. The handsome residences of the wealthy miners are usually enclosed in beautiful grounds, consisting of orchard and garden. This agreeable custom renders the place very attractive, especially when the trees, with their luscious fruits, are in full bearing.

From Colfax—the town of Vice-Presidential memory—we continue our journey amid varied and suggestive scenery, until we arrive, after a run of eighteen miles, at Auburn, the county seat of Placer County, a town of about 1,200 inhabitants. Here the care and neatness bestowed on the grounds around the handsome residences, as well as those belonging to public edifices, give to the place an air of comfort and repose, for which, however, Californian towns are usually noted.

The mildness of the atmosphere and the serenity of the skies in this portion of the State, render it one of the most attractive, as it certainly is one of the most healthy, parts of this rich and powerful empire. It possesses all the elements of true greatness —a soil of unsurpassable fertility, a temperate climate, with little or no excessive heat or cold, rich mines of precious metals, but above all a pushing, driving population of educated Anglo-Americans, who know how to utilize the great advantages offered to them by the very favourable locations of cities and towns on the coast, whereby foreign commerce— when unhampered by tariffs, one of the greatest sources of prosperity to a country —may be fostered and promoted.

It is to be hoped that now, having entered upon the second century of our national existence, loaded down with the experience gained during the first, specially with regard to the destructive effects upon our foreign commerce of the prevalence of false and delusive doctrines in political economy, and of the wrong and injustice resulting from putting them into practice, we may ultimately be led to adopt broader, juster, truer notions upon this very vital subject. In a word, let us build or buy our own ships, whichever process may prove the cheaper, regardless of any national prejudices. We shall then more readily encourage foreign commerce than we could by the adoption of the most stringent protective measures, whose real object is the enrichment of some small local shipbuilding interest, at the cost of our entire foreign trade. Commodore Vanderbilt once said, "If I had a line of steamboats which I could not run as well and as fast as any other line could be run, and ten per cent. cheaper, I sold out that line."

And so if we cannot build cheaper ships and as good as any other nation—which, however, remains to be seen—let us no longer attempt to lift ourselves up by the hair of our heads, for this is what a protective tariff endeavours most ineffectually to do, but rather let us shut up our ship-yards and buy where we can buy the cheapest. But no one at all conversant with the subject will admit that we cannot build ships quite as cheap, if not cheaper, than any other nation; for once remove the burdensome and comparatively unproductive taxes which are laid on almost all the materials which enter into the building of a ship, and then it would be at once demonstrated that we could build ships as cheap, if not cheaper, than any other nation.

Rapidly we arrive at and leave as rapidly five or six stations, and then with a whirl and a ringing of bells we dash into the city of Sacramento, California's handsomely built capital.

Large heavy buildings right beside us; a rush of many people of different climes; here a Chinaman, there an evident Mexican; your American arm-in-arm with the Spaniard, the Frenchman with his wife; many kinds of vehicles; much noise and bustle; many a craft on the river;—such is Sacramento.

The City of the Sacrament is situated on the east bank of the Sacramento river, south of the American. Here the latter river unites with, and becomes part of, the former.

With a population of about 18,000 it has all the appearance of a much larger city,— the public buildings combining with great size an air of solidity and strength, and possessing in addition the beauty of just proportion; the many handsome private residences, surrounded by beautiful gardens, in which abound a rich profusion of flowers and shrubs and wide-spreading shade trees; the broad streets adorned with rows of splendid trees;— the whole contributes to produce the impression of great extent.

The most conspicuous object, and indeed the first that strikes the eye, as you approach Sacramento from the east, is the CAPITOL. It is truly a very imposing structure. It is built in the centre of a piece of ground, which is one entire clock square. All the four sides of these grounds have three slight elevations, one above the other, in the form of terraces, which are reached by broad flights of steps. Planted with fragrant shrubs and well-trimmed evergreens, and brilliant with many-hued flowers, these terraces form a fitting vestibule to the grand edifice. Its front is 320 feet in length, and the main building is approached by a flight of granite steps 25 feet high by 80 feet in width, which lead to a front portico of ten columns. The visitor passes through this portico and then a large hall, to find himself in the rotunda, which is in the centre of the buildings, and forms a circle 72 feet in diameter. From this, in each story, through grandly arched hallways, the state offices are reached, on either side.

Five female figures adorn the front of the building, and are placed above the columns. The central one is standing, and the remaining four are in sitting postures. They represent War, Peace, Science, Agriculture, and Mining.

The first story, of twenty-five feet, is of white granite, from quarries in the vicinity. Above this the body of the main dome is surrounded by an open balcony, which is supported by twenty-four fluted Corinthian columns, and an equal number of pilasters. From these grandly rises the great metallic dome. From the top of this dome, again, rise twelve fluted Corinthian pillars, which support the final or small dome; and this is surmounted by the statue of California.

The interior is one entire mass of solid iron and mason's work. The panels and pedestals under the windows are of beautiful laurel, so celebrated in California for the exceedingly high and beautiful polish which may be given to it. The doors are of black walnut, with laurel panels, the sashes throughout the entire building being likewise of black walnut.

We now look forward with not a little sense of anticipated pleasure, to the end of our journey, "The Golden City," which is still 138 miles distant. The long journey already completed—some 1,800 miles from Omaha—seems as nothing to the 138 miles yet to be traversed. And thus it is in life; what we have accomplished appears of but slight importance in comparison to that which remains undone, while the pleasures already enjoyed sink from our memory in the anticipation of those which are yet to come.

The suburbs of Sacramento are very widely extended, and the environs of the city may be seen for a long time before we are entirely free of them.

The train courses along the river side, through a well-cultivated country, beautified by the industry of man no less than by the bounty of nature, until we reach Brighton, about five miles from Sacramento. At Brighton, the cars of the Sacramento Valley Railroad—managed by the C.P.R.R.—after running down the same track as the Central, branch off to several interesting places, among them Placerville, the county seat of El Dorado County, and forty-eight and a-half miles from Sacramento.

At Placerville, as all the world knows, the first gold of California was discovered, January 19th, 1848; which discovery created one of the wildest and most uncontrollable gold fevers ever experienced in this or any other country.

Passing six or seven unimportant stations, we come to Stockton, a place of some 10,000 inhabitants. The city of Stockton is surrounded by great level plains, which yield vast quantities of grain, and which product has indeed changed this place from a mere trading post, supplying the miners with the necessaries of life, to a great wheat centre, from which foreign populations receive their supply of bread. Like all commercial depôts where this great trade is massed, it has grown enormously, and will become still larger.

From Stockton a fine view of Mount Diablo may be had, which rises distinct and immense from out of the great level plains, and from whose summit the prospect is grand and impressive, taking in the country and towns around the bays of San Francisco, San Pablo, and Suisun, and likewise the valleys of the Sacramento and San Joaquin rivers.

Nine miles south of Stockton is Lathrop, at the junction of the new route (known as the "Visalia Division") to Yeo-Semite Valley and the Mariposa Grove of Big Trees. This road leads up to the SAN JOAQUIN VALLEY, which in extent alone far exceeds many a kingdom of the eastern hemisphere, while in the rich abundance of every element of wealth, but few empires in the old world could favourably compare with it. The products of this valley would readily support hundreds of thousands. The valley is over 250 miles in length, with an average width of 30 miles, its greatest width being 130 miles.

Here may be found millions upon millions of acres of the choicest and richest lands, not yet taken up, ready for tillage, awaiting the coming of the industrious settler.

The fortunate people who have already occupied and become owners of land in this delightful region, taking advantage of the beneficent operations of the Homestead Act, and having supplemented nature with work, rejoice in plenty and happiness,—the splendid climatic conditions contributing as much to the one as to the other.

Bantas, Ellis, Midway, Altamont, and Pleasanton are passed—the last-named being a town of some 500 inhabitants, beautifully located in a lovely valley—and we stop at Niles, so called, it is said, because the famous Egyptian river of that name is to be transported here from its native home by an enterprising company, through the means of a certain patent process, and when it is finally brought over, naturalized and Americanized in several dried-up beds of lost rivers,—which, like certain days, *vide* Tennyson, are now no more—and as it will necessarily be obliged to content itself with being cut up into divers small rivers, the only bed which would begin to accommodate it being now occupied by the Mississippi—the gentlemen named have therefore thought proper to adopt the plural form, hence "*Niles*."

This high sense of honour, which is represented in the desire to be so very exact and strictly truthful,—since anybody can see with half an eye that one Nile cut up into many smaller ones should certainly be designated Niles,—must go very far to confirm all the other statements of these gentlemen.

The above is given entirely for what it is worth, with some misgivings, however, as to whether any appraisement whatsoever could do justice in the premises.

And now we rush on through a country of marvellous fertility of soil, rich in every attribute of real wealth and substantial prosperity. The endless sweep of the fields many, many yards below us, greeting the eye with such a green; it seems really as if you had never seen green before,—that is, real green. And then the wayside gardens so picturesque; and away, away below, a little 'stream winding its way down mighty hills; and in the heavens, the sun, refreshed with slumber, pouring gold and glory on all it touches; then on through a country which might sometimes be Switzerland, sometimes Gascony with its vine-clad hills, sometimes bonny Scotland, and sometimes more pleasant and more beautiful Devonshire; and then on to a track of ground which had been cracked and torn by the coal-diggers, and, instead of the beautiful green and many-coloured flowers, shows the work of the devastators and the engines with which they had perpetrated their crime.

On through seemingly endless fields of glorious corn, over vine-clad hills, through gorgeous ravines,—on, always on, only stopping to get something to eat, and to drink a glass of native wine,—on to the Golden Gate of the Pacific.

At last we seem in front of the bay. Then soon we enter Oakland, which, with its proud churches, and large public buildings, appears such an extended place that we ignorantly a once ask whether we have arrived—if this i San Francisco; and then we run into the water—at least it seems so, for there is nought but water all around. Then we reach dry land again. Then, rushing out again into the water. we go ringing into a large building, from which two or three other trains come ringing out. This at last is the San Francisco Depôt, and terminus of the Central Pacific Railroad. I was quite surprised to see the number of passengers who had travelled with us, there having been four or five sleeping cars which we had not visited.

This wharf and depôt are built on a sort of marshy ground granted by the United States Government to the railroad, and when the appearance had been of rushing into the water, we had been simply running over poles which are placed in the water. The wharf was covered with people waiting to take the boat, and soon the enormous ferry-boats arriving, its occupants were allowed to pass off by one gate, while we entered by another.

These boats are larger than our New York ones, and are more gorgeously arranged. As the great machine puffed and sputtered into the water, and we passed the island in the harbour covered with its army buildings, and saw San Francisco rising majestically like another Malta from the bosom of the sea, our sense of attained goal, our feeling of rest after toil passed, and also the sense of having "done" America, gave us the pleasantest moment of self-complacency and contentment that we had enjoyed for a long time.

CHAPTER X.

Aspect of San Francisco—Woodward's Garden—Seal Rocks—Golden Gate Park—Indigestible Economy—From Merced to Coulterville—Dudley and Hubbards—New Acquaintances—Bower Cave—The American " Race"—Yeo-Semite Valley — Mirror Lake — The Clothes-Line — The Nigger "Lady of the Lake"—Perverseness of Guides—Snow's Hospice—Cloud's Rest—Departure from Yeo-Semite.

THE arrival in San Francisco is very strange to Americans. To see the signs in the stores in gaudy Chinese characters, or else in Spanish or Italian, to see many classes of people thronging the streets, the foreign look which everything wears,—all this is certainly strange to the American mind. We were driven in a gorgeous hotel carriage to the Lick House, one of the oldest and best hotels in the city.

In the evening my companions, the Anglo-American, and myself, went to the California Theatre. This is a large monumental building, the finest in the West. The decorations are very striking, being similar to the Pompeian style. The arrangement of the *audito-*

rium produces an impressive effect, not being made after the model of other theatres, and it is rather prettier on this account.

The play was "Bleak House," or rather an adaptation of "Bleak House," and the principal character was taken by Mdm. Janaschek. The performance was very striking, not such as you might have reasonably expected to see in San Francisco. Later on, we were shown that the San Franciscans are accustomed to the best of everything in their theatres. After the theatre, we were taken to have some California oysters; they are very small, much smaller than the English oysters, and not unpleasant. We then had a glass of California beer, which is thoroughly good, and one gets a taste of the hops very strongly, and it evidently has the properties of ordinary beer, making a cool and refreshing drink.

The next day, accompanied by my Anglo-American friend, I went to Woodward's Gardens. These gardens, originally the private property and pleasure-grounds of the wealthy and patriotic citizen whose name they bear, and who dedicated them to the public use in May 1866, consist of about five acres of land, laid out in the finest and most artistic style, possessing some of the rarest exotics and choicest flowers to be met with anywhere, besides the attractions of an Art Gallery, and a well-filled zoological department, with many specimens of curious as well as ferocious animals.

The place is bordered by a wind-fence twenty-five feet high, and is intersected by a cross-street, beneath which is a tunnel. This garden, though covering such an extremely small space of ground, is so artistically arranged that one does not notice its diminutiveness on entering. There is a museum of natural history, very well garnered with birds and reptiles of every species. Next comes the Art Gallery, and we see around us two or three statues and some fine paintings; next to this is a green-house, in which we find some very fine and rare plants. The green-house adjoins the Art Gallery; two or three picture-frames are filled with glass over which is painted "The Tropics." On looking at one of these pictures we see veritably a scene of the tropics, but find it on close examination to be only artistically arranged ferns and small palmettoes.

On a hill side is a large building, commencing at the bottom of the hill, with large courts and caves and artificial bosquets, in which one can have coffee served on rustic tables. Above this is the Turkish *café* and a very extensive restaurant, and still above this is a good-sized amphitheatre, where performances are held. On the top of the building is a Turkish minaret, and an observatory from which you get a fine view of San Francisco.

The division reserved for animals is spacious; you reach it after passing under the tunnel, the sides of which are covered with advertisements from all parts of the world. I was rather amused with one of them, which ran as follows:—

"Go to the *Maison au Coin du Quai*—you get your clothes at half-price!"

I thought it was rather funny that San Franciscans should be advised to go to Paris to get their clothes at half-price!

The first thing you see on entering this division is a gigantic soda-water fountain; next to it is a cage full of Australian kangaroos. Some of the animals were very fine; the lion, tiger, jaguar, etc., were the finest specimens of their kind. There was a black pig upon whose head a small monkey mounted and turned himself about, very much as a Hindoo guides an elephant, only the pig keeps going round instead of going forward.

We next saw the seals fed; the animal

chews the food, and then, if he finds it hard, he takes hold of one end of it, and beats the rest of it against the water till the flesh comes off, which he then eats, letting the bones fall to the bottom.

We visited the aquarium, which is very fine. Behind this there is a photographic gallery containing photographs of almost all noted parts of the world, and of great numbers of the most famous personages. Through the middle of the gardens runs a pretty stream, and near the centre of the grounds is a pretty lake with a Swiss *chalet* by its side; on this lake is a circular boat that almost completely fills it; in this boat people are allowed to take their children round the lake, which is accomplished without much danger to their lives; the rowing is done as in an ordinary boat.

The camels, elephants, giraffes, etc., are well selected specimens; very much the same as one meets with all over the world. The only thing that is truly remarkable is the massing of the animals; sometimes you see a card warning you to keep out of the way of some ferocious animal, and yet these animals appear to be perfectly at home with one another. So, people of essentially opposite dispositions, if forced to live together for any time, end by signing an armistice.

In the afternoon I drove out with my Philadelphian friend to Cliff House, which by land is seven miles from the city. The hotel is built on the edge of the cliffs, and commands the entrance to the Golden Gate. A fine broad macadamised road of five miles length leads from the outskirts of the city to a group of cliffs outside the Golden Gate, on the shore of the Pacific Ocean.

On either side of the road, the eye is gratified with a succession of low, grass-covered hills and mounds of golden-lined sand, which form together a fine contrast under the brilliant rays of the sun.

We get a glimpse of the Golden Gate and its impressive surroundings now and then, as we drive along; and just as we are near the end of the drive, a grand view of the Pacific, a glorious expanse of blue water, right in front of us, and here we are at the Cliff House.

This is a low, disconnected building, planted on these cliffs that rise suddenly from the ocean. From personal experience I can say the reputation of the Cliff House restaurant for excellence is well earned. The broad piazzas face the sea and afford cool, refreshing breezes, and an unexampled assortment of marine views, which you store away in your memory with no little delight.

The *bon vivants* of San Francisco often drive down here in the lovely morning and take breakfast. It is a great resort for young married couples, who are generally among the earliest comers.

Seal Rocks are close to the hotel, and consist of a series of bold rocks which rise directly from the water. These rocks are covered in great quantities by the slimy, bulky creatures from which they are named, and which flock about and bark at you in the most appalling manner.

Lounging upon the wide, shaded piazzas, it is pleasant to watch the seals basking in the sun, or wriggling their great clumsy bodies up and down the rocks. To the north lies the Golden Gate, through which vessels of every description sail in and out. Towards the south you see the beach, whereon the waves of the ocean beat unceasingly, bordering it with foam. Beyond, the endless stretch of water sparkles like a sea of diamonds.

From the piazza, when the sky is perfectly cloudless, the peaks of the Farralone Islands are visible on the distant horizon. The islands consist of a rugged mass of rock, in extent about 200 acres, and belong to the Farrallone Islands Egg Company. A large bird, the murre, resorts to these islands to deposit her eggs and hatch her young. In such numbers do they often here congregate, that a stranger would mistake them for a heavy thunder-cloud in that portion of the sky.

At the breeding season the Company robs the nests, and supplies the whole city and surrounding country, and, it is said, makes a very profitable business out of the plunder. A Company legally organized for "robbery" is a phenomenon among Companies; the ostensible *raison d'être* is generally very different.

The Golden Gate Park—the future "Central Park" of San Francisco—is just beginning to show the effects of the care and money bestowed upon it. This is a great undertaking for San Francisco. The earth, however, is all sand; nothing planted will grow unless fresh earth be taken to plant it in. Artistically, it is very well arranged, and one can see the beginnings of a very fine park. The ride back is very interesting, as you go down into the street from above, and get a complete bird's-eye view of the city.

The next morning at four o'clock, having provided ourselves with everything necessary, we started for Yeo-Semite. The trip as far as Merced, being on the railway, was easy and agreeable, with the exception of the dinner.

It is a remarkable thing that all through the West, where trains go so very slow, one has only fifteen or twenty minutes to dine. This tells severely on passengers who have to remain four or five days in the train. One would think they could accelerate the speed before arriving and after leaving, so as to give travellers time to eat; indeed, a full hour is always necessary, considering the slowness with which one is here served.

We remained at Merced over night, and were pleased to find a fine large hotel there.

The next morning we were called at half-past four, and having had coffee and cakes, were crowded into the omnibus. Being gentlemen, myself and my Anglo-American friend naturally got the worst seats, being placed with our backs to the driver. Two gentlemen, evidently Englishmen, who we afterwards found out were returning from New Zealand, had engaged a front seat near the driver, and the ill-feeling caused by this aristocratic superiority was not small—yet in one sense it was—in the bosoms of those inside the omnibus. Opposite to us were a German gentleman and his wife, and on the last seats a Western gentleman and his spouse. The

German was extremely funny, and his wife was not what the French call *cambrée*. The jolting during the whole trip was extraordinary, and the joking was very boisterous while the omnibus went dashing over flat plains, once barren, and now dusty enough in many places to furnish forth a small Sahara.

After the first stopping-place, where we got a glass of wine—an incident of more importance in Western than in Eastern travel—the country changes, and swinging down through magnificent ravines, climbing up the same, running round some rocky promontory, passing through great pine-forests, sometimes seeing a Chinaman washing sand for a profit of forty or fifty cents a day, we pass through Coulterville, a small village that almost resembles an Italian town. As we leave it, we meet a Chinaman dashing in at full speed on horseback, with the mail satchel over his shoulders and his pig-tail sticking out like a pump-handle.

At one time we all got a very perceptible chill, either by going over some "Corduroy" roads, or else by crossing the stream, there being no bridges, the carriages going over the round boulders. Mrs. *Deutcher* sitting on the outer side of the carriage, insisted on sitting on her shawl, saying she was getting all "pruised."

Having crossed a considerable amount of plain, covered with fine woods in many places, in others only used for grazing ground, we arrived at a town of which most of the inhabitants were Chinamen. Leaving the town about half-past nine or ten o'clock, we again reach higher ground. The scenery began to be very interesting. At twelve o'clock we reach the first stopping-place, or *ranche*. Before arriving at this, we had passed a place of family interment, the old settlers always having had the custom of burying near home.

Another stage had just preceded us, containing a very heavy load. We dined, and then pursued our journey. We now again enter upon really fine scenery, passing through some great pine woods, running along a ridge of hills with beautiful firs down into a valley, stopping every once in a while to refresh our horses, or to have a drink of wine, and then on again. At last, towards the evening, we arrived at a most enchanting site, beautiful in every way, great trees surrounding us on every side, the air balmy and soft. This place is called Dudley and Hubbard's, an unpleasing practical name for so romantic a spot. Sir George Aarney, who turned out to be one of the New Zealanders, and who was just on his way from New Zealand, of which he had been Governor, and afterwards Chief Justice, and who proved to be a polite and courteous gentleman, as was also his companion, the Rev. Mr. Bower,—both these gentlemen said this delightful spot reminded them of an English nobleman's park.

Having had a good night's rest, we started again, and having passed through the most beautiful and varied country, thickly wooded and very mountainous, we arrived at Bower Cave. Here the daughter of the proprietor of the inn showed us the mysteries of the cavern. She was a very pretty golden-haired Teuton (or Teutoness), but with a decidedly American accent in speaking English, and with very little knowledge of the German language. It is a marvellous thing how quickly the American "race," which is neither German nor Swede nor Spanish nor French, nor even English—begging Sir Charles Dilke's pardon —but American—it is marvellous, I say, how quickly it originates. I am aware that the English and Germans are still numerous in some places in the West, but they are fresh from their respective countries, and that after a ten years' residence at the same place; but their children growing up together, would at the age of twenty be neither Germans nor English, as we might naturally expect, but Americans in every trait by which race is distinguishable.

Bower Cave is evidently formed by volcanic action. The slopes on the rocks correspond perfectly to those opposite to them. It is but a hundred feet deep, and is formed by great masses of granite, which are collected in many places, so as to form galleries with balustrades. There is a small lake or pond at the bottom.

There is one thing that is very pleasant about California, and that is the homeliness and comfort of the wayside inns, where you get a glass of native wine.

At length, towards evening, we were told that we were approaching Yeo-Semite. Having passed a thick muddy stream, we were stopped by a man who wanted to know whether we would take to the hotel a wild goat, which turned out to be a deer. This proves how difficult it is to make any reservation or future game laws in America.

Passing through a thick wood, we arrived all of a sudden at the top of Yeo-Semite.

Imagine an enormous horse-trough, the sides of which are of solid granite, the rugged edge covered here and there with pines, vegetation running in lines along the sides of the granite; around the edge at intervals magnificent waterfalls, while at the bottom are beautiful green fields; imagine this, and you will partially have figured to the mind's eye what we saw on looking down into the valley.

Speaking from the limited knowledge of mountain scenery that I was able to get in Switzerland, the Engadine, in Norway, and the Pyrenees, I have never seen any scenery so thoroughly original in its character as that of the Yeo-Semite Valley. I have never seen an extended view so impressive and astonishing as that which we got from this point.

The road to the valley, although it is extremely rough and shakes people terribly, deserves mention for the rapidity with which it was made, and also for the almost perfect manner in which the work in many places was done. The way along this rocky ledge is certainly very fine, although we see that in many places the road has fallen down.

Opposite is the "Bridal Veil," truly deserving its name, a magnificent stream falling from a height of 940 feet without touching the rock on its way down. Long ere the water reaches the bottom of the valley, it is converted into a white flaky mist, which, caught by the gentle wind, is sometimes spread out, sometimes compressed and sways to and fro like a veil in the breeze.

The Cathedral rocks running just behind it, look as though they were really part of some gigantic structure, and the Fall seems but a rainbow resting on the side of it.

Opposite the Bridal Veil is a small stream of water which is called the Maiden's Tear; this also is appropriately named when once you know it; the continual gush is not at all unedifying.

Passing along the bottom of the valley, we have the Three Brothers; the Indian name of which, Pom-pom-pa-sus, means, according to Professor Whitney, "Mountains playing at Leap Frog." From below, the peculiar shape of the three rocks with their heads peering over each other strikes one as wonderfully like three frogs; the third pointed rock rises to an enormous height, upwards of 4000 feet above the valley.

What is specially wonderful about this valley is that though all the mountains are of solid rock, in many places on the sides of these rocks—it seems almost impossible to imagine it—we see trees growing. The reason of this has always been a mystery to me. Does the earth fall from above, or did the birds bring vegetable matter there? However, such is the fact; the trees grow where the rocks is hundreds of feet thick, right on its surface in the burning sun.

Passing on and recrossing the bridge we see the first building in Yeo-Semite, "——Hotel," kept by a German. I very much recommend travellers to shun his acquaintance. Two or three persons who were recommended there were not at all satisfied, and myself and my Anglo-American friend, though promised rooms, and those separate rooms, were about to have been forced into one small room together, but we rebelled and went over to Mr. Black's, where we were very comfortable.

That evening we walked down to the Cosmopolitan Bath House. This is a great institution where travellers can get an excellent bath of hot or cold water at any hour of the day, and where there is also a Gargantuesque blank book to receive and perpetuate their names.

From this point we have a beautiful view of the Yeo-Semite Falls; indeed, it is wonderful how they grow upon you. The first time you see them, you say, "Yes, they are very fine, but—;" and then you think of all the Falls you have seen, and you say, perhaps, to yourself, "After all, it is nothing so very wonderful;" but then as you take the height of a two-story house near by, and measure the Falls with your eye up to the top of the house, then measuring it again with the same—a seemingly endless wall over which a vast Fall tumbles—then continuing the operation up to a dizzy height, where water and sky seem to meet, and where from the bosom of the sky an inexhaustible stream appears to nourish unceasingly the waters that never tire of descending, and when you further remember that it takes two hours to get up there, and then think that in that position where the top Fall ends and the lower one begins there are said to be three square acres,—when, in short, you have realized in some degree the true magnitude of the cataract, you begin to alter your opinion.

Myself and the Anglo-American were billetted on a wooden house where the partition was made of linen. The effect of this was that some very noisy Englishmen, our neighbours, kept us awake a considerable part of the night. One especially was very demonstrative; after enlarging upon the inconvenience of American travel (though he had only seen San Francisco), he compared England with America, very favourably for the one, and very unsatisfactorily for the other. At length, having emphatically declared that

England was a great nation, he went off with a snore. *Requiescat in pace!*

The next morning we rejoined Sir George and Mr. Bowen at breakfast. After breakfast we found four saddled animals at the door waiting for us. Two of them were horses, the others mules. Mine turned out to be a very fine fellow, and carried me splendidly through three days of very hard work. Poor Sir George's mule was less governable and decent in his behaviour, and Sir George, accustomed to English thoroughbreds, failed to appreciate the advantage of using mules for equitation.

Having made a charge of five superior to that of the " Six Hundred " out of the village, we passed into a pretty grove where three or four charming *equestriennes,* evidently possessing small knowledge of the horse, but nevertheless looking very pretty with their hair and hats all blown back, went galloping past us. Following the finely wooded road, gradually winding up the valley, with a little pause here and there to enable us the better to admire the beautiful scenery, we kept steadily pushing forward.

We at length arrive at a beautiful lake, where, looking in, we are not quite certain whether we stand on our heads or our feet. This is the Mirror Lake, so named on account of the perfect reflection which it gives of all adjacent objects. It is surrounded by a beautiful growth of trees; in the distance are enormous rocks, looking like sentinels keeping guard over it. This is certainly as pretty as it is represented in the guide-books. The cottagers located on the borders of the lake, immediately called to us asking whether we did not want to see the "Clothes-Line," and were greatly surprised when we told them that we had plenty of clothes-lines in our part of the country—New York,—and that those who had the luck of living on the Hudson, and who took the Thirtieth Street train every day, were not strangers to that beautiful ornament of the landscape.

However, this celebrated clothes-line to which they referred was nothing but the effect produced on the rock where pieces had been broken off. The resemblance was sufficient to account for the unlucky designation. All through California we were bored by having such resemblances brought to our minds in the most delightful and romantic spots.

We then went off in a small scow under the guidance of a son of one of the cottagers to see the "Nigger Girl." This ebony beauty our young guide and oarsman talked of in a very familiar way.

"Have you been to see her this morning, Jim," calling out to a crony as he made ready to leave. "Does she stand it well? Was she half way in the water? I have no doubt you was greatly excited."

Mr. Bowen looked extremely shocked, and as though he wanted to go home.

At last we reached the further shore, and then, as we stood at a certain place beside the lake, we saw—not, as perhaps we might have hoped, jet-coloured nymphs rising from the waves in all the glory of African nudity, but simply the reflection in the water of a peculiarly shaped branch, which had the outline and appearance of a negress.

We returned to land disheartened, but were forced, nevertheless, to pay a "bit" apiece for this rare enjoyment.

Sir George wanting to pick some flowers, had wandered out of sight, so Mr. Bowen taught us how to make the Maori call, and we made the virgin woods ring with a whoop that might have resembled the war cry of their former inhabitants. Upon this Sir George making his appearance, we returned to our Rosinantes and started.

We had purposed going to the foot of the

higher Yeo-Semite Falls, but here as in Europe the guides are accustomed to do so much *per diem*, and though we explained very accurately to the guide who was with us what we desired, he kept telling us we had plenty of time, and that it did not take long, and that we must not be in a hurry, so that when we arrived at the foot of the bottom Fall he began to tie up the horses, and when we told him that he need not do so as we meant to go to the top, he replied that it would be quite impossible to do so that afternoon if we wanted to get to the house in the evening, as it took at least three hours to go up to the top of the Fall. On considering the time, we found we should have had ample time in the morning if he had not caused us to delay by telling us that we had such a superabundance of time.

Returning to the hotel discomfited, we had a hearty lunch and then started for Snow's, following a rugged track by the side of a beautiful stream.

At one time we met a gentleman and his son on horseback; the gentleman carried a many coloured snake twisted round his walking-stick, which he held at arm's length. This reptile, he assured us, killed the animal that it attacked by winding itself about it; sometimes it would wind itself round a deer's leg and craunch it.

In many places we had to put our horses in most awkward positions, sometimes with their fore-feet in the ditch-boulders, or standing away out on the edge of the precipice to allow other equestrians to pass us.

Having gone some distance farther on over a very poor track, we arrived at Vernal Falls. I think that this is perhaps one of the most loveable falls in the valley. I could imagine lovers or poets in rapturous contemplation of it. The exquisite gracefulness with which it glides over the cliff passes description, while its volume is very imposing. The effect of the falling water, together with the noise it makes in striking the rocks, produces an impression full of majesty, yet melancholy and poetic.

It has been well remarked that painting is inadequate to the representation of great mountain scenery; and it might be said that the inadequacy is directly proportionate to the grandeur of the scene to be represented. Even verbal description wearies more than it enlightens when it piles up epithets to describe a "matchless cataract."

Retracing our steps, we then climbed up the side of a mountain, having the Vernal sometimes in view, and at last arrived in sight of Snow's and the Nevada Falls. On the road up they had tried to levy a dollar from us for the benefit of Mr. Snow, the proprietor of the inn at Nevada Falls—he having made the road all through the valley. We are continually called upon to pay a dollar on very miserable trails, which in all probability had been made by the Indians long before the settlers came here.

The view as we came on the mountain side, looking down from a dizzy height from our left to the valley below in front of the Nevada Falls, with Snow's looking like a Swiss *hospice*, was very striking and beautiful, while still farther to the left a great round mass of rock rises majestically, and beneath, the Vernal tearing over precipices in its stony bed with a roaring as of caged lions.

The roads were very narrow, and in many places the earth had fallen down the mountain, and the thought that all the furniture and provisions at Snow's had to be taken over this road on mule-back rendered us very thankful that we were not obliged to sleep out in the cold. Passing down the side of a mountain on a winding road, crossing a yawning gulley, through which a river that forms the Nevada Falls goes tearing—passing this on a sort of bridge—we climbed the mountain the other side and arrived at Snow's, sorely tired and footsore, having walked and ridden a great deal during the day.

Snow's consists of a long building very much like the *hospices* in the Italian or Swiss Alps, while very near by a pretty *châlet*-like building is being put up. The workmen engaged upon it had nailed boards horizontally along the roof to rest their feet on as they worked, very much after the manner of the ledges on Swiss *châlets*, whereon they place large stones to keep the roof down, and which gives the building such a picturesque effect. I told Mr. Snow that by having some stones placed there, and letting moss grow over them, he would render the place very beautiful, perhaps the most attractive of its kind in the mountains, as otherwise the building was constructed to resemble a *châlet;* but he only said, "Ah! we are very glad to have anything we can get, and never give any thought for anything of fancy; all sorts of labour costs too much."

It is a very strange thing amongst a new people in a new part of the country to find the same stubbornness that one meets with amongst old and prejudiced people, the utter incapacity to see that one can arrive at an end without specially intending to do it from the beginning. I am sorry to say that Mr. Snow is not the only representative of this class. Otherwise we could not have desired a better landlord and landlady than Mr. and Mrs. Snow. They were Massachusetts people, and had been in the West a considerable time.

Sir George and Mr. Bowen had climbed up from the foot of the Vernal Falls with a guide, and arrived some time after. Poor Sir George was very much pleased with his climb, describing the view from his side as extremely beautiful.

There being a good many guests in the house, we were put on what Mr. Snow called short rations, but they were really as good as, if not better than, what we had recently been accustomed to, consisting of chops, steaks, and tomatoes, and some very good California Hocheimer. We were shown into a cosy sitting-room, where a pleasant fire was yet burning in the stove, as the evenings at this altitude are cold. We spent a very agreeable one. Sir George gave us a description of the Maoris, the native New Zealander race; he spoke of them as very fine fellows, perhaps finer than Cooper's Indians. He told us of the trial of a Maori chief. It appears there is an arrangement between the English settlers and the natives for selling land, but sometimes the native, after selling, claims the land back again, and gives warning to the English to leave it. They gave two or three of these warnings, and then if the land is not vacated they sometimes commit murder openly. Our hero had been compromised in a rising which had ensued from a discussion of this kind, and had been condemned to death by a court-martial.

Sir George, thinking the condemnation unauthorised, had suspended the execution of the sentence, and recommended him to call for a trial by jury. The jury, however, found him guilty, and he was condemned to death, and this time to be hanged. Sir George described his indignation very finely; the condemned man rose, and striking his breast, said, "When English soldier makes war on Maori, Maori captures English soldier, the Maori judges him and kills him as a soldier; but your chiefs have already condemned me, why did they not kill me? I am a dead man already." He waxed very indignant that he should be tried and condemned like a thief, so that when he was being led to prison, Sir George, thinking it hard that he, a chief, a man of great importance, should be degraded, and that the policeman should put handcuffs on his great strong wrists, and make him walk through the town,—Sir George ordered them to a carriage, saying he would pay for it if the town would not.

When the time came to retire, we were shown to a nice clean room and comfortable bed. The next morning we awoke surrounded by a dense fog. After breakfast—it being Sunday—we had service in the sitting-room, and then held a consultation whether we should push on to Cloud's Rest that same day. We came to the conclusion that if it were clearing by one o'clock we would go. During the morning, the Anglo-American and myself, who had not seen the Vernal Falls from the top, retracing our steps a little along its steeps, and turning off from the head of the Falls, after climbing over some slaty stone, arrived near a pond surrounded by what is called poison lilac. It is said that sheep die from eating it. It is a plant of a very pretty fair tint, and has a very pleasant odour. Presently we came to the head of the rock, over which flows the Vernal. I have never seen such a gorgeous and imposing effect produced by water.

We see water going smoothly over, over

into the valley beneath, and a strange longing seizes one to throw oneself into its bosom, and be carried over with it, one knows not, cares not whither. You seem to think that it will take you to some other land, where your soul will find that something which every soul yearns after, and which none can define.

Gazing over and down into the green valley, imagination peoples it with other beings, other forms—more fitting denizens of this lovely region. Can the dwellers in it be the low, drunken, brutal characters which are seen along the railroad stations as one comes West; must one, looking down there, imagine them occupied in some horrible rites of grovelling human debauchery, amid these sylvan scenes of more than mortal beauty. No! oh no! Rather let me dream of the primitive people who once perhaps lived here in pastoral simplicity; yonder, I might imagine, near that group of noble trees, a chief stood, high above the rest, while two young lovers stand taking oaths of fidelity before the supreme chief of the tribe, and then a shout—not resembling the war screech which their poor degraded descendants are made to give at some New York charitable entertainment, but a shout of joy because two pure and loving hearts are united on earth.

A thousand fancies of this kind came crowding upon me as I looked over and pondered, and it was hard for me to believe that I did not hear the voices of the people, and that in the woods underneath I did not see the faces of the lovers with their arms locked in each other, while they slowly passed through the woods, and that the voices—but only the roaring of the Falls, and the surging of the winds through the pines were all that remained of the betrothed ones, and the horsemen of my day-dream, pushing past on lightning steeds, were only the play of the sunbeams through the branches.

Returning to Snow's, we visited the Nevada Falls at their lowest point. They are several hundred feet high, and are very beautiful; one part of the Fall is deflected towards the middle by a ledge of rock which expands it to a width of 175 feet.

On returning to the house, we entered into a consultation and determined to try the ascent. Taking our luncheon with us, we started. The mist had begun to rise, and the ground in every place was wet. We wound up the side of the Nevada Falls, up a ravine where the rocks had broken off into great boulders, and where roads had been made with great ingenuity. A dollar's toll was certainly due on this piece of trail. At the top we thought we must have lost our heads and had been going down hill instead of up, as we found ourselves in what seemed to be the Yeo-Semite Valley, on a smaller scale. This valley is known as the Smaller Yeo-Semite Valley. It was evidently snowing or raining higher up the mountain, so we did not attempt to climb immediately, but had a delightful gallop through the valley. In the middle runs a pretty river that forms the Nevada Falls. Here and there are ponds in which game and fish are found. It was certainly a pleasant gallop over the soft sod, the fresh cool air giving new vigour to one's lungs, and I enjoyed it as though I had been following the hounds in Lancashire.

Retracing our steps, we began the ascent of the valley. The climbing was very steep. Our guide was not a good one; he did not seem to know his way. In one place he went down the road to take an easier cut, as he said, but he carried us by a very steep incline over soft ground with a precipice by the side of it. As we mounted, the sun began to fall, and as we pushed our way through bending branches of evergreen, we might have thought ourselves in the midst of a California winter; but such air! our lungs seemed to sing a Te Deum in breathing it. Soon it began to snow.

About two o'clock we came to a ranche, but a deserted ranche. The desire to be a proprietor and householder in the valley was awakened within us, and so we entered and took possession of it at once.

We were lucky enough to find an old demi-john which was used as a water-pitcher, and plenty of pine boards with which we made a roaring fire, to which I added a large log which I had found under some wood in the snow. We had a pleasant luncheon, of which we all partook heartily. Where we were, indeed, I knew not, but the oddity of the situation was pleasing. The log burned away at a great rate, and the snow-flakes falling on it produced a crackling and a sputter as with fuel on the fire. Indeed, we were quickly alarmed for the poor settler's hut, as the chimney was very low, and the fire blazed away like Vulcan's furnace.

The shelves on which the inhabitants were supposed to sleep were made in berths, two on two sides of the room. I imagine that here must have been spent many a pleasant evening over a pipe and a chat. As for us, we were very soon hurried away.

The continual riding had begun to tell upon us, and our knees and backs were very tired and sore. Mounting again our poor Rosinantes, who seemed very forlorn and not quite certain what to make of all this "bother," never perhaps having had to do with such extraordinary people, who gave them double food and made them do double work, we commenced the ascent again in the face of the snow. The guide began to grumble very seriously, and said if it got worse he would not go on. In the track, the snow was beginning to lie very thick, and all signs of trail were lost in the morasses, in which were large pools of snow, and we were surrounded by a dense cloud of falling snow. The guide now refused to go on, and said he would not risk his own life, the mules, and us, and that it was not the same here as in England, that he did not know his way and could not find it. We told him pretty sharply to come on, and Mr. Bowen and myself wanting to "do it" if possible, pushed ahead and kept along the elevated ground. God knows how we got along! Every once in a while we came to an empty space between two rocks. We had not the faintest idea where we were going to, only knowing that we intended to get to the top if possible. We passed bear and deer tracks. We could hear the voices of our three companions away down in the track, and every now and then a vigorous call, "Come back!" but we had gone thus far, and intended to go to the end.

Continuing on, we came to a very rough stony place where ice had been formed, and where the horses slipped at every step. We were now on a ledge of rock about thirty feet broad, with precipices on both sides; and the snow was coming down like hail in our faces. This ledge kept narrowing until, after some twenty yards, it was not more than ten feet wide, with precipices of great depth on either side. Here we dismounted, and putting both reins of the horses under a heavy stone, pushed along the ledge. In most places the ledge was covered with snow and ice, and our passage was obstructed by large boulders. Often we went on our hands and knees, holding to pieces of rock hanging over precipices more than a thousand feet above the valley. Sometimes even we preferred getting on the ledge formed on the sides of the precipices by the top of the rock breaking off; sometimes we straddled the ledge and worked along for a way; and all this with the snow beating in our faces and on our hands. I was not very happy, as, expecting to find warm weather even here, I had only brought low shoes with me, and had on light cotton socks, which were pretty well soaked.

At last we arrived at a peak from which we could see a stone crane built on the highest point a little farther on. Although I had had some pretty difficult climbing before, I found this sufficiently hard work, as this ledge came to peaks each of which makes one think oneself at the top. But here we saw a peak still farther on, which we climbed to, and soon to another. Still one more spirt, and clinging on to the rocks, pushing ourselves on with sheer force of determination, with a last energetic grab we found ourselves on the top.

Hurrah! Surely this is Cloud's Rest! And a tremendous cloud was resting on it to-day. We were shivering and wet through and through, our coats all buttoned up round our ears, our hats pulled down over our noses, and looking probably very much like a couple of chimney-sweeps who had slid down a factory chimney into a water trough.

We did not stop long, but began to work our way down again. This was no easy work, as the natural propensity was to slide downward. Nevertheless, by making use of every cranny, we let ourselves down gradually.

Suddenly a happy thought struck Mr. Bower,—" Let's write our names on a penny, and put it up there!"

The next thing was, where to find a penny, as the circumference of our cent is not large enough to show much writing within it. Strangely enough, I found one amongst other pieces in my pocket.

Poor thing! it little knew when it was stamped that it was going to pass through the hands of many filthy peddlers and traders in old London to find its way into the hands of a scoundrilly Yankee, and last of all to meet its grave on the top of one of the highest peaks in the land of that heathenish people, more than 200 feet over the Cap of Liberty, with the name of a good-for-nothing American on its back.

On this piece of money of "Her Noble, Gracious, Serene, Royal, Imperial Majesty,* Mr. Bowen, with great care and some difficulty, scratched the inscription:—"Your humble servant's name, his own, and Cloud's Rest, June 13th: six inches of snow: very hard work." Then the question was, who should go and put it on the crane, as the snow was falling very fast. We both wanted to go down, and it needed some stoicism to remain still longer in the piercing cloud. We

---

* A lady addressed the Prince of Wales very much in the above style during his visit here, New York.

had not implicit faith in each other, and neither cared to be the one to go up with the penny, for surely it would be a very dreary, unpleasant place to be left all alone in. What should we do but squat right down in the snow and ice, and play heads and tails with this marvellous penny. Fair *demoiselle* Fortune smiled upon me, and poor Mr. Bowen had to go climbing back and put the penny on the crane, and then come down again.

After having slipped two or three times in very unpleasant places, and got down as best we could to where our horses were, our hearts were light within us, and if any man who at any period in his life had professed Voltairism ever felt less Voltairian than I did at that moment, and proves it to my satisfaction, I will give him that memorable penny, which he can then go and get at Cloud's Rest.

We had some difficulty in getting our horses off the ledge where we had left them, but once off, I can assure you, we were not long in getting into our saddles and pushing our horses with all convenient speed down the mountain.

We soon saw three spectres, black as night, flying off on the wings of the wind in front of us. The coat-tails of one were standing out behind him as he dashed ahead in his desperate hurry. He proved to be my companion the Anglo-American, and I will say that at that moment my love for him was not very great, though he made a whole series of excuses, and the guide was very insolent, and told me that I must not imagine we were in England, and that they did not climb mountains that way in America.

That was too much for me, and I gave him a decided piece of my mind, assuring him that I belonged to the *libre Republique*, and that I considered him an extremely poor specimen of my countrymen, and that I was glad to say I knew some who had climbed that and many worse places without resting; and I also further assured him that he had behaved like an insolent scoundrel. This and a great many other pleasant things of a like kind I thought it desirable to tell him,—all of which he received with the utmost complacency.

We then put ourselves in line and began the descent. As we passed the cabin the fire we had lighted was just going out, the snow about melting, and it was beginning to be fine. I requested the guide to take us down the right trail this time, which he did, and we were soon in the Little Yeo-Semite Valley.

Very little incident happened on the road down; the snow had begun to melt near the valley, and the sun was coming out beneath the clouds. As we wound our way down, everything looked fresh and new, as if waking from slumber, and it appeared to me as if I had spent fully twelve hours in the mountains, and was coming out on another day.

We were very glad to get back. When I walked I could not quite feel whether I was walking on my feet or on some part of the bone of my leg. My feet did not seem to exist; as for my knees, they felt as if they had an enormous pair of thumbscrews on them, and were being unmercifully tortured.

The red isinglass of Mr. Snow's stove had a very pleasant and cosy effect, a pair of fresh warm stockings and slippers and a good wash seemed to be heavenly gifts, while a pleasant supper, served as only New Englanders can serve a supper, cheered our hearts within us, and, later on, the bed was not at all unwelcome, although, from over fatigue, I slept very little. Cloud's Rest is 6,450 feet above the valley.

The next morning we were up again at half-past four o'clock, and taking the same road by the side of the Falls, and turning to the right instead of going down the Yeo-Semite

Valley, entered into a dense forest. We must have been two hours in these woods. Mr. Bowen, who is something of a botanist, described to us the different species of trees. On emerging from the woods we found ourselves in an open country, covered by a growth of stunted trees, amongst which the most common and noticeable was the manzanita. Winding on like Indians, a projecting branch every once in a while carrying away one's cap or something else, at last, by two o'clock, we found ourselves at Glacier's Point. Here Mr. Bowen made the acquaintance of one of the ladies who had arrived in our party, and it was very pleasant to see how well the English and completely Americanised women get on together. So far, indeed, as I have been able to notice, a thoroughly well-bred Englishman seems to agree perfectly with the ordinary American, all national idiosyncracies notwithstanding; and as for Americans, it is only those who impose on Americans themselves, that impose, perhaps, a little more on the English.

Leaving this point of the valley, we pursued our journey to the east of the Yeo-Semite Fall, until we came in sight of the Royal Arches, a vast wall of solid rock several thousand feet in height, having its side perfectly perpendicular; the top, however, is scooped out, and is not inappropriately named the Shade to Indian Baby-basket.

From this point we get a charming view of the Nevada Fall in the distance, Cloud's Rest looking much less formidable than it did when we made the ascent of it, but still quite sufficient to make us feel proud of our success, considering the weather we had. Down into the valley the view seemed more than earthly; indeed, we felt very much in the position of one of Milton's angels perched on a cloud and looking on a pigmy world beneath us, from an immeasurable height.

To describe the effect produced on the mind by standing on a perfectly perpendicular wall of smooth granite 3,000 feet high, and looking straight beneath you into a beautiful valley all surrounded by walls of the same height, with lovely rivers tumbling over them here and there—an abode of peace, happiness, and security, secluded from all the worry and bustle of the outer world—to attempt a description of this is more than I will undertake to do. We stayed here but a short time, sufficient to gloat our eyes on the enchanting scene, and then pushed on still higher to the Sentinel's Dome. From here the view is simply glorious; the mountain of rock forms a perfect dome; from it we scanned the whole of the valley, with its surrounding peaks, and the Nevada chain in the distance. From here also we got a look to the back of our position, and we found mountains in every direction. To any one ignorant of the peaks that surround him, it would seem that he was here on the highest point for miles around. Even on the top of this mass of granite, a tree grew that overlooked a little basin of water collected in the rock, and which formed quite a pretty little lake on the stone surface.

Going down the mountain side to where a beautiful stream winds into the valley, we had a thoroughly rustic luncheon, after which Mr. Bowen called forth our admiration by making up his mind to do a thing that he had been proposing to do all the morning; this was to go to Inspiration Point, about twenty miles distant, and that all by himself, without a guide. This is one of the most famous points of the Yeo-Semite, because it has probably been more written about than others equally magnificent.

Mr. Bowen got a fresh mule, and having had the way explained to him by a guide, he started. For our part we began to wind our way into the valley, having made an engagement to meet Mr. Bowen at the Bridal Veil Falls.

About half-way down, we met the German gentleman and his wife, whom we had not seen for several days, and whom we were very glad to see, as we had plenty of things to tell.

They were very much amused at our adventures, which would have been more amusing to ourselves but for the state of our feet and legs, and the abnormal lumps in the throats and abdomens of our poor horses; indeed, my poor trustworthy mule was so fatigued that he could hardly put one foot before another, and as he did so, it was with the greatest care and precision; nevertheless, he slipped considerably in some places, and when we had to go round corners—the zig-zag trail making rapid curves—he would place his two hind-legs on the edge of the precipice, and stand perfectly still, and as he refused to go on, I was afraid to force him, lest out of stubbornness he might back over the edge and carry me into the depth beneath.

However, we were lucky enough to get down without any accident. I immediately made for a bath, in which I steeped myself for an hour, much to my advantage both physically and mentally; then, with my companions and the German and his wife, went in a carriage to the Bridal Falls.

This cataract is certainly beautiful in the

true sense of the word—graceful, magnificent, imposing, not sternly sublime. On my way up to it, I fell down two boulders, and hurt myself rather sharply in the wrist,—the only accident I had met with as yet.

Coming back to the carriage, we found Mr. Bowen just returned, seated on his mule with a fine specimen of a beautiful indigenous plant attached to his saddle. He looked over wearied. He said he had had some difficulty about the way, and had met with some Indians who had indicated it to him by signs.

He had, indeed, done more than he had at first intended, having visited one peak besides Inspiration Point. Altogether, bearing in mind what he had already gone through, this expedition was no slight thing.

Returning to the hotel, we passed a very pleasant evening with Mr. Hutchings, who was one of the earliest explorers of and the *first settler* in the Yeo-Semite. He gave us some very interesting information about the valley, and was very much scandalized at the behaviour of our guide.

Having concluded to leave this by stage the next day, we were uncertain about our places until we learned that another party who had secured seats had relinquished them, intending to go by another road. We were then lucky enough to be accommodated with seats. Travellers, although assured beforehand by the parties who sell them tickets, that if there be not places in the stages running, additional ones will be put on, often have to wait two or three days before they can get down the valley, as the stage lines nearly always refuse to put on an extra omnibus, even if they have one they could easily spare. And this disappointment is certain to occur when, as in our case, it happens that tickets are procured beforehand, as the proprietors know that the prices of the tickets being secured, you cannot, to their loss, go by the competition line; so that all the supposed advantages of getting a through ticket are not only illusory but positively a detriment, as you get bad guides, bad horses, and bad seats, or none at all, in the omnibus, besides being always obliged to take the one line. By taking your tickets separately for each successive part of the trip, the whole may cost you a few dollars more, as it may also cost you a few dollars less, and then you are perfectly free to go or stay, to take one road or another, to choose one guide or another, to select your horses and your saddle, and in general to feel yourself perfectly at liberty, which is the very essence of all travel for amusement.

CHAPTER XI.

Pioneer Laundry—Ferry Boats—A Wayside Inn—*Digito Monstrari*—Sonora—The U.S. Mail—Muscular Christianity—Intemperance of Miners—Calaveras Grove—An Aristocratic Innkeeper—Change on the System of " Heads I Win, Tails you Lose "—How to see the World—Big Trees—Postprandial Eloquence—Poor Farming.

WE were called from our sleep at the same unearthly hour, half-past four o'clock, and after a hurried breakfast found ourselves again squeezed into that species of tumbril known as the Yeo-Semite stage-coach, and were soon off on our way to the Calaveras Big Trees.

Passing along the valley we again wind up the sides of its cliffs, and soon find ourselves in front of a building called the Pioneer Laundry. Just as one is coming down over dangerous roads into the valley, we see these ominous words branded in black letters on white boards, attached to the pine trees:—

> How would you like to have a Broken Neck and a Dirty Shirt on? Go to the Pioneer Laundry. ☞

Our party in the omnibus is made up of some Australians, Sir George, Mr. Bowen and the Anglo-American, Mr. and Mrs. C—— of Philadelphia, whom I think I have already mentioned, and the present writer.

Mr. C—— told us that having been sent by a person to whom he had been clerk at Philadelphia, to a Mr. Junot, on arriving at that gentleman's house he had been ushered into a room of which the walls were covered with arms, and among which he had particularly noticed a large sabre covered with black. While his attention was occupied with these arms, a dark, scowling, fierce-looking man came in and spoke to him about them in a way that alarmed him not a little. When he got home his employer asked him how he liked Mr. Junot, and seemed very much amused at the fear he had been in, telling him that this was the famous Marshal Junot, the hero of so many fights. In general great men do not amuse themselves by frightening little ones, but the taint of vulgarity, whatever form it assumes, is no doubt ineradicable, and Marshal Junot is said to have been conspicuous among the rest for the republican vulgarity of his manners. The memoirs of the *vie interne* of some of Napoleon's *protegés* and notably of Napoleon himself, do not much enhance our idea of the essential superiority of the military *caste*.

Mr. C—— also told us about the sale of Jerome Bonaparte's pictures. It seems strange that these people, accustomed to the pomp of European courts, should have settled down in a place like Philadelphia.

Mr. Bowen entered into conversation with the Australian gentleman, and from the conflict of their opinions we learned something about two countries.

This road, I think, was the roughest that we had yet travelled over. At midday we had luncheon in a long low cabin. As we were looking in at the door, a great broad-shouldered, heavy-moustached man called out in a loud rough voice,

"Come in and eat; don't stand there staring; we haven't got no time, you fools."

This was a little shock at first, but we found out afterwards that this was our driver, which of course explained everything satisfactorily.

As we were getting into the stage we heard him speaking in a very loud voice to an unfortunate gentleman who had the appearance of being an Englishman.

"I guess you'd better let me have that there hat; it's moighty fine, it's just splendid, it's the finest thing I ever saw." The hat that brought forth all this admiration was a pith hat belonging to the Australian traveller, and which he quickly handed to the driver, who wore it jauntily all the rest of the way. Some distance further we stopped to change horses, and in this little out-of-the-way inn I found all the walls covered with photographs of Capoul, Mdlle. Patti, Mdme. Ilma di Murska, and others.

After leaving this station a miner of enormous dimensions asked to be taken up, and was put on the same seat with Sir George and myself. He took up a great deal of space, and as I do the same, poor Sir George feeling very unwell, and being on the outside into the bargain—our friend the miner pushing vigorously all the way, and making himself as big as possible,— I was obliged to hold against the seat of the waggon with all my might in order not to pulverise poor Sir George.

This man had done mining in many parts of Australia and New Zealand, and had travelled a good deal; but he had abandoned his old occupation and was now a groom, and seemed to be perfectly satisfied with his humble position in life, and was going to San Francisco to get higher wages. It was very amusing to hear him speak of Australia or New Zealand as a New Yorker would of Massachusetts.

Here we saw one of the ferry boats of the kind generally used, I am informed, in this part of the country. They consist of a raft made of strong boards, having a chain attached about one-third of the way down the side, and a pulley on the end of this chain; the pulley is fastened to an iron rope which is stretched across the stream by chains from it. On this the pulley runs, and such is the force of the stream against the sides of the boat or raft that it pushes it along. This ingenious contrivance replaces the bridge very advantageously.

The drive down was through a very beautiful country, indeed more like Spain than anything I had seen in America; vines growing on the hills, and muddy torrents rushing at the foot of these.

About five o'clock a tremendous rain-storm began furiously to pelt us, large hail-stones being mixed with the rain. All the seats were soaking, and naturally those that sat on them were partially soaked too. The leather sides were let down, but the rain beat in between the crevices. The driver's seat was naturally the most exposed, but the possessors of that seat of honour made a gallant defence. The miner, Sir George, and myself had a small shower-bath down the back of the neck. The miner I didn't so much care for, but Sir George and myself—you can understand—it was different; a question of *esprit du corps*. Luckily we got to a stopping-place not far on, and a very cosy stopping-place it was. A German kept it. A little piano in the corner of the sitting-room, purple papering on the wall, handsome volumes of Schiller and Goethe on the table, with a pleasant stove in the corner — all told of comfort. An old-fashioned dining-room downstairs, with the kitchen opening into it by means of a window through which the food was passed, old plate and glasses ranged round on the shelves and at the bar, all contributed an air of comfort that made your beef-steak doubly acceptable. As I was leaving the dining-room, I saw our friend the driver with a lady, whom I took to be his wife. As I passed she said to him in a very loud voice, while staring at me from head to foot,—

"Is this the big boy you were telling me about?"

At this, dear reader, yuo can imagine how

my soul revolted within me. But there was nought to be said; she belonged to the fair sex, and he was our driver. What could you say against a demi-god, a creature that takes all the letters, carries all the parcels, and so forth? I say, what could be done against a force like this? Indeed, if she had desired to flay me alive, I must, I suppose, have submitted. I was born, it is plain, with a special faculty for the recognition of power.

After strumming a little on the *claviar*, I went to my room, and heard a whole oratorio on an instrument of different size and different power—that is, not the wind organ, but the nasal organ, an instrument which is more generally understood and more commonly played on with facility and perfection than any other that I am acquainted with. Having had my ears charmed with this delightful melody wafted on night's soft breezes, and having looked under the bed to see whether there were not hidden there a hundred robbers, more or less, although the border of the bed came down to within two inches of the floor, and having looked into the bed to see whether there were any *avant-gardes* or dark-coloured picket men, I jumped into it myself, blew out the candle, and—good-night!

The next morning we started early, and had a beautiful drive during the forenoon, passing under two or three long tressel bridges made to support the hydraulic pipes across the valley for mining purposes.

Passing through pretty little villages, which had most of them a Spanish look, we noticed one town which had been built by miners, and near which the earth was turned up in enormous circles of barrenness, giving it the appearance of the side of Mount Vesuvius, or of some torrent-wasted district in Switzerland. About midday we arrived at Sonora. This is a very considerable town, having three or four churches of Spanish architecture, and altogether presenting an appearance of age very agreeable in some respects in a new country.

Passing through the streets, we stopped at a butcher's, and saw a couple of Indian women catering for the tribe. They seemed pretty sharp at this work, and went in for quantity not quality, taking all such parts as other people don't touch, and continually asking the butcher for another small piece, which he would throw to them disdainfully. His butcher's blocks were pieces of sequoia, or big tree. The town is, generally speaking, pretty. We had an excellent glass of ale here.

The people have a decided Spanish cast of countenance. While we were here a violent hail storm came on, which took us greatly by surprise. The stones were of the size of rifle bullets, and all equally large and smooth as if made by some machine. This ended in a violent rain-storm. The country during the rest of the journey was very pretty, the scenery resembling, a good deal, that of the Pyrenees. As we were winding along the sides of one of the hills, we saw a man, evidently a farmer, coming towards us in a large tent waggon. As we carried the U.S. mail, the waggon had to pass on the outside. This rule, which breaks the law of the road, would, in the case of the stage with the U.S. mail and only the driver and one passenger meeting a conveyance with nine or ten persons on board, oblige all of them to run the risk of breaking their necks—for the chances are very often little less than this.

Our friend the farmer did not seem to understand this work, for, instead of backing to the side of the road, he went sliding backward over the hill, holding his reins all the time, and looking at us meekly, with a melancholy expression on his face, as much as to say, "You see I cannot help it, I'm going over, no help for it. Isn't it funny? D——

the U.S. mail!" and over he went, and gracefully slid into a small oak tree, which prevented him from going down the precipice. He soon made his appearance from under his waggon, with his face gashed but no limbs broken. We helped him with his waggon to the other side of the hill, while he never once swore nor got angry, but took everything in perfect quiet and thanked us for our aid. Having seen our friend on his road, we started off ourselves.

Sir George told us of Bishop Selwyn, late Bishop of New Zealand. He said that Selwyn preached at three very distant places on the same day. He told us also of an adventure of the Bishop's with a settler. This man had appropriated a piece of ground, belonging, it appears, to a Maori. The Bishop remonstrated with him about it; the settler, getting very angry, said he would like to see any Maori or any other man claim the ground from him. Having said this, he was greatly surprised to see the ecclesiastic (who had had more than one fight at Eton) take his coat off and attack him in a very scientific way. He was still more astonished to find himself completely thrashed, and it is said he returned the land to the Maori, and went to seek his fortune elsewhere.

If we only had some Bishops like this in the West, to help Bishop Whipple in defence of the Indians, the agents, I think, would have more black eyes and less "green-backs." Surely muscular Christianity is a very good thing. Holy Paul himself would probably have adopted it for the conversion of Maoris and Indian agents.

From the scene of the upset to Murphy's, where we stopped for the night, we had but a short drive. Murphy's is one of the mining settlements, and a place of considerable size. Lounging after dinner, we got into conversation with a miner. One of our party from the West joked him about the habits of miners, asking how much a miner could drink. To this the miner replied that when he first came to the mining country men thought very little of putting away a couple of bottles of whisky, but now they are becoming very degenerate, and very few could manage more than one at a time. We asked him whether he did not think that all this alcohol would have an injurious effect upon his intestines. He said he did not think so; it would, he thought, if he took California wine. I am sorry to say we differed from him in opinion. His cheeks were all sunken, and he presented, generally, a cadaverous appearance.

What a horrible thing this vice is among the people who have to work as these men do. How is it that Americans and Englishmen cannot find out the exact medium between the use and disuse of stimulants?

Our hotel was a specimen of the peculiar Spanish sort of building we meet with so often throughout California; low and square, with enormous iron shutters. They are said to be very efficient against fire.

The next morning we were up betimes, and had one of the most charming drives through a beautiful country to the Calaveras Big Trees.

At one of the roadside inns that we passed we saw two young fellows on horseback, very plainly dressed, in old blue pea-jackets and tight trousers tucked into high boots. They rode fine, strong-looking horses.

We made various surmises as to whether they were Americans, Englishmen, or Australians. Sir George was of the opinion that they were Australians or New Zealanders.

We arrived at Calaveras Grove about two o'clock. The hotel was a very comfortable one for this out-of-the-way place, and I was quite surprised to find that it was kept by a Frenchman—a *soi disant gentilhomme*, very elegantly dressed, with a large open collar and long waistcoat.

With a very affectionate ardour he hugged two or three of our acquaintances in a charming way; he assured me that he had bought this hotel simply because it was a very pretty residence; that coming down from the valley the situation struck him so much that he thought he would like to have a dwelling there, but instead of living by himself he had determined to keep an hotel, so as to see visitors; that he had made absolutely no money—that was not his object—that the more he interested himself in the place the more he was cheated.

A small boy wanting horses to go to the Grove having said to our marquis, "I think I shall want horses this evening," the nobleman's wrath was roused, and he said, "No, you shall not have one horse."

Notwithstanding his declaration that he had made no money, he had little rings made out of the bark of the big trees, and these he sold for a *long bit* each, viz., twelve and a-half cents.

I may notice here that all through California they have a method of calculating small sums more convenient to the selling than to the purchasing party. If you get a glass of ale which costs you one "bit," and you give in payment ten cents, it is refused, while if you give fifteen cents you do not get back any change; then if you take another glass of ale and give ten cents, the barkeeper makes a principle of not remembering the former transaction, and makes you pay again fifteen cents. I asked a Californian if this was always the case; he said he did not think so, but I found it so invariably.

Here we met the horsemen of disputed origin whom we had encountered on the road. They turned out to be two young Englishmen, both of them of excellent family and position in England.

They were travelling here with very small purses. They told us that they had bought their horses for thirty dollars apiece, and that when they should have done with them they intended to travel by rail. They not unfrequently sold their horses at a good bargain, and bought others. They told me they had spent the winter in Colorado, up among the mountains, hunting, etc., sometimes living in "ranches," taking care of sheep, or else hiring themselves out to do cooking or other work. What a grand thing it would be if we could get some fellows like these to come and settle here! With all this show of roughness, they had both passed through the English

Universities with honours, and were perfectly polished and gentlemanly in every way; they said that although they had travelled otherwise, they really preferred this to any other mode of seeing the world. Altogether they made a most pleasant impression on me.

I then went to visit the trees. It is said that these trees are, some of them, nearly 3000 years old. The most remarkable tree, and the one whose size I appreciated most, was one which had been cut down, and on which a small summer-house had been built, the floor being perfectly polished like a *parquet*. The stem measures twenty-five feet in diameter with the bark on; the labour of two men for twenty-four days was required to cut it down, and the work was accomplished by boring it through with pump augurs. It is said that four sets of Lancers—that is, thirty-two persons—can dance on it without coming into collision. Over the fallen tree there was, up to within a short time, a bowling alley.

Strange to say, these trees spring from a very small core, not larger than a hen's egg. Twenty of these trees are seventy-five feet in circumference, or more. One stem, which is hollow, is called the miner's cabin, and is large enough to admit twelve or thirteen persons inside. One of the trees is designated the " Mother of the Forest." I was informed that the tree was so called from the fact of its having breast-like protuberances. This maternal parent has a circumference of ninety feet. The highest tree in the grove is called the " Keystone State," and is 325 feet in height. One of the trees near this, that was lately felled, occupied five men for twenty-one days, constantly at work, in bringing it to the ground. After the trunk was severed from the stump, it took the five men three days, using ponderous wedges, to topple it over.

The largest tree ever discovered in the world was found in this grove, and was called the " Father of the Forest." It is now prostrated, and measures 110 feet in circumference, and 435 in length. All of the most noble trees have received names, and the following will give some idea of this tree-nomenclature :—

" Hercules " rises to the majestic height of 320 feet, with a girth of 95 feet. The " Hermit " keeps company with the " Three Graces," near the " Husband and Wife," while the " Old Bachelor " is attentive to the " Pride of the Forest;" the " Old Maid " looking up for protection to the " Two Guardsmen," who, or which, like the others named, are of gigantic proportions. It would be tiresome to enumerate them all, with their several measurements; most of them have been more or less appropriately christened. The sight of them raises an immensity of wonder, but their beauty is less remarkable; they are all stem, or nearly so; but branch and foliage count for something in our estimate of the beauty of trees.

We had here the first digestible food we had eaten for a long while. As every one I had seen belonging to the house was French, I suppose the cook was too; at any rate, the dinner seemed to taste as though it might be so.

We were served by a young Frenchman, who wore spectacles, and looked like a medical student, or something of the kind.

We started on our return journey by two o'clock, and in due time arrived at Murphy's, where we dined, and where one of the passengers told us a little anecdote about a gentleman who was a great admirer of Queen Victoria, proposing her health at dinner. The gentleman being a very poor speaker, delivered himself in the following manner:—

"Gentlemen, I am requested to propose the health of Her Majesty. You all know, gentlemen—you all know, I say—you all know that, what I have to say—I mean to say, gentlemen, that—the less we say about her the better."

The next morning was the last day of the trip. Most of the road was down hill; we crossed the plains at Minton, at which place we took train and went as far as Stocton, a line we had not yet visited. Most of this region is rich for farming purposes, but unluckily the people here abuse it grossly—overworking it sometimes for nine years without giving it a year's respite or change of produce.

We arrived that afternoon at San Francisco pretty well tired out, and not sorry to find ourselves again in the city.

CHAPTER XII.

Sunday Amusements — New Palace Hotel — San Franciscan Hospitality — Reckoning without One's Host — Starr King — Chinese Opera — Home, Sweet Home !— Chinese Society — An Opium Den — Leper's Den.

The following day being Sunday, I went to church—one of the largest Protestant churches on the Pacific Coast—and was very much pleased with the service and music. In the afternoon I went with a friend to Woodward's Garden, where I found that quite a performance was going on in the skating rink; admission twenty-five cents. These people were enjoying themselves on Sunday just as Frenchmen or Italians are accustomed to do. As the majority were neither Frenchmen nor Italians, but simply Americans, their light-heartedness appeared to me of course extremely wicked. But reflecting that the Spanish element in the population, or at least Spanish traditions, might account for the anti-puritanical spirit of their amusements, I did not think it incumbent on me to remonstrate with them.

In general it may be observed that habits of mind associated ith wreligious dogmas, increase like gravitation towards the circumference, while diminishing to zero at the centre of the sphere within which they operate. Nowhere is catholicism so intensely catholic as in America, which has always been the chosen abode of a puritanism too sullen for Europe, and of every quasi-religious or irreligious Church ever spawned in the old world's heresy. Is it that the original "inventors" are naturally the first to discover their mistakes, while America buys up the old patents, and by exaggerating makes them her own? It must not be supposed from this that California is conspicuous for religious bigotry. The dominant religion in California, as in the Western States at large, is *Dollarism*,—generally very tolerant, but with a leaning to Revolverism on some points, with a sprinkling of Bowie-knifeism, etc.

In the evening I went to see Ristori as Marie Antoinette. Altogether this is one of the most European cities of the Union. The next day I was at the Exchange, and that evening went to see the new Palace Hotel. This is a mammoth building, very ugly in appearance, having been built for the comfort of families spending the winter in San Francisco. Most of the rooms are made in *suites*, while every window in the house is square-bowed. This is probably the largest hotel in the world. The San Franciscans indeed are getting very ambitious. One of them has just put up a Turkish bath which is to be the largest and finest in the world, even more magnificent than Hamman's, in Jermyn Street, London. The town, indeed, is finer in many ways than our eastern towns. The side-walks are paved with wood, and all are kept in very good condition. One street which runs up a very steep hill has cars which run on a continuous rail worked by a motive power on the top of the hill; when the car goes up it attaches to the rail, when it has to stop it undoes the attachment.

The San Franciscans are naturally polite and hospitable, and I received invitations to many of the clubs, which rendered my stay very pleasant. I was also invited to dine, which gave me opportunities of studying the habits and peculiarities of the San Franciscans. They are very free and familiar in their intercourse with one another. Going into one house I laid my hat and coat on a coat-stand, and on going out, I found them on the floor, and another gentleman's coat and hat in their place; asking for an explanation, I was told it was probably the Chinaman. This to anyone who knows the habits of that inoffensive people, will seem rather funny. The San Franciscans eat frogs with great gusto, and the gentleman of the coat told us he was very dexterous in cutting their heads off to prepare them for cooking; generally it is the other extremity that is guillotined. There was a wonderful amount of anecdote during our game of cards; one anecdote was especially noticeable. I believe it is told by some new Bret Harte. The hero who relates it was one of the first miners; he tells us how having set out in hopes of making money, and having but little if any with him, and being extremely hungry after a day's travel, he noticed on arriving at the diggings a man who had placed three or four barrels with boards across them, on which impromptu tables he served coffee and meals to the miners. He knew it was very hard to get " tick " at the " diggings," so he sidled up to this man the whole time; whenever he got into a quarrel, he always took his side; whenever he had anything to do, he did it for him; whenever he said yes or no, our friend was his echo. From time to time he thought he saw a smile of approbation flit across his grim features, till at last, as the shades of evening drew near, about dinner-time, the restaurant keeper, whom our friend had pretended to mistake all day long for a miner, went into the house and came out with a double-barrelled gun, and then going out in front of the house fired one of the barrels off. Our friend said he knew he wasn't shooting at bears, because there were not any there; as the rabbits were game, the ground was all worked up by the miners, and there wasn't any cover for them; he did not see a man anywhere around, and he couldn't be firing out the snow as the gun had been fired a quarter of an hour before, so he asked him innocently,

"What are you firing that gun off for?"

"Oh!" the man answered, with a grin, "I keep a sort of restaurant, and that is my dinner-bell; the miners here are scattered around for two or three miles."

"But," says our friend, "they mayn't hear the first one; why don't you shoot off the second?"

A wicked smile passed over his grim countenance as, looking at our friend, he answered, "I keep that there one to collect the price of the dinner with;" and our friend lost his appetite.

We were entertained with many other stories, but I spare you them, as you are sure to find them some day in some other book.

As we reached home about one o'clock in the morning, we passed in our way the church where Starr King had preached up to the time of his death. In front of the church, on a small plot of grass, was a long large marble monument or shrine, where Starr King lay, with the moonlight pouring down on it. And there I was told the story of his life; how, on the breaking out of hostilities between the warring sections, he had spoken up for the North, and had kept the Californians, who were very uncertain, from going over to the side of the Seccessionists; and how on his death military honours were paid him, orders from Washington being sent here to that effect, the fortress guns booming in the harbour—an honour that has never, before or since, been shown to a simple civilian.

One day after dinner in the evening, I made my way to the police station, to see if I could get an officer to accompany me to the Chinese quarter, as on a former occasion I had only seen it with friends. I had not seen the theatre and other places of interest. I was accordingly taken to the theatre. The building very much resembles a small country hall or concert room; not unlike the Newsboys Theatre in New York, which, by the way, the wise and benevolent city fathers have thought proper to shut up, because they were making money at two cents a head, and yet persisted in saying that they had not enough to pay a license with.

The appearance was orderly on first entering, but I soon discovered that the filth was something terrible. The spectators appeared to be completely wrapped up in the play, but of my other American co-citizens, who were spoken of as audiences slow to applaud, two or three appeared to be slightly under the influence of opium. In the place reserved for ladies, there were some pretty or at least young Chinese women, and not a few horrible old sorceresses, more hideous than all the goblins, giantesses and dwarfs that figure on the stage. The music was not wanting in melody that slightly resembled Richard Wagner's, the melody being hidden and taking an extremely long time to develop itself, and indeed needing particularly sharp ears to find it out at all, and when it did develop itself, breaking out in thunderclaps of harsh, squeaky noise.

The scenery appeared to be stationary, the furniture only changed. The room was decorated with many colours, strange forms, and papered great long boards, or placards falling parallel with the walls, resembling the figures that are seen outside of Chinese or Japanese stores.

The plot was laid in one of the early Tartar dynasties, and one had the singular chance of seeing a Chinaman with a long beard on. I found out afterwards, that only kings and noblemen had a right to wear hair on their faces. The plot opened in a time of war, a young king, beardless and effeminate, ruling in state, when a clamour was heard, and four or five savagely-dressed creatures (evidently the Chinaman's barbarian) were dragged before him, their necks and backs bending under the load of the equally savagely-dressed Chinese noblemen, who had evidently conquered them. They were made prisoners; that is, chained in the room. After having submitted thus to a long lecture from His Royal Highness, who got a little into a rage, and sang a great deal, these poor creatures having squatted with semblance of being fettered to the ground, and placing their heads in sign of humiliation between their lifted knees, the kings and courtiers with one accord rushed to the front of the stage and sang a chorus to them, screeching, pirouetting, making frantic lunges with their swords and sticks, stroking their beards, and finally forming, marched round, evidently very much to their own satisfaction.

Afterwards, their wives came to claim their vagrant spouses, and appeared to quarrel a little with them, very much after the fashion of the more gentle and civilized wife. That reminds me of a story. On the road to the Geysers, a gentleman from Boston told it to us. It appeared he had been travelling somewhere west, and being very tired, stopped at a farmhouse to ask for a drink of milk. Leaning up against the door was an enormous bearded individual, whose face and hands were all cut and scratched, and bunches of hair were on different parts of his clothing, which was in fact torn to tatters in many places. In the garden hoeing was a perfect western Venus Genitrix. Our friend approached her, and having got his glass of milk, said with a sweet smile—

"I suppose this is your husband, Madam? He seems to have fallen, or been run over, or to have been scratched by a pole-cat, or to have fallen into a blackberry bush?"

Venus smiled.

"Oh, he ain't had no accident. He knows what it is;" and the sweet hand was clenched, and the beautiful eyes darted flames in the direction of her mutilated spouse, and then with a sweet smile she told the stranger,—

"Him and me have had a little discussion, that is all, sir."

Mais laissons ces gens du Far West, and let's go back to the pigtails.

By the way, a good many of the actors did not wear pigtails; but I cannot account for this; plainly they might have had them. I am sure they cheated me out of a yard of entertainment with diabolical *malice prepense*. But, as I have said before, let's come back to our mutton chops. The reason I say this is, that Eve was produced from one of Adam's ribs, therefore I suppose that Chinese women are produced from Chinamen's ribs, and if I wanted to say, Let's go back to the Chinamen, I should have expressed it, "*Revenous à nos moutons;*" and, very naturally and logically, in speaking of their wives I say, Let's get back to our mutton chops. And very disreputable mutton chops they were, too, for no sooner had their virtuous spouses gone to bed than they were down in their *robes de chambre*, and making most demonstrative and passionate love to the prisoners, who also were equally unfaithful to their spouses. After which they took off their shackles and set them free.

Having lived some time in Paris, and there perfected my morals, I could abide no longer, but left them in peace—or rather in discord, for the peaceful spouses were quietly cutting their wives entrails out—and retired to the back of the scenes. Here I was shown the costumes. They were most of them gorgeous; undoubtedly each one of them worth a small fortune. The principal material was velvet; all the designs were made to stand boldly out, most of their *relief* being worked by hand in different coloured silks. I was also shown into the laboratory, where I had the pleasure of witnessing three simple young men painted to resemble beautiful young Chinese misses; likewise some gorgeous beards and moustaches pasted on to gentlemen whose countenances were as smooth as the palm of your hand.

I also had the pleasure of seeing the other side of all the dragons and dwarfs, which when on the stage always kept their fronts towards the audiences. Most of these creatures were simply enormous pasteboard masks.

The gentlemen actors were extremely familiar, and felt the material that the cloth of my coat was made of, very much to my disgust; while the lady *artistes*, at least the painted ones, smiled at me in a way that pleased me highly.

From this place I was taken to a restaurant.

The restaurants are extremely clean, and are, to all appearances, well managed eating houses, I went into the top rooms, which are the better part of the house, and which are gorgeously finished in the highest style of Chinese workmanship. I was also introduced to the host and his partner, both of whom were reclining on a divan placed in a small alcove, inhaling at their ease the delicious fumes of opium; while two charming little wives, neither of them more than thirteen years old, sang love ditties to them, and played on a sort of Chinese guitar.

We were received with great politeness, and the youthful spouses smiled at us charmingly, and in a much more tantalizing way than the more highly-coloured actresses.

I was next conducted through dirty by-streets and alleys. At last my guide knocked discreetly at a low door, sunk a few steps below the level of the alley. For a few seconds we heard a confused chattering of Chinamen, and one of them made his appearance. After a few words interchanged between my guide and our yellow friend, the former patting him on the cheek familiarly the while, we were admitted into a filthy, low, stinking passage.

One miserable oil lamp was dangling from

the wall. Slime and filth were visible on the ceiling everywhere. Leading us down a flight of stairs, our guides ushered us into a large cavern-like chamber. On entering, the atmosphere almost stunned me. My first impression was that the Demon of Human Trouble had whirled me back on board of one of the slave darbiers of the Nile, and that all the occupants had been imbibing too freely of the date liquor, and were smoking off their drunken fits in their respective berths. Line above line of just such berths as one has seen in Egypt, and in them creatures benumbed, frenzied with the fumes of opium.

Look at that horrible man in the corner, with his eyes slightly open, his lips and nostrils convulsively moving every time he draws his breath, as though breathing was a business of itself and needed all his energy; his filthy pigtail passing under the cavity of the neck as he lies on his breast, and with convulsive movements shakes his hands and feet; from time to time there is a change of the position of the body, and sometimes a gasp as if he were going to die outright, and an appealing movement.

Well, let us leave this man. Look at this other, who in his slumber seems to be deliciously ruminating. You see in his eyes a whole legion of snails, slugs, chicken, cakes and tea,—a real epicurean's repose! What monarch or satrap in Egypt's palmy days, or since, basking indolently in Egypt's sun, sleeping off the effects of his copious draughts of Cyprus, could boast himself happier than this poor wretch?

Thence on to that man who, to all appearances, is labouring under some awful disease, and who now sees himself young again, happy and clean. Perhaps at this moment his imagination takes him to some garden near Pekin, where little Chinese girls enter, quaintly dressed, and bending low at their gardening, slightly turn their heads towards him, their almond eyes looking up at his and firing his soul again to life and setting it free from that miserable vessel of clay. From that horrible condition of filth and degradation, from that sickness and horror, from toil and debasement, his immortal soul goes out and lives again.

Pass we to that old man, who, under the influence of the laudanum fumes, sees himself a boy again, knows that he is sitting on his father's knee, who teaches him to carve and paint, while the mother looks on pleased at his improvement, and he is indeed at home again. Doubtless many more beautiful dreams than these are dreamed, and many terrible ones; many a wretch who has sweated and toiled looking as to a goal when laudanum would free him from all misery, and yet in its cold embrace had only found horror worse than all that real life gave him. But the filth and fumes are too much for me; I must get to the open air, or suffocate.

I am next conducted to the Leper's Den, a still more frightful abode, on entering which one is nearly tripped up by the rats and other horrid creatures running across one's path, and skipping between one's feet. Entering a low den where the quintessence of the Hotel Dieu and Bellevue Hospital appear to have met and fraternized in horrible decay—— But this is too much for me; horrors I can take, but not so much at a time.

I left the Chinese quarter after having spent time and money with, on the whole, considerable satisfaction.

CHAPTER XIII.

THE CHINESE ON THE PACIFIC COAST.

Every Chinaman of the labouring class is consigned to some one of the Six Companies—great corporations founded somewhat on the type of the East India Company. These Companies make their head-quarters in San Francisco.

The agents of the Companies are scattered all throughout the interior of China, visiting large tracts of country; and wherever they find a poverty-stricken old couple, sinking under the burden of a large family, they mark them as fit subjects for their machinations.

Having ascertained which is the most sprightly and gifted of the sons, they prepare a trap, into which the old father easily falls. A creature of the agent either picks a quarrel with him, or has him arrested on a false charge, or some abominable intrigue of the kind is used. Being miserably poor, without friends or influence, the unhappy father of, perhaps, a dozen hungry mouths, dependent for food upon his daily labour, is thrown into prison. The agent now awaits to allow the pangs of hunger and distress to do their inevitable work with the unfortunate family, now deprived of its head. He then appears on the scene as a deliverer, and offers to procure the freedom of the imprisoned father, besides paying a large sum of money down, on the condition that the son whom he has selected shall be bound over to him, for service beyond the seas, for a certain term of years.

Stern necessity compels the father to consent to the hard bargain, and the son signs an agreement containing the most horrible penalties against father, mother, brothers and sisters if he should fail to observe all the conditions of the contract. The agent on his part agrees to return the bones of his slave (for he is nothing else) to his native land should he die before the term of service has expired. This condition is indispensable, as no Chinaman would leave China if he thought he would die and be buried in the land of the barbarian.

The agent now ships the victims of his machinations to a seaport, where the contract is assigned over to the Company in whose employ he is, and the young Chinaman is freighted across the Pacific with a numerous company of his fellows to San Francisco, or to Australia, or wherever else that his master may think his labour can be made available.

The term of service is lengthened in various ways. The passage-money across the Pacific must be paid for in a long period of labour; and moreover, these Companies exact an insurance or protection fund from each emigrant, in case of injury or illness.

These Companies are said to hold almost despotic sway over the Chinese labourer. It is difficult to ascertain to what extent this authority is exercised. It is believed, by those who are best informed, that there is not a Chinaman working in the mines, on the ranches, in the depths of the forest, at points the most remote from civilization, whose movements, plans, and prospects, are not regularly reported to his Company in San Francisco. It is stated that various infractions of our laws are condoned by these Companies, and felons and even murderers are protected by their power and influence from arrest and punishment. It is currently reported, with considerable appearance of truth, that there are secret tribunals organized and sustained by these Chinese Companies, who sit in judgment upon the differences between Chinamen, and whose sentences involve every degree of punishment, from the smallest fine to the infliction of the death-penalty.

From the decision of these tribunals there is no appeal, and no Chinaman, on pain of death, dares to reveal their existence.

Much of the food consumed by the Chinese in this country is brought from China. It is commonly believed that a Chinaman's bill of fare consists almost exclusively of rice and a few other articles of very plain diet. While this is doubtless true of the very poor classes and of the "boat people" in the home districts of Canton, a walk through the Chinese quarter here, and more particularly an observation of the market stalls and provision shops with which it abounds, will serve to correct the notion that the celestial appetite is rigidly moderate and severely simple. The ample array of fresh and cooked meats, of fresh and dried fish, the little mountains of poultry, the endless coils of sausage and the large quantities of hashed meats in great variety, powerfully and conclusively bear witness to John's carnivorous tastes, after he once gets accustomed to our climate. Roast pig—the excellence of which is said to be a celestial discovery—may be found on sale, most exquisitely prepared, at all the meat shops Not unfrequently, they roast a half, and sometimes a whole hog, from which any desired quantity is cut for the almond-eyed, pig-tailed customers. In the drying and curing of fish, fowls, oysters, tongues, beef and hams, the Chinese are found to be exceedingly skilful. Oysters, shrimps, and shell fish of all kinds are dexterously preserved, and ducks, besides wild game, dried so that they will keep any length of time. There are numerous other comestibles exposed for sale in a Chinese market, which I do not feel called upon further to particularize, the various and peculiar toothsomeness of which is, doubtless, well understood and appreciated by the skilled and initiated heathen, who does the marketing for his fellows. Tradition, however, has so indelibly impressed on the mind of the barbarian epicure the rat, mouse, and puppy theories in the formations of the main pillars of the celestial larder, that the "Melican" marketer is exceedingly distrustful of the spiced, seasoned, and disguised mixtures with which the Chinese provision-dealers tempt him.

Rice, tea, dried and preserved condiments, are all imported from China, and it is a noticeable fact that the tea in common use among them is of a very superior quality, and far better than that which is usually sold to Americans.

In the first class Chinese restaurants, tea is used that cost from three to five dollars per pound. Conserves, a great variety of which are prepared by this people, are extensively used, while almost the entire range of kitchen vegetables enters into their daily food. The beverages used are but few, and by no means of heroic strength. There is only one alcoholic liquor — to any extent — manufactured in China. It is distilled from rice; its use as a beverage is so limited that intoxication rarely, if ever, results from it. But John, in addition to his native "fusil-oil," has acquired a taste for cheap "Melican" whisky, besides gin and rum, though drunkenness, except that peculiar kind resulting from the use of opium, is a vice from which John is almost entirely free.

Now and then an epicurean taste crops up among them, manifested in occasional "swell" dinners at some of their choice restaurants. These dinners, it is said, sometimes cost from five to eight dollars a head.

Among the better classes, especially those who have abundant leisure, from one to two hours are consumed at the dinner-table, while all Chinamen eat slowly and with moderation.

There is among them a system of pawnbroking very similar to that in vogue among us. There is no banking system, such as may be compared to ours, yet there are a few brokers and money-changers. A certain class of Chinese business men in San Francisco, belonging to the upper ten, can easily effect loans from these brokers, without note or security of any kind. But these borrowers are not only well-known and of good credit and standing, but they are subjected to special odium and loss of social position in case they make default in payment of a loan of this kind. The average Chinese labourer, however, has little use for cash, thousands of them spending less than a dollar in coin during the week, all their physical wants being supplied to them by their employers.

Viewed as business men, the Chinese differ very greatly from the American, English, French, and German merchants, and in some respects are very inferior to them. They exhibit none of that wonderful enterprise and daring which characterise the Caucasian race in many of their commercial ventures, and which so often approve the judgment no less than courage of their projectors by resulting in the rapid acquisition of great wealth. The celestial man of business undoubtedly makes money, but he does so by the exercise of excessive caution, and by the practice of a most rigid and exacting economy. Not a dollar is expended for useless luxuries, and the expenses of living are reduced down to the lowest possible point. They never indulge in speculative ventures, outside of their gambling practices, for which, however, they show a decided predilection.

Now and then a Chinaman, throwing off the habitual caution of his race, will try his luck in the stock market; but these instances are rare, and are looked upon among them with disfavour. Go into any of their leading stores in the Chinese quarter, and you will fail to notice that bustling activity and promptitude in serving and attending to customers which form so marked a feature in the "barbarian" establishments, and is, perhaps, one of their secrets of success. On the contrary, there is an apparent apathy and indifference among partners, clerks, salesmen, and porters,—as if none of them had yet gotten over their last opium "spree"—which if found to exist in the remotest degree in any of the stores which line Market, Kearney, or Montgomery streets, would speedily drive away the customers and cause a total suspension of the business.

But this deliberation, this composed, almost dreamy exterior, is in consonance with the

Oriental character, and especially in keeping with the training of the patient Chinaman.

As traders, the Chinese are far in advance of any of what is called the semi-civilized nations. The Persians, Arabians, and East Indians cannot be compared with them for industry, frugality, and thrift. The Chinaman may accumulate money slowly, but the process is sure, and when he has once made it, he knows how to keep it. He has learnt the secret of clipping the proverbial wings which riches are said to generate for themselves. In San Francisco there are quite a number of Chinamen who are reputed to be worth from one hundred thousand to two hundred thousand dollars. But they are probably leading officials in the famous Six Companies, where the opportunities for money-making, it is well known, are not lacking.

The Chinese trader has a system of book-keeping and of reckoning utterly incomprehensible to the ordinary outside "barbarian," and by no means easy of solution to the skilled mathematician of the same persuasion. But it seems to answer all purposes, and is as accurate as our own.

On every counter in a Chinese shop there is a small computing case, consisting of movable balls on wire, not unlike "the case box" arrangement used in the American faro game. With the aid of this peculiar reckoning machine,—if I may so call it,— a Chinaman rapidly adds, multiplies, subtracts, or divides; but that quintessence of keenness popularly called a Philadelphia lawyer, could not solve the process, or even "see through it," in a twelvemonth. A few rapid movements of the balls on the wires, as though marking billiards on a small scale, a few cabalistic characters dotted down perpendicularly, and the result of the sum is declared. It is found to be invariably correct according to our method of computation.

The paper used in their books of account is the thin light-brown material manufactured from rice. The use of pen and ink is of course unknown. A fine pencil brush with a small point, and a small bottle of India ink, constitute, with the books of rice-paper above mentioned, the writing materials of the celestial book-keepers. With these the entry clerks make their entries and the correspondents write their letters. In their dealings, the Chinese merchants are said to have many crooked ways; but in their correspondence, no one has ever accused them of being anything but straight up and down.

It is, however, as a mechanic that John has achieved, perhaps, his greatest success; more especially in those trades which are learnt by the exercise of the imitative faculties. Here lies his strong point. To illustrate the skill of the Chinese as copyists, it is related that some years since, on the arrival of one of our famous clipper ships at Hong Kong, her captain employed a Chinese artist to copy a beautiful oil painting of the vessel. The picture had been torn by accident across its face, and the rent, a few inches in length, had been sewn up. In due time the copy was finished,—a perfect imitation in all respects, even to the sewn gash in the original.

Almost any mechanical trade they pick up with surprising facility. The manufacture of cigars in San Francisco has passed entirely into their hands, several thousands being employed in this branch of industry alone. Knowing nothing whatever about the manufacture of boots and shoes, they have made such rapid advances in mastering this extensive and difficult business, that no other class can compete with them. The result is that in no place on this continent are boots and shoes sold so cheaply as in San Francisco, since the cost of production is reduced perhaps one-half. As carpenters, manufacturers of furniture, and workers in all kinds of wood, they have supplanted an army of white labourers, who have been crowded out of their respective walks because the " heathen Chinee " can do their work quite as well, and at greatly reduced rates of wages because he knows how to live so much cheaper. It is no doubt very hard for the white workmen, who thus suffer from competition with " Chinese cheap labour," but it is precisely what happened upon the introduction among us of labour-saving machinery, which caused misery and starvation among large masses of people who lived wholly upon the labour of their hands. Gradually, after a great deal of suffering, they adjusted themselves to the new order of things, and it was found that the production of articles of utility at the lowest possible cost was a blessing to all alike—a self-evident proposition now, which was then combated fiercely, since the daily bread, for the time being, of large numbers was dependent upon retaining the old order of things undisturbed.

The problem of " Chinese cheap labour," which must sooner or later agitate the land, is but a repetition of that disturbance which followed the application of labour-saving machinery to almost all forms of industry. Whole families were then " thrown out of work by machinery," the same as now large masses of native men, and even women, are superseded by the Chinese.

But to return to John. With all the uses of the sewing machine he has become thoroughly familiar; it is not uncommon for him to sit and work at the machine for a space of twelve or fourteen hours without ceasing. Few men of the Caucasian race, and certainly no women, can compete with him in untiring industry. If there is any work, of whatever kind, in demand, he is sure to be on hand, offering his services at such rates that no other race, white or black, can contest the field with him. The trades or professions into which he has not yet entered are so few that you may count them on your fingers. He has not yet figured as a preacher, doctor, lawyer, journalist, legislator, car-conductor, or auctioneer; but the time may not be very far distant when even these callings may feel the effects of his competition.

But in all the departments of servile labour John's supremacy is unquestioned. As cooks, house-servants, waiters, scrubbers, gardeners, porters, he and his numerous "doubles" crowd out the Caucasian, and in every position they fill give entire satisfaction to their employers.

Perhaps the largest branch of business in the hands of the Chinese in San Francisco is laundry work. In almost every part of the city their wash-houses may be seen, every square block, so to speak, containing from four to six establishments of the kind. They do the washing for nearly all the hotels, and that of nearly all the families of the city is done by them. A system prevails among them by which the rent of their premises is reduced to a very low figure. Two wash-firms will occupy the same shop, and use the same tubs and appliances; one firm working there during daylight, and then surrendering the place to the other firm, which works there during the night. By these means they effect a saving in fuel and other material.

As a general thing, Chinese laundry-men are better ironers than washers. This may arise from the use of Chinese starch, which gives the clothes a peculiar gloss and a very decided stiffness. The prices which they charge are of course much below those fixed by others. All the work is done by hand, the average Chinaman having no taste for the mysteries of steam, nor does he care to understand the intricacies of complicated mechanism. Even the soiled linen is collected in bundles and carried on the head to the respective laundries; while the "wash" is returned in the same manner in clothes-baskets neatly covered with white napkins, not one of these establishments having a waggon. In addition to their regular business, most of these laundries derive a small revenue from the sale of lottery tickets, being the sub-agencies of the lottery schemes maintained here by the Chinese.

Another branch of personal service which they have perhaps wholly monopolised is that of the tonsorial artists. The Chinese barber-shops in San Francisco are very numerous, and, as a rule, handsomely fitted up.

The toilet of the Chinese dandy is not considered complete if it does not include the close shaving of a greater part of the head and neck, a thorough cleansing of the eyes, ears, and nostrils, and even a trimming and pencilling of the eyebrows and lashes. Razors, probes, and lances of peculiar construction constitute some of the instruments used by these skilful artists in conducting these delicate operations. The cleaning, combing, and braiding of the cues consume no little time. The closely-shaven cranium must be scraped very often, and each time very assiduously, in order to preserve that much-desired shining appearance of perfect smoothness which, next to the secure possession of his cue, is the acme of celestial felicity. This service necessarily requires, in a city so largely populated with Chinese as San Francisco, the constant attendance of a small army of barbers.

It is noticeable, not only in San Francisco, but in all the other cities on the Pacific coast, that the Chinese are crowded together into one portion of the town, generally known as the Chinese quarter, or, facetiously, as "Little China." This quarter in San Francisco is six large blocks square, and when you are well within its precincts, you might imagine yourself, with no great stretch of fancy, especially at night, in the midst of a thickly-populated Chinese city. For, in lieu of gas, rows of various-coloured paper lanterns, placed along the houses and shops, serve not so much to illuminate the streets as to robe all objects in a curious twilight dimness.

The beginning of a Chinese quarter in a town is a striking illustration of the law of "national affinities." A landlord rents a single house in a street to a Chinaman, who proceeds to fit it up as a lodging-house, which he overcrowds to a degree absolutely impious to the Anglo-Saxon mind. Ordinary rooms, say about ten or twelve feet in height, are furnished with false floors, half way up to the ceiling, and each floor in that room is filled with lodgers to its utmost capacity. They sleep in bunks placed along the walls two high, like berths on board ship, on the floors, in hammocks slung just above these, anywhere wherever a human being can be stowed away. Every room in that house that can be devoted to sleeping purposes is served in the same way; thus the lodging-house keeper drives a thriving trade.

From this excessive overcrowding of human beings, a sickly odour is generated, which pervades the entire neighbourhood. The celestials do not seem to mind either the overcrowding or the bad smells thereby created. But the Anglo-Saxons living in the adjoining houses on either side are quite overpowered and speedily vacate their dwellings, which can be let thereafter only to the Asiatics, who finally get possession of these houses at their own prices. They then continue the same process, until at last the whole street is abandoned to them. In a short time the opposite side likewise falls in value, becomes useless for renting to white occupants, who will not live where Chinese live, and thus the entire street on both sides is wholly devoted to Chinese occupancy.

When they have gotten full possession of

their quarter, they build and excavate to suit their own fancies. Their houses are often as many stories under ground as above. Not unfrequently they penetrate two or three stories beneath the surface. Here are situated their gambling-houses and opium-cellars.

The Chinese are perhaps the greatest gamblers in the world, whilst the vice is well-nigh universal among them. In one of these subterranean gambling hells often may be found eighty or ninty Chinamen of all classes seated around tables and betting. The eager, yellow faces, the dark gleaming eyes, the lithe, lazy figures clad in a dark-blue nightgown sort of garment, the dimness of the light, the crowded place, the stifling atmosphere,—the whole combines to present a scene interesting from its singularity, though scarcely deemed attractive by the "barbarian."

There is nothing very complicated in their mode of gambling: someone throws a handful of copper coins on the table, and after putting up stakes, they bet whether the number of coins is odd or even; then they count them, and declare the result. Often in a single night they will gamble away one or two months' wages.

The celestial smoking-houses are likewise situated, deep down, underneath the ground.

Each one of these delectable establishments is divided off into small apartments, which are fitted up with small cupboard-like enclosures. Each enclosure contains eight shelves, and every shelf accommodates its opium-smoking celestial, who stretches out at will in dreamy blissfulness, with a wooden box for a pillow.

They smoke in companies of two; that is, while one is taking a peep at paradise through the medium of the opium sleep, his neighbour, above or below, is preparing the pipe and opium, takes his smoke, hands it to the first, who having got through his cat-nap, in his turn prepares the pipe; and so it goes on backward and forward until they are both thoroughly saturated with the fumes of opium, and fall into a deep, drunken sleep, most effectually " shelved." They take the smoke into their lungs, retain it there as long as possible, and finally eject it through the nostrils.

It is estimated that there are upwards of 30,000 Chinamen now in San Francisco; and not less than 150,000 in the Pacific States, 60,000 of which number are confined to California, leaving 90,000 distributed among the other States and Territories.

It is freely admitted that these figures are very liberal, yet if they are now not quite exact, they not only very soon will be, but such is the steady rate of increase in our yellow population, that in a few years the numbers here stated will be far below the truth.

Not a little apprehension is expressed by our Californian fellow citizens—I might say all our Pacific neighbours, did not the term involve a direct contradiction, in this particular connection—at the rapid growth of the Asiatic element of the population. This apprehension grows into bitter antagonism towards the yellow man the deeper we descend in the social scale and question there the state of feeling. This antagonism breaks out occasionally into mob-law, and fierce and sanguinary riots result.

If we look deeply and dispassionately into the cause of this trouble, we find its source and origin in the fact that the Chinese are able to work not only as well but much cheaper than their white competitors. Here is the head and front of their offending; this extent it hath, no more.

This agitation is but a repetition, as stated before, of the disturbance of the currents of labour which followed the introduction of labour-saving machinery, intensified by the added fuel of race-prejudices, which always burn the fiercest in the bosom of the uncultured man of the Caucasian race, who has little else to boast of, perhaps, besides the accident of being born of white parents.

The demagogue is ready to take advantage of this race-hatred in his endeavour to wield great masses of voters, in the interests and fortunes of himself and his party. It is, unfortunately, too true that the demagogue is often successful in his schemes,—always, however, to the ultimate detriment of his dupes, for whom he cares little or nothing intrinsically, his interest in them being solely confined to their weight in numbers at election time, by skilfully throwing which in the scale he is enabled to gain place and power; and thus the poor starving workmen, "ruined by Chinese cheap labour," for whom he has been screeching on many a hard-worked stumping tour, are really his unconscious cattle who turn his political grinding stones whereat he sharpens his numberless axes.

After the demagogue has shrieked the wrongs of the working man for a certain period of time, after the working man has been ridden by his master, whom he is made to think is his servant, without arriving at any definite destination, fed meanwhile on chimeras, deferred hopes, and countless systems for the amelioration of the "labouring classes," sprinkled profusely with denunciations of the Chinese, the truth will no doubt finally dawn on the mental horizon of the victim of demagogueism, that if he would compete with the Chinaman he must work as cheaply, drink less rum or none at all, and learn to live on celestial diet.

These are hard terms for the Anglo-Saxon, but they are the only ones open to his acceptance. Like his ancestors of the labour-saving machinery days, he must be prepared to suffer much; but he will also be benefited, like them, in the cheapening of all articles of consumption, and so if he earns less in new and untried fields of labour, he will also require less.

The best friend of any class of men as of every man individually whom hard, unyielding circumstances have almost squeezed to death, is he who will tell both sides, or all sides, the exact truth regarding their respectives cases.

The Darwinian theory of the "survival of the fittest" (the "fittest," it being taken for granted, are those who "survive") is nowhere so strikingly illustrated as in the sphere of labour,—the word being used in its widest acceptation. And the "fittest" in this connection are those who produce the most and consume the least.

CHAPTER XIV.

Oaklands—Restaurants—Growth and Civilization of San Francisco—Its Natural Advantages—Bird's-Eye view of the City—Mission Dolores.

The day following my visit to the Chinese quarter, we went to Oakland, just across the bay, where we spent a very pleasant afternoon. Many of the San Franciscans live here. The residences are very pretty, while some may be designated magnificent. This is a very pretty town, of considerable size; most of the houses are built solid, in stone or brickwork. I was rather astonished to find two or three buildings kept to rent for French flats, a thing not seen in the more populous San Francisco.

The large new buildings surrounding the square in the middle of the town, give it a very important look, which the more scattered and sparsely-settled part is quick to belie to the eye of the careful visitor.

The thoroughfares are broad and well paved, which appears to be the case in most of the Californian towns; indeed, the visitor is often astonished in the midst of a wilderness to see two or three ill-built wooden houses in a line, and between them running an macadamized avenue that would do honour to the Central Park, New York, or to the Boulevards of Paris. This evidently shows a wholesome state of the borough government, and I hope I shall be excused for saying this, as I did not intend to reflect upon our Eastern roads.

There is one stupid thing about their system; it is this: they only carry the boulevard to the limits of the town, while our longer-headed city governments in the East have seen the stupidity and extravagance of this plan and have placed their boulevards on the outside of the town, where obviously they will not get worn out so quickly. Indeed the Californians have quite upset all the principles of city government.

One surprising feature in California is seen in the beautiful wooden mansions which adorn most Californian towns. In their elaborate and rather extravagant decorations, they much resemble Genoa filigree work, in their minuteness and perfection of detail; and the grand old trees, which have been growing for ages without any of man's tending, with the clustering grape vines and gorgeous flowers and beautiful shrubbery, give the place more the appearance of some Italian or Sicilian nobleman's elegant mansion. Indeed, of all people I have ever met with, the Californian, for all questions of outward luxury, seems the most *exigeant*.

In my walks in San Francisco, I could not help noticing the very large number of restaurants of every description, and which present for the most part a very inviting appearance.

Few cities either in the old or the new world have so many restaurants where so many different styles of cookery may be found.

If you are cosmopolitan in your table habits, you may here, if you choose, dine every day in the week in the prescribed mode of as many nationalities.

From the early habits of the first settlers in the town, of eating in restaurants, the custom has perpetuated itself, so that you often find whole families taking their meals together seated in a restaurant at little round tables, covered with spotless white cloths and napkins (the last usually protruding out of the cut glass tumbler, and fashioned into some fantastic shape), while all the table furniture is of the most faultless descriptio n.

The Englishman may here rejoice, and rest satisfied with his roast beef, mutton chops, "half and half," and plum pudding; the Frenchman may have his truffles, his frogs, and his red wine; the Spaniard his *olla podrida*, his garlic, and his olive oil; the Italian his macaroni, his toothsome stews and his native wines; the German his *sauer kraut mit speck*, his beer and his Rhine wine; the Russian his caviar, his national strong drinks, and his peculiar brand of tea; and as a matter of course, the Chinaman not only may but does have his puppies and his fat rats prepared and cooked under the experienced eye of one of his own celestial countrymen, learned in the noble art of baking puppies and frying rats.

Like the chop houses of London, you may go into one of the eating houses known as *rotisseries* and select your own dinner raw, and have it cooked before your eyes; for, on one side of the room, great cooking ranges are placed, the fires kept always bright and ready for use, while in the spacious show-windows or on the broad counters may be seen a fine stock of steaks, mutton chops, birds, game, and other edibles in a crude state. From these the epicure makes his choice, and gives his directions to the polite attendant regarding his preference in the matter of his meats being "well done" or "rare."

During this process he reads the paper that comes nearest to hand, and there is usually a large number on the table, for these chop-houses generally take the leading periodicals, such as *Punch*, *Figaro*, and the German and French journals of the same class; having already swallowed a "pony" of fine cognac, or some other concoction, recommended as a "stomach corrector," but generally disguised under the unostentatious and quasi-medicinal designation of "bitters."

The rapid growth of San Francisco is certainly one of the marvels of modern times. In 1848, its inhabitants numbered about 1,000; they are now certainly understated at 150,000.

"Other things," writes an intelligent observer, "than the increase of the population and the enlargement of the city have made the growth of San Francisco an event without parallel either in America or in any other quarter of the habitable globe. Its name had become synonomous for all that was most shameless in profligacy, for all that was basest in depravity, for all that was wanton and brutal in ruffianism. In the open day men were murdered with impunity; at night the property of the citizens was at the mercy of the lawless.

"The scum of Polynesia, desperadoes from Australia, bullies and blackguards from the wild State of Missouri, Spanish cut-throats from the cities of the Pacific Coast, dissolute women and reckless adventurers from the slums of Europe, congregated in San Francisco and there plied their several avocations and followed their devious courses in defiance of the prohibitions of a law which had lost its terrors for them, and in disregard of any other check save the revolver or the bowie-knife. At that time, San Francisco was one half a brothel and one half a gaming hell. There came a crisis in the annals of the city, when the action of the law was forcibly impeded in order that the reign of law might be restored. A Vigilance Committee discharged the fourfold functions of police, judge, jury, and executioner. A short shrift and lofty gallows was the fate of the criminal whom they took in the act of committing robbery or murder. The remedy was strong and dangerous, but the symptons were so threatening as to inspire fear that what men call civilization would cease to exist, and no peril incurred in applying the remedy was comparable to the risk of allowing the disease to spread and become intensified. Never, perhaps, in the history of the world, did the result more completely justify the means employed than in the case of San Francisco. The Vigilance Committee discharged its duties with unrelenting severity, so long as professional thieves and systematic murderers were at large triumphing in their crimes.

"As soon, however, as order was restored, the Vigilance Committee decreed its own dissolution, and the dispensers of summary justice became conspicuous for their obedience to the administrators of the law. From being a by-word for its lawlessness and its licentiousness, the city of San Francisco has become as moral as Philadelphia, and far more orderly than New York."

As the practised eye of a good general recognises at a glance the field he would choose for a great battle, so a statesman—if such there were among the little band of Europeans who were the first to gaze on the spot where now is seated the fair city of San Francisco—must inevitably have come to the conclusion that he was looking upon the natural site of a future great city. Given an energetic population, here must certainly be its great metropolis.

Perhaps the best view of San Francisco

is to be had from the summit of " Telegraph Hill,"' which is 290 feet high, and situated at the northern extremity of the city. The prospect is superb. It embraces at once the wide circling city placed throne-like on a range of hills which form almost a crescent; the entrance to the bay and both its arms, apparently well filled, but within which there is yet room for all the commerce of the globe; Yerba Balna (now called Goat Island); the mountains of Marin in the county on the north, with the Peak of Tamalpais 2,600 feet high, and the Contra Corta Range on the east, with the majestic Monte Diabola rising in the back-ground, grand and awe-inspiring, to the height of 3,700 feet.

Along the entire length of the extensive water-front of the city runs a broad avenue, 150 feet wide. Here may be seen the great sea-wall of San Francisco, now near completion, which will extend the whole distance —some 8,500 feet—which makes the frontage of the city. This great piece of work will cost, according to the latest estimates, upwards of $3,000,000.

This wall is 100 feet wide at the bottom, the foundation being firmly laid twenty-five feet below low-water mark. The top, which is sixty-five feet wide, and which will form one of the most attractive promenades to be found anywhere in the world, is on a level with the city grade, and is laid out with three-inch plank, a large portion of which has been subjected to a process which renders it comparatively impervious to the weather.

Mission Dolores is three rides south-west of the city, and is one of those old Spanish mission stations to be met with all through California, founded by the Jesuit missionaries nearly a century ago. Instituted for the conversion of the native Indians, the uses and objects of these stations have long since been changed. Many of them being situated in the most beautiful and sequestered localities, are now used as nunneries and conventual retreats.

Mission Dolores is an adobe building in the old Spanish style, and was erected in 1776. Adjoining is the cemetery, where sleeps many an Indian convert and Jesuit brother. The church near by has been enclosed in wood on three sides to save it from utter ruin. The ancient front remains bare to the gaze, its simple but quaint façade recalling to mind some village fane in old Spain. Service is still held in front of its now almost ruined altar, and beneath its time-worn roof.

The adobe buildings which adjoin the

church and which were the abode of the simple Indian converts, are now profaned by being used as shops, and one is turned into a station room shabby and dilapidated. Opposite is a large brick three story building in the modern style, surrounded by a high fence enclosing well-kept grounds. This structure is devoted to the purposes of education by the nuns of the order of Notre Dame.

CHAPTER XV.

Nappa City—Lunatic Asylum—White Sulphur Springs—A Civic Dignitary of California—Mémoirs pour servir—Popular Ignorance—Petrified Forest—Hot Sulphur Springs—Odious Comparison—Discounting the Future—The Geysers—Californian Wine—Santa Rosa—Return to San Francisco.

I HAD received an invitation to pass a Sunday at White Sulphur Springs, and likewise to visit the Geysers.

Leaving San Francisco, we pass some of the most charming scenery one meets with in all California, less grand but more pleasing in many ways than the more highly lauded scenery of the State. Sailing down through the Golden Gate—which at one time was supposed to have been bound in by land—and having crossed the bay, we at last arrived at Vallejo,—a distance of twenty-eight miles from San Francisco. Here we take the train to Nappa City and beyond.

Nappa City well deserves a moment's attention. It is situated forty-four miles from San Francisco, and is certainly one of the liveliest towns in the State. Its population is nearly

4,000, and it is located in the midst of a country famous for the softness and geniality of its climate, the unbounded fertility of its soil, and especially the great productiveness of its vineyards.

The city is very prettily laid out, and the buildings, like most Californian towns, are situated in gardens. As we pass along in an open space, I see a lordly edifice going up. I think perhaps it is a State house, destined at some future time to hear the voices of California Websters and Clays ringing through its arches. But no; it is the abode of moral death, and only madmen's screeches are to raise the echoes within its walls.

Already California possesses an enormous receptacle for the insane and idiotic at Sacramento. But this is not sufficient. Imagine barracks—enormous barracks—such as are to be seen either here or on the other side of the Atlantic, and then imagine a building stretching over an enormous expanse of ground, a building turretted and portcullised like some old feudal castle, and capable of receiving three or four such barracks within its walls, and you will then have some small idea of the residence now being erected here for the demented of California.

Visiting a gentleman in San Francisco, who

had just received a letter which seemed to amuse him, I asked him what it was.

"Oh, nothing," said he; "my tailor's guardians want to put him in the asylum. He's gone mad again, poor fellow!"

So here this calamity, which in most parts of the world is looked upon as the greatest misfortune that can befall a man, is regarded as a mere casualty. A physician whose opinions are of considerable importance in San Francisco, told me that there are few old men to be met with in that city. And no wonder when we consider the Pandemonium in which they live, the continual rush from extreme wealth to the fear of losing everything; the desperate eagerness with which fiery liquids are consumed, and those of the most mischievous kind, the looseness of morals generally, the nearly complete absence of intellectual culture,—all these are the ingredients from which mental disease and early death are distilled.

Nevertheless, since there is such a demand for this kind of habitation—a dwelling for mental darkness—it is as well that the government and arrangement of it should be in the hands of the State, and not left to the voracity, imbecility, and cruelty of private speculation; and it is also well that the exterior and general appearance of the building should not be so sad and melancholy as such buildings generally are, that the minds of the inmates should be cheered and lightened by having pleasing objects to rest their gaze on; while it is also good that those merely viewing it externally should not be too much oppressed and frightened by it, as through excessive fear of madness people have often gone mad; moreover, since it is advantageous for the human mind to familiarize itself with every condition of humanity, so as to be able to judge between what is natural and healthy and that which is abnormal and strange, it is wise not to make a bugbear of anything.

This is an utterly republican and anti-monarchical place. Monarchy always seeks to intrigue lookers-on, so that it may have a life apart from the every-day existence of the world, and which the world may not understand and therefore be awed by it; while an utterly republican spirit seeks to make institutions comprehensible by everyone, so that, knowing them, all may cherish and uphold them.

From Nappa City we went through the charming Nappa Valley, which is covered with gigantic oaks and other large trees, such as we may see in most parts of England. Soon we arrived at the railroad station, where we got out to go to the Springs. We found a large omnibus waiting for us, into which we were stuffed, and then we go on again for the White Sulphur Springs. Following a pretty road which winds through delightful valleys, we at last arrived at the Springs, as night was coming on. The hotel with all its adjuncts is owned by one man, and he has put everything in the most perfect order, at the same time giving to the place a very picturesque look. A large reflector placed among the trees, throwing light through the branches, makes a very pretty effect. Dancing goes on nearly every evening.

I was introduced to one of the chief city officials of San Francisco,—a very insignificant Irish-looking creature. To this person I had a letter of introduction, which I had sent to his house in San Francisco, and had waited four or five days for an answer, refusing other invitations, so as to be able to accept any politeness he might show me. On being introduced I said,—

"I had a letter of introduction to you, dear Mr.———, which I sent to your house in San Francisco; I suppose you did not get it, being out of town?"

"Oh no!" he said, "I got it four or five

days ago, but you understand, not being at home——"

I did not understand at all. Just think of an Irish creature like this representing the society of a city like San Francisco. Imagine a Mayor of a large town in Europe knowing so little of etiquette as to do a thing of this kind. Supposing him to be called upon to receive a brother dignitary from France or England, just fancy the awkwardness and *gaucherie* with which he would acquit himself. Imagine, for instance, a state occasion, such as a reception of a representative of another country; try to conceive him placing the hospitalities of San Francisco at his feet. With what grace he would do it! But enough of him.

Dancing was going on, and I had the pleasure of being introduced to some of the notables of San Francisco, and of dancing with some of their descendants.

The waltz is different from that to which we are accustomed in the east. Instead of a slide, it is a very fast hop. Most of the people I saw here were people of vast wealth, and yet they live at this watering-place with astonishing simplicity.

I stayed here on Sunday. In the evening I made the acquaintance of a gentleman who had travelled a good deal, judging from what he said of the many places he had visited, and who spoke as though he knew a little about everything. During our conversation, we touched on the subject of the Hon. U. S. G. He said that he remembered him drunk, lying on the steps of the Court House of St. Louis, and that after he left West Point he was so lazy and unable to work for himself, that he went to his wife's father, who supported him for a long time. What glory for the descendants of the men who fought at Bunker's Hill and New Orleans, to know that their country is governed by men such as these! I will not vouch for the accuracy of this story, but give it for what it is worth.

Later on, another gentleman, who spoke as though he had seen a great deal of the world, asked me some question about the French Government and the state of affairs in that country. When I disavowed Louis Napoleon, and expressed my admiration for Louis Philippe, stating my opinion that he had been the real organizer of the army which fought in the Crimea and in the campaigns in Italy, and that the same army had degenerated under Napoleon III. so as to be beaten in the war with Prussia, he appeared to be very much edified, and said in a jovial way,—

"Yes, yes, Louis Philippe was a fine fellow; he and Lafayette helped us through a good deal."

Is it not strange that a people who laugh at the French for their want of education, should be thus ignorant of simple facts which are so closely entwined with our history, which is so very short, and of which Lafayette, together with Washington, may be looked upon as the originators. Indeed, I have very often been astonished in France to find a good deal more knowledge of American history than is current in America. History, it seems, does not pay; if it did, we should certainly know more of it than any other people.

The day was very warm; the hotel, being situated in a small ravine, and being closed in on both sides, was very hot, so much so that we were very glad to sit and talk and do nothing all day.

In the afternoon, I had a sulphur bath, which I found truly delicious. As I was going to bed, the gentleman I had been introduced to said,—

"Can I send you a *mint-julep* in the morning?"

I said, "Yes, thank you," and went off to bed.

Effectively, in the morning by five o'clock,

there was a gentle knock at the door, and a waiter made his appearance with a large glass full of *mint-julep*, with two straws in it, and the gentleman's card. No wonder Americans have bald heads at their early age.

That day I got as far as the Hot Sulphur Springs at Calistoga.

Here we were surprised to find two large paintings, one of which resembled the style of David, the celebrated French painter. We were told that this had been given in remembrance of the assistance rendered by the proprietor of the hotel in the French war, by some society in Paris.

The proprietor had a German name, so I thought it was from some of his German friends, who had liked the looks of it, when on a warlike visit to Paris, and fearing that somebody might envy them its possession in Germany, had made a present of it to their beloved cousin in America.

In the afternoon we drove to the Petrified Forest,—another California wonder well worth a visit. The keeper of the forest is an old Swede, who has travelled all over the world. He told us the history of his life. We had been told that cholera was coming into the neighbourhood; he said he had been four times in the midst of cholera, and at one time had had the disease. He had visited almost every populated part of the globe, and had lived with most people, and yet he had come here at last and had undertaken the care of this forest, and seemed likewise perfectly content. His only companion was a Billy-goat, whose head he invited all his visitors to try to put to the ground, and which I succeeded in doing. He seemed mightily pleased at this, and kept crying at the goat all the rest of the time, saying,—

"Well, Billy! you are beaten at last, aren't you?"

The trees appeared to be of the species *sequoia*, the stumps being extremely large. One of the stumps was nearly thirty feet long and fifteen feet in diameter.

On our way to the hotel, passing through a very beautiful country, we reached soil completely untilled and unworked. It seems wonderful that people do not go and squat, fencing in the land and living upon what they could plant with ease, until the time prescribed by law to give them possession elapsed, instead of dying in London and Berlin for want of a dish of beans. It has never seemed to me surprising that so many emigrants come to this country; I only wonder that more do not come.

The Hot Sulphur Springs of Calistoga are

very favourite resorts in some seasons of the year, but those that frequent them are not so *recherché* as those that come to the White Sulphur.

The buildings are large; a good many small buildings are attached to the hotel, besides the large ones used for the baths.

We were given a small villa, where we were as at home.

The next morning we were off betimes in a large rickety omnibus. The proprietor having driven in with his buggy, gave it to a young gentleman of the party to drive on in front.

A mile's distance from Calistoga, he went off at a good pace on the wrong road, and we had quite an exciting chase after him. We found him at last speeding into the yard of a farm.

But the road soon began to climb the sides of mountains. Every few hundred yards we passed quicksilver or lead mines, the shaft of one of which we visited. But most of this country is a garden.

We heard two or three rather fine jokes on our drive. One story is told about a discussion between a Californian driver and an Oregon man. The Californian saying "Well, it's a nice country, Californy is—a very nice country —a beautiful climate, plenty of this, and all sorts of that—magnificent scenery—indeed, we'd be perfect, if we'd only plenty of water and good society," the old Oregonian screwed his plug around his cheek, and looking right into his eyes, said,—

"Waal, I guess if they had good society and plenty of water in hell, they'd find it perfect."

We stopped at a house placed on the ridge of the mountain over which we were going. This place was situated near to a large quicksilver mine, and we were shown pieces of the quicksilver, as large as the last joint in your thumb.

I forgot to mention one of the cities we passed through. Only the map of it, which we saw at this house, brought it to mind. As we were driving along on a dry plain, we saw a few trees cut down, and on one of them a board fastened with "De Clootz Avenue" upon it, and indicated in the same way at regular distances in blocks, "Munroe Avenue," "Washington Avenue," "De Bar Avenue," "Madison Avenue," "Fifth Avenue," and so on, and the cross streets marked out, and named, First, Second, Third, Fourth, etc.

We came to one place, with a small brook running through it, and where a large board was put up with "City Park" on it. The only buildings standing as yet were two small wooden shanties. On the map, all this was represented beautifully painted with a park drive along it. The two houses that were built were put down, but with the word "suburbs" affixed. There's enterprise for you with a vengeance! *E pluribus unum.* Excelsior!

We arrived at the Geysers about five o'clock, thoroughly tired out. Although it was very hot, we climbed and had a look at them. The devil seems to be well supplied here with all sorts of baths, inkstands, seats, ovens, etc., as every bubbling of water or strange formation of rock has his name prefixed to it, and some service assigned to it, *auprès de sa majesté Satanique.* One very curious freak of nature is the pond where a cool delicious water is put out one moment, and where a boiling inky substance goes bubbling up the next. Indeed, very often at a very short distance from the boiling water there springs water clear as crystal and cold as ice; and this is the more strange that the whole of the mountain side seems to be burning away.

After dinner I had quite an argument with the Englishman who had travelled with us from White Sulphur Springs. The discussion was about the right of men to fight in defence of their country without being enlisted, but in aid of a standing army. I supported the Prussian system of treating the "*Francs-Tireurs;*" he, on the contrary, said that it was the first time anything of the kind had been done, and he thought it could never be looked up to as a precedent, it being practically an abuse of power on their part. If "the essence of war is violence," as Macaulay assures us, it will be hard to prove that the Prussians were wrong; if, on the other hand, the horrors of war may reasonably be expected to diminish with the increasing civilization of the world, the Prussians may fairly be charged with having done their best to delay progress. The reader is welcome to either horn of the dilemma.

During the afternoon I found that I had letters to some of my travelling companions which I had been unable to send to San Francisco; so I introduced myself, and we had a good laugh over the chase after the buggy, which I have already mentioned.

The next morning the impossibility of all going in the same coach for the one trip was apparent to us; two gentlemen and a lady and her child had to follow us in a gig, which belonged to the proprietor of the hotel. The men who were ousted took it very quietly, although they had perhaps more right to the places than those who ousted them. The former were plain people from Boston. The other two were going another way. One of them was an *attaché* to the embassy X——, and spoke in a very dictatorial way. I asked an explanation of this, and was told that he had contracted the habit of ordering in the civil service.

That is not one's ordinary idea of the diplomat, but rather of a person who receives orders.

The drive was very pretty as far as the place where we had to stop for dinner. On the road my attention was called to a purple rock supposed to look like a Turk.

After dinner we visited the house of a gentleman, a German, who had built a charming homestead near this place. The house was low, long, and with deep gables like German houses. The grounds and flowerbeds were kept in perfect order, with trees neatly trimmed, tables and swings disposed throughout the grounds. There you could drink wine out of enormous barrels, each of which, to our unaccustomed eyes, resembled the celebrated butt of Heidelberg. The wine was excellent. The ladies were given a light sweet wine, with which they also were pleased.

This gentleman told us that it would be possible to make just as good wine in America as elsewhere, but the growers could not afford to keep it very long, and the consumers drank it "right away." This is much to be regretted; a bottle of good wholesome wine at a reasonable price, in all parts of the United States, is still a great desideratum. In the afternoon we took the train as far as Santa Rosa; from Santa Rosa to San Francisco, only one days travel. Before leaving, we saw some very peculiar Texan spurs. They are Brobdignagian, the spur having an enormous curve standing out fully two and a half inches from the heel, and having the rowel fully the size of an English penny. This machine is attached to the foot by immense leather straps; altogether it has a very Quixotic look.

We saw also some very curious saddles and bowie-knives, revolvers, and other firearms of all shapes, besides other articles of accoutrements for horse and guide. It is wonderful that in this new country, and in this new part of it, they should have arrived at all the small trifling perfections such as are prized in Switzerland and Italy. The guides always assure you that it is indispensable for you to have a pair of these spurs, also a flask, and you must absolutely have a box of new cartridges.

Santa Rosa is the county seat of Sonoma County, and contains a population of about 2,500. It is situated in Santa Rosa creek, which is a tributary of Russian river. From the cupola of the Hotel de Ville you get a magnificent view of the lovely Santa Rosa valley, celebrated for its wondeful fertility, especially in the yield of wheat. The valley contains about 5,000,000 grape vines, producing yearly about 350,000 gallons of wine and brandy,—the largest yield of any county, with the exception of Los Angeles, in the State.

The sail across the bay is very enjoyable. As we were going along, we heard the guns of the fort firing to salute the *City of Pekaho*, one of the China line of steamships, as it steered majestically out of port. It was only half an hour afterwards that I found out we had passed within one hundred yards of a dire tragedy. As the steamship came down, the order was given "No. 1., No. 2., Fire!" Accordingly the two guns fired. The cannoneer of No. 3, thinking in the smoke that all three guns had gone off, began to clean his gun. Just at that moment the ship passed, and "No. 3, Fire!" was ordered, or perhaps the gun was discharged by electricity. However this may be, the gun went off, and the ramrod with the upper part of the man cleaning the gun was shot a thousand yards out to sea. The passengers on board the steamboat knew nothing of this awful drama. How often it happens that spectators know nothing of the fearful things that are occurring within a few yards of them. For instance, the applause of the spectators at the death of Viami did not stop from any knowledge on their part of the fact that the American revolver is not used as an instrument of suicide in "*Phèdre*."

Our journey back to San Francisco requires no special mention. The periodical stoppages, with the usual number of small accidents, took place, and were forgotten five minutes after their occurrence. We duly swallowed our meals and washed them down with California wine regularly three times a day, with a punctuality that bespoke a thoroughly normal state of the digestive functions, which must be largely attributed to our having passed so much of our time in the open air, in active exercise, free from all mental anxiety. We arrived at San Francisco very much pleased with our trip, and began to turn our thoughts eastward, in which direction we were soon to bend our steps,—if travelling homeward in a Pullman car with all the modern conveniences might be thus designated.

Several gentlemen met me at the ticket office, and to make their hospitality, of which I had fully partaken, complete, they accompanied me across the harbour, saw me installed in the train, and did not leave until the whistle blew.

Of all the hospitality I have ever experienced, theirs was the most gentlemanly and thorough.

CHAPTER XVI.

Travelling Bores—" Great Mill "—The Pullman " Chicken "—Won by a Foul—Proficiency of the Pullmanites in the Noble Art—Second Visit to Chicago—Detroit—Central Freight Depôt—The Canadian Side—Falls of Niagara—A Short Essay on the Sublime and Beautiful.

The ride as far as Sacramento was not new to me, having been over it already, but after Sacramento I was able to see parts of the country through which we had passed during the night time on the westward journey.

For long stretches, the country lay bare. Small grey peaks rising up everywhere gave the appearance of a perfect glacier of earth; then we went over hills beautifully green in all the luxuriance of western vegetation; passing through towns and villages commenced and left to grow up in the track of the locomotive.

As we passed through the different forts or villages adjoining military stations, soldiers in an equivocal condition were to be seen hanging about, for it was the great national holiday, the Fourth of July.

24

In some places we saw attempts at fireworks, none of which were very satisfactory. On the train we managed to amuse ourselves pretty well, as most of the travellers were Californians going through to the east, and we had much more unreserved communication than we had going west.

There was one lady with a family of children who had at some distant period resided in New York. Her children assured me, and likewise all the other passengers, with the utmost gravity, that when they lived in New York they had hot and cold water all over the house. Later on, their mother assured me of the same interesting fact; she objected very much to the eastern people's habits, especially of the gentlemen being compelled to wear dress clothes in the evening, affirming in support of this objection that our ancestors had never worn them. In the case of Adam and Eve, to whom she doubtless referred, she was certainly correct, but since the tailoring operations of our first mother, the cut and style of clothes have altered somewhat.

This style of creature, very proud of hot and cold water, but averse to evening coats, is one of the travelling disgraces of the American people, both here and abroad.

On the morning of the fifth, we were called

at five o'clock, to have coffee. We found the train at the station, and every one near the track; we were told that a fierce war was being waged by the opposition coffee-sellers, one of whom was an old woman of some seventy years, whose privilege to sell coffee, she maintained, had been secured by the Company.

Arrived at Omaha on the 7th July, and there Mr. S. and myself left the rest of the party, with the intention of returning by the Chicago and North-Western Railway.

As a general rule in travelling I had secured a double berth in the Pullman car, but on this occasion the ticket-master assured me that they were not allowed to give them without two tickets, one for each berth.

Being comfortably seated in our place, engaged in conversation, we were disturbed about nine o'clock by a negro who came and, without asking permission, let down the upper berth, just over our heads. This of course rendered sitting underneath the reverse of agreeable.

I asked him if this was necessary, as I knew the upper berth was not taken. He told me he was tired, and as he was going to bed he intended to make up the berths now; if I did not want mine made now, I should have to wait for the conductor to do it. Not caring to give trouble, Mr. S. and myself went to the end of the compartment, where we were continuing our conversation, when the negro made his appearance, and began the same operation with the berths above us. When we remonstrated, he said that that was his berth and he was going to bed. We thought we would move to the small room at the other end of the car, but we found every seat in it occupied, so that, highly discontented, we were obliged to go to bed. Seeing the upper berth made, and as it is always very stuffy, I pushed up the bedding. I was just passing into Elysian dreams when, with a tremendous thump, a rude voice called out to me,—

"Don't touch that berth, young man!"

I remonstrated, but with no avail. Two or three times during the night the conductor came to satisfy himself that the berth was all right, and made so much noise at each visit that I was several times woke up from my slumbers and was at last made so nervous that I could not go to sleep at all. Anybody who has travelled in a Pullman car, and has slept in a lower berth, will remember the difficulty he has had to adjust his apparel without putting his feet outside the curtains, and when it is remembered that this time it was the case of a person six feet three inches in height trying to dress in a box measuring in length but six feet one inch, one can imagine the added difficulty. At last I was obliged to put my feet out, and I had no sooner done so than I experienced a crushing sensation on one of my corns and saw my friend the negro "Blondinning" over it. I requested him, if he had no serious objection, to dance somewhere else.

"I have got to pass somewhere," said he.

"Certainly, only please don't walk on my feet."

I was trying assiduously to get dressed, so as to be out of the way, when he again gave a slight tap on my over-sensitive foot. This, with the accumulated injuries of last night, in addition to those of the morning, was too much for me.

"Be careful where you are walking." I said this very sternly, as if I was a master on my own plantation. I thought I had put an end to everything, and I was quietly dressing behind my double-buttoned curtains—there being two loops to each button—when I was again marched on. This was too much; I gave him a vigorous push, which sent him spinning into the opposite sleeping compartment. What was my astonishment when I felt two or three hard blows rained upon me through the curtains. I had done a pretty fair amount of pugilistic work, but had not practised in this way for a long time; besides, I was taken at a disadvantage. The blows continued, all the people in the car crowded round, some kindly calling out, "Give it him." By "him" I suppose they charitably meant me; I considered he gave me enough. I tried to unbutton the curtains, or tear them away, so as to get through, which I had no sooner succeeded in doing than I saw him bring his right fist up to his shoulder, and before I could ward off the blow, he hit me with his full force in my eye. Not a person in the car had tried to prevent this disgraceful scene, and I heard only such ejaculations as "Bully for you!" "Give it him, Darkey!" from the lady occupants. Immediately on receiving the blow, my eye and the whole of my face was suffused with blood, and my temper was thoroughly aroused, and I admit, had I been able I would have given him a thrashing. But I could not see, and though I have in my life had hand-to-hand fights with the lowest class of people, and sometimes even with animals, yet the disgusting idea of this filthy, stinking brute, who a few years ago was perhaps a slave, and but for the life-blood of our brothers and our fathers would be a slave still—the thought that this creature could touch me fairly took away the little spirit I had for the struggle, and added to my incapacity to carry it on, maimed as I was. Besides, the coolness and evident experience of my antagonist soon put me *hors de combat*; and I found that I was at a point where the best that I could expect was to be mutilated, as I was receiving all the blows and could not see. I called out to hold him off, and ran to the middle of the car. The rest, instead of doing as I requested of them, reiterated their cries, "Give it to him, Clem," and other such expressions, the conductor being amongst the number of his adherents. I caught hold of a berth to see where I was, and was going to wipe my face, when I was hit again; I turned to defend myself, but suddenly I felt a loathing come over me; the horrible creature had put its thumb under my upper lip, passing it away up towards the left, so as to take in the whole fleshy part of the face, while its finger nails were strongly impressed just above my left eye. The wretch had escaped thus far. I saw that his evident intention was to maim me in a most horrible manner.

Others have told me that in moments of danger I have great power of self-command. One thing is certain—I had my Derringer in my right-hand pocket. To have taken human life would be to me under any circumstances extremely repugnant, particularly the life of such a thing, against which I could not feel any real anger. My right hand was free and on my pistol. I knew that if he scratched he would affect the pupil of my eye, most probably cause me to lose the use of it (my eye has been affected, as it is continually tearful). If he had scratched, I should most certainly have killed him.

"Stop!" I said to him. Whether he understood the threat, or obeyed the command, I do not know, but he certainly took his hand away. While I was occupied washing my sanguinary countenance, the conductor came up to me, and asked me in the most kind-hearted way what I meant by knocking about a small man like that. I requested him to observe our two countenances.

Mr. S—— was very much astonished that I did not, as he tersely put it, get a big club and knock the d—— rascal's black brains out. But his was the only sympathy I received, all the other passengers unanimously taking the negro's part. Mr. S—— recommended me strongly to have him "run in" on arriving at Chicago; this, however, I did not do, business possibly preventing me. I went to Dr. Jones, the celebrated oculist in Chicago; he assured me that I had received a very severe contusion, but which he believed would not prove serious to the eye. He gave me a letter to one of Mr. Pullman's *employés*. The next morning I made my complaint at the office. They all seemed to be highly amused at my account, and I have no doubt "Mr. Clem" is striving to do his best to please travellers in the Pullman cars even to this day. I hear that an occurrence of this kind is no unfrequent one.

A gentleman told me of one case in particular, in which a gentleman had been roughly handled, four or five years ago, by one of Mr. Pullman's porters.

I have also heard of frequent cases of their opening curtains to look into ladies' berths, and calling their comrades from the next car to have a look too.

Fighting amongst the porters is regarded as the smallest of faults, and Dr. Jones told me that his coloured man, having sent his wife to visit her relatives, took a berth for her in a Pullman car. The porters tried to deprive her of the use of it, and she trying to retain possession of it, had been horribly knocked about and bruised by them. It is a disgraceful thing that people who pay for luxuries should get in return nothing but discomfort and danger; it is also poor policy on the part of the monopolists to abuse their power. As it is, the three cars are not satisfactory on the New York Central, nor on the Union Pacific Railroad; and everybody who has travelled west will uphold me in saying that the comfort is very much greater on the Central Pacific than on the Pullman sleeping cars.

A Company that depends on the suffrages of travellers, should see that travellers meet in every way with the comfort which they have a right to demand, and for which they pay.

I passed a week at Chicago, principally occupied, however, in recuperating. In my walks about the city, I found what had escaped my attention on the former visit, that they are substituting tunnels for bridges in traversing the three sections of the Chicago river intersecting the city. The bridges are found to be, in many ways, far from perfect means of intercommunication between the several divisions of the city. Being drawbridges, pedestrians are necessarily debarred from crossing while the vast fleets of vessels of all descriptions are passing up or down; which process occupying, from the great number of craft, such a large portion of time, was found to incommode beyond endurance the rapid moving Chicagoan.

In order to obviate this difficulty, the determination was arrived at to construct tunnels under the several branches of the Chicago river.

To Chicago belongs the honour of constructing in this country the first river-tunnel, which was commenced in that city in the month of July, 1867, and completed in December, 1868, at a cost of nearly half a million dollars. The whole length of the road-way is three-tenths of a mile. The diameter of the tunnel is $19\frac{1}{2}$ feet at the entrance, and increases to $20\frac{1}{2}$, at 150 from the river centre.

There are ventilation shafts 110 feet from the entrance, and lights from 40 to 50 feet apart. There is a double carriage way the whole length of the tunnel, each one being 11 feet wide and 15 feet high.

Many improvements have been made in the subsequent tunnels constructed since this initial one, and it is thought that in process of time the bridges will be entirely done away with, and that the tunnels will take their places.

Already great relief is found alike by pedestrians and the traffic on the water, and it is argued that the entire abolition of bridges will still further benefit all parties, though the sentimental loungers upon the bridges on moonlight summer nights already begin to make themselves heard in tones of loud complaint, while young lovers, who haunt these resorts at the same witching hour, are likewise beginning to murmur, while that large proportion of the population chronically disposed towards suicide, who find a leap from a bridge so very handy, are thoroughly disgusted, and more bent on self-destruction than ever.

If Boston is the City of Suburbs in the east, Chicago must be so regarded respecting the west.

There are certainly not less than between forty and fifty little towns surrounding Chicago, which must be considered as its suburbs. Numerous special trains convey to and from the city their respective inhabitants, composed almost exclusively of persons engaged in business occupations in the great city by the lake. It is estimated that the aggregate population of these suburban towns will reach nearly 50,000. A charming variety in climate and in the conformation of the land exists among these places, so that the intending settler may pitch his tent in the forest, or prairie, or on the bluff, lake-shore, or river side.

Millions of dollars are being spent in improving and beautifying these pleasant retreats from the incessant roar of traffic in the great city, by which means these suburban homes are becoming daily more and more attractive.

At last I said good-bye to Chicago. The ride thence to Detroit was one of the most interesting that I had had during all my travels in America. The country very beautiful and variegated; all the flowers and vegetation in full bloom. I got to Detroit about six o'clock. It is a very old-fashioned place, resembling somewhat a French provincial town. The City Hall is very striking. I found here a large opera-house being built. Not only is the place old-fashioned, the people themselves seem to belong to some past generation.

It is matter for wonder, in travelling through America, that, wherever you are, you find an opera-house, provided the town numbers 20,000 inhabitants and upwards. When we think of the rarity of an opera troupe finding its way to these places, it is a mystery how the lessees of an opera-house can make its livelihood through operatic performances. My own opinion is that the negro minstrel predominates and eclipses the Latin songster. Another thing that surprises travellers is, that one gets amusement at almost any of these places.

Few cities in the west—I may even say in the country—can boast of a higher antiquity than Detroit, for the records of the town relate that it was founded in the year 1670 as a French missionary station, when the sites of most of the great cities of the plains were part and parcel of the howling wilderness.

The "City of the Straits" (an exact rendering of its name), from its situation on the banks of the Detroit, a lordly river, or rather strait, twenty miles in length, connecting Lakes St. Clair and Erie, affords the best harbour on the whole chain of the Great Lakes.

The Detroit river is not subject to any great variation in its level, while its width varies from one-half to one mile; its waters being celebrated for clearness and purity, and likewise for the abundance of its fine fish, of which the Detroitians are justly proud.

The city is built along the river's bank for about three and a half miles, and extends back from the water for nearly three miles more. The streets near the river are some what hilly, the ground at that point marking a gradual rise; but soon reaching the top of the eminence, the city stretches out fair and level, the streets being very broad and as a rule well shaded by many giant trees, many of which formed the original forest which here, as tradition has it, once sheltered the early missionaries from France.

The numerous shops are large and well-stocked, and bespeak a very extensive trade. Many beautiful churches and other edifices adorn the city, while the dwellings of the wealthy citizens give evidence of taste and culture; for not unfrequently you find them surrounded by spacious grounds filled with beautiful trees, flowers, and shrubbery.

To a certain extent, the almost invariable rule for the laying out of American cities—a rule which might be aptly denominated the great American *checker-board* plan, as nothing but great squares are allowed—has been departed from in the case of Detroit, as a portion of the city is built up on the plan of a circle, with avenues radiating from the centre, like the spokes of a wheel. This manner of constructing a city has resulted in a certain degree of intricacy to the American accustomed always to what I have called the checker-board arrangement;

but he soon learns to find his way, and the little extra trouble is more than compensated for by the numbers of small triangular green spots—hardly large enough to be called parks—which ornament and diversify this portion of the town.

The noble river furnishes in summer a never-ending source of delight to those who take pleasure in aquatic sports. Daily excursion parties throng its waters, while the owners of private boats and yachts and the numerous boat clubs are organized as the Detroit River Club. Several times during the season, grand reviews of this "Navy" take place, when between 200 and 300 of these beautiful river crafts, of all sizes and descriptions, but all disposed in good order and sorted as to kinds, form in line, and headed by a small steamer with a band on board, pass up and down the river, accompanied by many large steamers; all combined forming a water-pageant which is gazed upon with no little delight by great throngs upon the shore.

The principal park of the city is called the Grand Circus, from which common centre radiate the avenues I have already mentioned.

Among the numerous public buildings, the House of Correction is worthy of note from the fact that it is one of the best reformatory prisons in the country; and likewise because there stands directly opposite this prison, and in full view of the convicts, a home for discharged female prisoners, who are received here and furnished with work until places can be procured for them, thus placing them out of the reach of the malign influences which formerly surrounded them.

Michigan has ever been foremost in introducing the humanatarian and reformatory element into her modes of punishing and restraining the criminal classes, and in none is she entitled to more praise and, I may say, gratitude, from every lover of his kind, than in this effort to save the female criminal from persistence in evil courses. The very existence of an institution of this kind is an indication of an advanced moral development among the people.

Here is situated one of the greatest freight depôts of the whole West—the Michigan Central Freight Depôt. It is 1,250 feet long, 102 feet wide, and is covered by a self-supporting corrugated iron roof,—not a pillar nor partition of any kind in the whole immense room. This is justly considered a perfect marvel of mechanical skill.

The day after my arrival in Detroit being

Sunday, I desired to occupy the day in visiting a relative who resided at *Grosse Isle*,—a favourite suburb of the city, situated on a small island some eighteen miles down the river, and which overlooks its main channel.

I got up at an early hour to catch the boat. The first individual of whom I asked my way told me to go up to a certain wharf; there they told me to go on three blocks, and then turn to the left; here they sent me back to the old wharf to where I was first directed, notwithstanding my remonstrances that I had just come from that very spot. Some sailors I met sent me still farther off, so I gave up Grosse Isle in despair; and as I had nothing to do, I took the ferry and crossed to the Canada side.

One could see a different look about everything. There was only one line of horse cars, and that very carelessly made; the car itself was of American manufacture; the streets were badly laid; everything bore the backwoods appearance for which Canada is noted. Two or three of the passengers were Americans, some of the others English or Canadians, and between these there arose a pretty brisk discussion.

The British were routed on their own soil

—more properly speaking, on the American car. There is a certain disadvantage an Englishman would always meet with in arguing with an American, and that is the assurance and affirmativeness with which your American sets down his opinion and makes you believe in it, whether you want to or not, even if he does not believe in it himself; while your Englishman defends his opinion with a certain timidity, as if asking you yours, although he may be most firmly convinced that his own is correct.

We passed on the road a large convent. The bells were ringing for service; it was a fine quaint old building, standing all by itself in the midst of the open country.

I had come thus far pretty well without knowing whither I was going. I had heard the conductor calling out something about White Sulphur Springs; I had not quite understood what he meant, but on arriving at a way-side inn, and seeing a good many people, evidently out for a holiday, I discovered that this was a kind of Sunday resort. There were carriages of every kind: I was told that one paid one dollar here in hiring a carriage for what one would have to pay five dollars on the American side; as may be readily imagined, the ferry does not take over many carriages to the Canadian side. English ale is drunk here in very large quantities; also a horrible preparation of American drinks, all ready for use, as the Canadian bar-keeper is evidently unable to prepare them himself; also large quantities of iced cream were being eaten.

I was trying to eat some of the latter, when a countryfied looking man slouched in, and taking a seat beside me, asked me what I was eating. I told him it was ice-cream; then he wanted to know whether I thought it was good. He told me he had just arrived from Texas, that he had come to New York with his cattle, and had come up in that direction to see some relatives. He wore a large brimmed hat, such as are much worn in Texas; so I took him at his word, and we had quite a conversation about Texas. He said he had been in Detroit only two days; he mentioned the hotel he was staying at, and then proposed that we should go out in the woods, where I saw that a picnic was going on. Effectively, out amongst the poplars, we went, on the banks of the river, old Fort Wayne * opposite; dancing and merry-making were the order of the day.

---

* *Fort Wayne* is a bastioned redoubt standing on the bank of the river completely commanding the channel. It is situated three miles below the Michigan Central Railway Depôt.

There were there a good many French Canadians, and I heard "*Vive Henri IV.*" and two or three other French songs which are hardly ever sung out of France. They sing very correct French, but when they speak it is a very different thing; it required a good deal of attention to understand them.

Among their amusements was an old airgun, kept by a Scottish-looking man, who spoke very bad English. I asked him if he was French. He said, "Oh yes, I am not ashamed to own it;" he said both himself and his wife were French. I asked him his name, and he told me MacGregor, and his wife's name O'Connell.

I said they were very fine names for French people. He told me his wife had been living among French people for fifteen years, and that she would never consent to speak a word of English, but his own father was a Scotchman, and his wife's father Irish. I thought that they were the funniest pair of French people I had ever met. The police tried to stop his shooting, saying it was a species of gambling; upon which my Texas friend waxed wroth, and eventually the Franco-Scotchman was allowed to go on. Seeing some other men, who, my Texas friend told me, came from his hotel, he introduced me to them, and then told us the story of his adventures in New York, how he had brought all his cattle from Texas, and having sold them, had remained in New York to have a little fun with the money he had made.

He took out a large roll of bank-notes from his pocket, and said that was all he had left of the original sum, as he had been introduced to some men in New York who had made him bet on some cards which they threw over "in this way." Here he proposed to explain the trick with some cards procured from the restaurant. In the beginning he was very awkward at it, and some of his friends made, to all appearances, a good deal of money out of him, and I was called upon two or three times to join.

At last, I took up a bet, and immediately his playing improved. I was very much inclined to believe him a sharper, particularly as I afterwards found out that he had a farm near this place, and was not at all *en voyage*.

It is strange how these fellows find their way into every nook and corner. It is still more strange how people will let themselves be repeatedly fleeced. I was initiated into this game at Cairo; next I lost £60 crossing the English Channel; and at last, on my way home, to be taken in by a pretended Texan at a country merry-making near Detroit! But on the whole I did not regret the few dollars, as the originality of the man and his imaginary anecdotes quite made up for the small pecuniary loss.

I returned to Detroit with the sun sinking behind old Fort Wayne, and many boats crossing and recrossing us as we passed over the river. I was rather late for dinner, but I gained by this, as I had a neighbour also late for dinner,—a Hollander, who was travelling on business, and who turned out to be an extremely agreeable and entertaining man, and a great admirer of Detroit. We took a walk together after dinner. He took me to two or three large German Bier Houses. These were generally music halls, with a large orchestra, and they seemed to be patronized almost equally by Germans and Americans.

The next day I took the Canadian Central, going through the beautiful environs of Detroit, and crossing the river on a fine iron bridge, found myself in Canadian territory.

The change in everything is truly wonderful. One no longer hears that continual chatter, nor sees that sprightliness, which is so natural on the other side; people seem to be more composed, and to have less interest about things in general.

Two real English "reverends" got into the car; English with the exception of the roughness which they had acquired by their residence in this rough country. At one station I was aroused from my peaceful slumbers by the entrance of a Masonic Society, with their banners and insignia; and all this in an American car, run by an American Company.

Two stations farther on, our friends the Free Masons were received by a deputation of the citizens with cheers and acclamations, and they passed in double file through the midst of their entertainers, fresh plaudits welcoming each pair as they stepped off the platform.

The rest of the trip is rather monotonous, as we pass through, seemingly, never-ending forests of gigantic trees, with here and there a small village of wooden houses, and here and there a farm, all of a sudden, striking out of this wilderness into a beautiful piece of pasture land, cultivated and gleaned as in Devon or Somersetshire, and then back again into the same monotony of woodland.

At six o'clock I arrived at the bridge to await the train going to Niagara. While waiting for the train, I had a conversation with a Canadian gentleman, of evident English origin, about the railroad system, and about Canada in general, and asked him whether the Canadians were not peculiar in having most of the railroads run by American companies.

The idea seemed never to have entered his head, and I was surprised to find that when speaking of news or impressions, he generally spoke of New York, or America, and the word "Canada" hardly occurred in our conversation, except when mentioned by myself. All this country, though near the United States, bears the stamp of sloth and ill-cultivation, the farms appearing to be carelessly tended. In one place I saw a farm of perhaps thirty acres left to grazing land, although the man had only two cows and three horses.

When in America, one is but too likely to see many faults which have grown up with the sudden growth of civilization over an immense territory. When, however, one goes into a country analogously placed, and then compares the improvement there with that of one's own country, he cannot but be proud and happy to be an American, and glad to excuse the faults which must necessarily follow such rapid and abnormal growth.

The train for Niagara soon put an end to my conversation, and I was whisked off through the darkness towards that great wonder of American scenery.

About nine o'clock, looking from the car, I saw a stream as of molten silver rushing into an immense cauldron; the moon was shining beautifully; I saw the water come rushing down on the American side, and as I passed right on to the English side, the water seemed to be turned into real silver. I had seen the Falls as a boy,—I had just come back from the gorgeous scenery of California, from the Falls of Yeo-Semite, 1,400 to 1,600 feet high. Well, as I stood in front of the hotel, and looked on that fearful mass of water, I was bewildered and amazed; the glory of the scene was more than I could have imagined.

Sir Charles Dilke, with characteristic love of paradox, denies that sublimity can properly be attributed to Niagara, the nature of the forces at work being so plain and obvious. If sublimity arises from a certain blending of the terrible and beautiful, it will be hard to say where these primary elements are found in greater perfection or more happily combined than in the Falls of Niagara. It may be quite true that the Falls are not so sublime as the Atlantic Ocean, but they have a dynamic power, an eternal persistence in their flow, that take the imagination captive and leave us nothing with which to compare them. It may seem ridiculous to argue a point on which all tourists, with the exception of Sir Charles Dilke, are probably agreed; but a good deal of mountain scenery merely grotesque, and far away, is often foolishly characterised as sublime. In this category most assuredly we cannot place the Falls of Niagara.

I was up betimes next morning, and spent most of the day visiting the beautiful scenes about Niagara. That which most impressed me was the open basin known as the Whirlpool; here the river makes a sudden curve to the right; between two perpendicular banks the water comes rushing down in wild confusion, with timber, branches, planks, while the *debris* of the floating matter is caught by the ebb, and carried with a continual whirl up the river, where it again meets the current with fresh supplies; dashing down again, it is again caught by the ebb, and thus this whirl goes on continuously. Every now and then some piece from the mass detaches itself and goes on down the river.

It was through the very midst of this cauldron that three men carried the "Maid of the Mist." The action was a disgraceful one, as it cheated the Canadian creditors out of their lawful dues, but as a piece of nerve, daring, and pluck, its equal has seldom been seen. Those only who have actually viewed the river with its shallow rapids and its fierce torrents, can have an adequate idea of what these men did. Of the three, two died within the year, and the third lost his reason.

I returned to Niagara just in time to catch the train for Buffalo, where, after a pleasant ride through a beautiful country, I arrived just in time for the hotel dinner. The hotel was invaded by a number of German Jews, and their conversation was truly entertaining, especially when their energy led them to occasional outbursts of patriotic zeal, leading them to the conclusion that it was " a zame this gundry could not be better cuvened than it wass," the general tenor of the sentiment being far less faulty than the language in which it was expressed.

But after my rush through Canada, their interesting conversation did not prevent my leaving them to obtain a little rest; and in mercy to my reader I will now leave him to do the same.

FINIS.

www.ingramcontent.com/pod-product-compliance
Lightning Source LLC
Chambersburg PA
CBHW022112290426
44112CB00008B/642